STREET CORNER SECRETS

NEXT WAVE: New Directions in Women's Studies

A series edited by
Inderpal Grewal,
Caren Kaplan, and
Robyn Wiegman

STREET CORNER SECRETS

SEX, WORK, and MIGRATION in the CITY of MUMBAI

SVATI P. SHAH

DUKE UNIVERSITY PRESS   DURHAM AND LONDON   2014

© 2014 Duke University Press
All rights reserved
Printed in the United States of America on acid-free paper ∞
Designed by Heather Hensley
Typeset in Chaparral Pro by Copperline Book Services, Inc.

Library of Congress Cataloging-in-Publication Data
Shah, Svati Pragna
Street corner secrets : sex, work, and migration in the city
of Mumbai / Svati P. Shah.
pages cm—(Next wave : new directions in women's studies)
Includes bibliographical references and index.
ISBN 978-0-8223-5689-9 (cloth : alk. paper)
ISBN 978-0-8223-5698-1 (pbk. : alk. paper)
1. Prostitutes—India—Mumbai. 2. Prostitution—India—
Mumbai. 3. Rural-urban migration—India—Mumbai.
4. Women—Employment—India—Mumbai. I. Title.
II. Series: Next wave.
HQ240.M86.S43 2014
306.740954'792—dc23
2014000765

Cover image by Chitra Ganesh

To Sojar Bai,
who talked to me for no good reason,

to my mother,
Dr. Pragna Nina Shah,

and to the loving memories of
Dr. Madhukar Kantitlal Shah and
Dr. Sid (Uday) Madhukar Shah

CONTENTS

The project from which this book emerged developed out of a three-month internship in 1996, when, as a master's student in public health, I worked with an international nongovernmental organization (NGO) devoted to preventing HIV transmission in the main red-light districts of Mumbai. At that time, NGOs focusing on sex work in India had been operating for less than ten years, spurred into existence by the flow of new international funding streams that had become available to organizations working in Asia, Africa, and Latin America on the heels of the first decade of the AIDS pandemic. Funds for HIV-related work from the European Union, Sweden, Norway, and Canada to India, funneled through then relatively new entities like India's National AIDS Control Organization (NACO), provided the infrastructural support for both governmental and nongovernmental efforts to surveil, control, and eventually treat HIV infection and AIDS. Local organizations had emerged and used these funds to provide HIV-related services to sex workers, men who have sex with men, and *hijras* (people assigned male sex at birth who live as a "third sex" in the feminine range of the gender spectrum). At the same time, an antitrafficking framework—composed of laws, policies, and theories that tied female gender with prostitution—was taking hold within some governments, within some segments of some governments, and within segments of the United Nations system, as a primary lens for understanding sexual commerce. Although this version of the antitrafficking framework has been repeatedly criticized for conflating human trafficking with prostitution, and for failing to provide clear parameters for tracking the phenomena it aims to describe, it has, for the moment, become a significant but contested lens on sexual commerce for the international policy establishment, especially with respect to interventions crafted for countries in the Global South. The highly controversial ascent of this antitrafficking framework, as well as the increased significance of prostitution in the global image and imaginary of India (usually as the dark foil of India's buoyant economic growth rates), unfolded over the period I spent developing and researching this book. By the time my formal fieldwork for this project had ended in 2007, "prostitution in India" had become a categorical focus for charitable organizations, an object of study for filmmakers, a worthy cause for politicians and celebrities, and a Wikipedia entry. This was not due to the discourse on HIV per se, nor was it due to an increase in the proliferation of HIV in India (the national rate of new infections decreased by half between 2000 and 2009).[1] Rather, the increased significance of prostitution to the idea of India itself was linked with the increased global significance of this antitrafficking framework. To be sure, this framework is far from being hegemonic, or even unequivocally dominant, in managing and understanding prostitution. At the same time, the increase in its significance in the halls of international policy formulation has helped to articulate prostitution as somehow being of particular importance to understandings of women in the Global South. The familiarity of this articulation notwithstanding, the rise in the significance of the conflation of trafficking and prostitution has been convincingly linked to a number of historical developments. These include the ways in which discourses of venereal disease have figured female sex workers as infectious vectors since the nineteenth century. They also include the altered conditions for labor migration brought about in the late 1980s and early 1990s by the adoption of neoliberal economic policies in many parts of the world, the well-rehearsed histories of feminism and pornography debates in the United States, and the confluence of interests between governments and some segments of women's movements in seeking to eliminate illegal and undocumented cross-border migration.

My own engagement with the questions that I raise in this book began before the international discourse on "prostitution in India" was so profoundly shaped by debates on human trafficking, during a period when the primary critical lens for understanding prostitution was that of HIV/AIDS. This project was initially motivated by an impulse to argue that a theory of sexuality must also be a theory of political economy, and by the idea that this could be argued effectively by examining prostitution through a critique of the infrastructure of HIV/AIDS-related interventions. Having "grown up" on the immigrant and leftist fringes of the LGBTQ movement in the United States, I found the possibilities of a critical ethnographic project on sex work in India deeply resonant, primarily because the debate on sexual commerce seemed to afford a discursive space to elaborate on the political economy of sexuality in a new way. Questions of economic class and the material conditions necessary for survival had been increasingly abdicated and ignored by mainstream Western LGBTQ movements, writ large; the identitarianism of LGBTQ politics in the United States, while affording some spaces to speak of "class," seemed to result in relegating any focus on the political economy of sexuality to the status of an afterthought, at best. At worst, the elision of political economy within discourses of sexuality reproduced the idea that sexual freedom, autonomy, expression, and even sexual subjectivity are all luxury goods, available only to those whose access to food and shelter is secure. This form of the depoliticization of sexuality politics in the United States and elsewhere has attracted much scholarly and activist attention, as well as criticism from the mainstream left, to be sure, but also from the LGBTQ left. In my view, a sustained scholarly engagement with sexual commerce in the Global South would not only offer a way to critique prostitution per se but would also demonstrate the kind of discussion of sexuality, politics, and power that is possible when sexuality is not primarily or exclusively understood as a valence of individuated, innate human expression.

As the call for federally recognized gay marriage has gathered pace in the United States, LGBTQ political discourse has increasingly reified a narrative of origins, in which same-sex erotic desire is seen as individual, hardwired, a state of being, immutable and historically ever-present. In this narrative, sexuality simply exists, without any interference from social forces, and all aspects of sexuality are phenotypically explicable. As my own research project in India gained momentum, it became apparent that this narrative form was also in effect in discourses of sexual commerce. As the project grew and shifted, I observed that, over time, women and girls selling sexual services were increasingly becoming sub-

ject to a discourse in which prostitution is a state of being from which
they must simply be rescued; in this discursive trajectory, sexual commerce was never figured as a livelihood strategy that is part of a complex
set of negotiations for daily survival.

As identitarianism marginalized questions of political economy with
respect to LGBTQ politics, so too is the conflation of selling sexual services with human trafficking deprioritizing and, in some spaces, disappearing the question of survival with respect to sexual commerce. Both
ways of framing these respective tropes and issues have focused on the
idea of origins, on the moment in which an individual subject *knew*, *came
out*, was *forced*, was called into being, within a fixed subjective matrix.
In a sense, this book is part of this other, related debate as well, on the
consequences of framing sexuality in the terms of identitarianism, and
within the politics of choice and privilege.

Ultimately, this book is neither a critique of identitarianism per se
nor a direct rebuttal of a particular antitrafficking framework. Rather,
it is an attempt to situate, within the frame of sexuality, questions and
critiques pertaining to sexual commerce that can be mobilized neither
under the sign of identitarianism, nor within the rubric of human trafficking, nor even under a unitary notion of what the terms "prostitution" or "sex work" may signify. From its early incarnation as a project
dedicated to migrant sex workers, this study became an ethnography of
the layered negotiations for economic survival among three groups of
migrant women in Mumbai, who solicit sexual commerce as one of several other forms of day wage labor. The result is a book that begins with
the question of sex work and ends with the question of the city, and the
ways in which migrant workers negotiate survival within it.

ACKNOWLEDGMENTS

This book has a long genealogy, having begun as an idea in the mid-1990s. Given its very long gestational period, there are too many people to thank for their contributions during the course of this book's production. Nevertheless, this is my attempt at doing so.

My teachers and mentors at Emory University's Rollins School of Public Health, where I was a master's student in international health, provided the impetus for my first trip to Mumbai as a student intern for an organization working in one of the red-light districts there. I am especially grateful to Stanley O. Foster and James Setzer, as well as Enid Bulboff Sullivan and my classmates at the time, all of whom contributed to the development of my scholarly interests and to my skill in addressing them. The project continued to develop afterward as a PhD research project while I was a graduate student in the Department of Sociomedical Sciences in the Mailman School of Public Health at Columbia University. Under the auspices of this interdisciplinary program, I had the benefit of working with mentors in both the School of Public Health and the Department of Anthropology. I am especially grateful to Carole S. Vance, my adviser and mentor, without whom I can imagine neither myself as a scholar nor the life of this project. I am also grateful to Nicholas Dirks, Anupama Rao, Radhika Balakrishnan, and Richard Parker, who served on my dissertation committee with Dr. Vance. Phillip Oldenburg gave invaluable feedback as I was beginning to apply for external support for the project, as well as explaining the ways and history of South Asian studies in the United States.

In addition to supportive teachers, I have had the great good fortune of classmates and cohort members from whom I learned a great deal. I would like to thank the fellows of Columbia University's Program for the Study of Sexuality, Gender, Health and Human Rights, 1998–2005, especially Ali Miller, Sealing Cheng, Penelope Saunders, Douglas Crimp, and Oliver Phillips. My friends and colleagues in the Department of Sociomedical Sciences included Marysol Ascencio, Katrina Karkazis, Rebecca Jordan-Young, Pardis Mahdavi, Alicia Peters, and Sahar Sajdadi. My classmates and cohort members in the Department of Anthropology included Amira Mittermaier, Ruchira Chaturvedi, Christopher Lamping, Karin Zitzewitz, Katie Meroc, and Lisa Mitchell. Thanks also to E. Valentine Daniel, the Departments of Sociomedical Sciences and Anthropology at Columbia University, and the Institute for Social and Economic Research and Policy (ISERP) at Columbia, which afforded me the time and space to write after I returned from fieldwork.

The American Institute for Indian Studies (AIIS) funded the most extensive period of my fieldwork in India from 2002 to 2003 and has consistently supported my research over many years. Thanks are especially due to Frederick Asher, Elise Auerbach, Purnima Mehta, the trustees of AIIS, and the AIIS offices in Chicago, New Delhi, and Pune.

I am also grateful to the countless friends, colleagues, and teachers who read or heard various drafts of these chapters and gave invaluable criticism, comments, advice, and support. They include Kamala Visweswaran, Ashwini Sukhtankar, Peter Rosenblum, Lucinda Ramberg, Christian Novetzke, Sunila Kale, Naisargi Dave, Biju Mathew, Anjali Arondekar, Geeta Patel, Srimati Basu, Lawerence Cohen, Denise Brennan, Ratna Kapur, Kamala Kempadoo, Jo Doezema, Kerwin Kaye, Elizabeth Bernstein, Junaid Rana, Vanessa Agard-Jones, Christina Hanhardt, Anne Rademacher, Vijay Prashad, and Nicole Constable. Special thanks are due to Shekhar Krishnan and Eric Beverley. I am especially grateful to Debra Liebowitz and Susana Fried, who provided both material and intellectual support during my research, as well as Prantik Saha, Trishala Deb, and Abbie Illenberger. Thanks are also due to Sharmila Rege and the University of Pune for institutional sponsorship for one last summer of fieldwork in 2012, to Gayle Rubin, and to Rajeswari Sunder Rajan, who generously read through an initial draft of the book and said that I was on the right track.

Thanks are also due to the numerous venues and institutions where I had the opportunity to discuss insights that emerged from this project. These include the American Anthropological Association; the Annual Conference on South Asia at the University of Wisconsin, Madison; the South Asia Institute at the University of Texas, Austin; the Stein Rokkan Centre at the University of Bergen; and the Institute for Gender and Women's Studies in the School of Global Affairs and Public Policy of the American University, Cairo. Special thanks to Itty Abraham and Kamran Asdar Ali (Austin), Dag Stenvoll and Christine Jacobsen (Bergen), and Martina Rieker (Cairo). Thanks also to the University of Nottingham for several opportunities to share my work there, and especially to Srila Roy, Steven Legg, and Julia O'Connell-Davidson. Thanks also to SARAI in New Delhi, which organized the unforgettable 2003 City One Conference, and to the organizers of the 2003 International Conference on Women and Migration in Asia at Delhi University and the Developing Countries Research Centre.

I have also had the great good fortune of finding institutional and individual support for this project from colleagues and teachers in India. I am especially grateful to Uma Chakravarti, Nivedita Menon, and Shohini Ghosh, whose support and feedback have been helpful beyond measure. Thanks also to Geeta Misra and all at Creating Resources for Empowerment and Action (CREA), New Delhi, and to the numerous participants of the Sexuality, Gender and Rights Institute. Thanks also to Partners for Urban Knowledge, Action, and Research (PUKAR) in Mumbai, where I was invited to share an early iteration of my argument while I was conducting fieldwork. Shilpa Phadke and Rahul Srivastava provided feedback at key moments during fieldwork and after. Naresh Fernandes provided a host of initial contacts in Mumbai when the project was in its conceptual stages. Geetanjali Gangoli's early work on Kamathipura provided context for this project, and her insights during the formation of the project shaped my understanding of the ethnographic possibilities.

This project was also supported and sustained by an engagement with numerous organizations within the world of Indian social movements, including the Indian autonomous women's movement, LGBTQ movements, and the sex workers' rights movement. Thanks are especially due to Forum Against the Oppression of Women (Mumbai) and Saheli (New Delhi), two long-standing organizations within the autonomous women's movement. At the time I was engaged in research for this project, the members with whom I interacted the most about this project included Chayanika Shah, Shalini Mahajan, Apoorva Kaiwar, Meena Gopal, Swatija Manorama, Flavia Agnes, Sunita Bagal, Nandita Shah, Nandita Gandhi, Sandhya Gokhale, Chatura Patil, Vani Subramaniam, Deepti Sharma and Ranjana Padhi. Thanks also to Leslie Esteves, Jaya Sharma, Manjima Bhattacharya, Kalpana Viswanath, Pramada Menon, Alok Gupta, Vikram Doctor, Elavarthi Manohar, Arvind Narrain, Gautam Bhan, Arunesh Maiyar, and Satya Rai Nagpaul. I am especially grateful to Sunita Bagal, who took me to the rural districts from which many migrant workers in Mumbai had originated, and whose patient explanations of daily life there were illuminating. Deep thanks to Surabhi Kukke, who traveled to India with me, and witnessed the trials and tribulations of the eighteen months I spent learning how to conduct ethnographic research in wholly unexpected ways.

I also owe thanks to the organizations that offered help and support in Mumbai at various moments. These include Nirmaan, which works at Mumbai's *nakas*, and especially its director, Vaijayanta Anand. All who worked at Nirmaan over the years provided essential early contacts at the nakas. The Nirmala Niketan College of Social Work in Mumbai, where Nirmaan is based, provided institutional sponsorship for my fieldwork. Social Activities Integration, especially Vinay Vasta and Vinod Raipure, and the organization Prafulta also provided essential support as fieldwork commenced.

My initial student internship in Mumbai in 1996 was hosted by Population Services International (Mumbai), then directed by Dr. Shilpa Merchant. Anand Grover of the Lawyers Collective and Mihir Desai, then of the India Centre for Human Rights and Law, both lent critical advice, as well as providing a further institutional context for this project. Meena Seshu, founder and director of the Sampada Grameen Mahila Parishad (SANGRAM) in Sangli, Maharashtra, and Dr. Smarjit Jana, founder and former director of the Durbar Mahila Samanwaya Committee (DMSC) in Calcutta, both provided critical feedback on and insights into the workings of the sex workers' rights movement in India. Thanks also to Maitreya Maitreyan, whose confidence in differential ticket collection on Indian Railways facilitated my first trip to meet activists in the city of Chennai.

I owe thanks to the activist networks and communities in the United States of which I have been a part. These include the South Asia Solidarity Initiative (SASI) in New York City, the Sex Workers' Outreach Project, the South Asian Lesbian and Gay Association, the Audre Lorde Project, and Queers for Economic Justice. Special thanks to the members of the erstwhile Youth Solidarity Summer in New York, especially Surabhi Kukke, Biju Mathew, Sangeeta Kamat, Rupal Oza, Ragini Shah, Saadia Toor, Prantik Saha, Prachi Patankar, Tej Nagaraja, Ali Mir, Prerana Reddy, Ash Rao, Yalini Thambynayagam, and Aleyamma Mathew, as well as Sangay Mishra, and Jinee Lokaneeta of SASI.

The Program for Gender and Sexuality Studies and the Department of Social and Cultural Analysis at New York University, as well as the Wellesley Department of Women's and Gender Studies, were my institutional homes during and immediately after the initial writing phase of the project. Carolyn Dinshaw and Lisa Duggan read early drafts of the book while I was at NYU and provided several opportunities there to share work from the project. I also served as a postdoctoral fellow in the Program in the Study of Sexualities, housed in the Program in Women's Studies, at Duke University, in 2008–9. The fellowship afforded time to think and write that would not have materialized otherwise. Ara Wilson, director of the Program in the Study of Sexualities, and Ranjana Khanna, director of the Program in Women's Studies, provided essential intellectual support during this time, as did the vibrant community of fellows and students there.

My colleagues and students in the Department of Women, Gender and Sexuality Studies at the University of Massachusetts, Amherst, have offered an engagement with this project that has been nothing short of moving. My colleagues in the department include Laura Briggs, Alexandra Deschamps, Banu Subramaniam, Miliann Kang, Ann Ferguson, Angie Willey, Tanisha Ford, and Jacquelyne Luce. I am also grateful to other current and former colleagues at the University of Massachusetts, including Janice Irvine, Barbara Cruikshank, Jackie Urla, Arlene Avakian, Whitney Battle-Baptiste, and especially Dayo Gore, as well as the graduate students from numerous disciplines who have participated in my annual Feminist Theory Seminar. All of these colleagues, students, and friends at UMass have offered spaces for sharing my work and have served as sounding boards for key aspects of my argument.

Many friends supported this project, and me, in an individual capacity over the years. They include Lipika Banerjee, Sandhya Luther, Farah Vakil, Lesley Esteves, Javid Syed, Jayanth Eranki, Bhavana Nancherla, Ashwini Sukhtankar, Peter Rosenblum, Penelope Saunders, Flick Ansell, Samina Baig, Seema Yasmin, Yasmin Halima, Tonia Poteat, Sarita Khurana, Seema Agnani, and Malu Marin. Special thanks are owed to Vivek Divan, Jasmin Jagada, Shumona Goel, Shai Heredia, and Ashim Ahluwalia, who witnessed much learning while I was in Mumbai. Thanks to Laurie Prendergast, who agreed to make the index when asked at the eleventh hour.

Thanks also to the series editors of Next Wave: New Directions in Women's Studies, Inderpal Grewal, Caren Kaplan, and Robyn Wiegman; to Duke University Press, and to the two anonymous readers, whose invaluable feedback has indelibly shaped the public face of this book; to Liz Smith, Heather Hensley, Jade Brooks, and Christine Riggio for solid editorial and production support; and to Ken Wissoker for his unwavering support.

Thanks are due most of all to the many, many people at the nakas, on the street, and in the brothels who spoke to me for this project. I am especially grateful to Sojar Bai, who was my primary interlocutor at the nakas, to the Shah family, to Krishnan Ganesh and Bina Gupta, and to my partner, editor, cheerleader, and dearest friend, Chitra Ganesh.

Thanks to all for their support of this project, any shortcomings of which remain my own.

Shortly after completing an eighteen-month research stint for *Street Corner Secrets*, I returned to India to attend the 2004 World Social Forum, held in Mumbai that year, and to present a preliminary paper on this project at a conference on migration and labor in New Delhi. After the conference, I returned to Mumbai via the Rajdhani, the express train that runs daily between Delhi and Mumbai. Passengers embark from one city in the early evening, arriving in the other by eleven o'clock the next morning, a journey that, on a nonexpress train, would take at least twenty-four hours. Before budget airlines had taken hold in the Indian market, the Rajdhani was the preferred means of intercity travel for the relatively affluent. Affluence was marked in a number of ways on this train. Every car was air-conditioned, for example, and many of the conversations on the train, like the one I relate here, happened in English.

As with most long-distance train journeys in India, a lengthy trip intersected with passengers' desire for "timepass."[1] Combined with a shared understanding of train etiquette that includes helping one another alleviate the boredom of the journey, random conversations between strangers traveling in the same compartment became inevitable. Each railcar was divided into four or five segments, each with eight beds, five of which collapsed during daylight hours. With the collapsible beds and the narrow passageways, the railcar felt much like a ship, bobbing along the tracks.

The conversation in our compartment of the train eventually began in earnest, taking on a round-robin quality, in which each of the eight passengers would have a turn being the focus of discussion and questions, for the entertainment of all within earshot. The conversations began in Delhi, as we embarked, interrupted by sleep and an early breakfast. I chose to remain quiet throughout, without inviting conversation, a habit I had picked up from airline travel in the United States. Eventually, the man sitting opposite me decided that it was my turn. "So," he said, "what do *you* do?"

Having been asked this question many times during the course of my research, and being fresh from speaking extensively about "what I do," I still hesitated before I answered. After a moment I said, "I'm doing research on . . . migrant workers who come to Mumbai and try to find work from the *nakas*."[2] Both the questioner and the man sitting next to him looked expectant, wanting more of a story. We still had more than an hour until we reached Mumbai, and everyone else had been wrung dry of talk. "It's a research project," I continued, "about day wage workers. It's about women who get work from contractors to work on building construction sites."

Both men exchanged surprised expressions. One looked at me and said, "Hmmm . . . yes . . . there are women like that near where I stay. They're building that new flyover [overpass] in Andheri."

After providing a brief description of exactly which flyover, how long the construction had been going on, and in which local slum the workers of that flyover were housed, my two interlocutors asked me to continue describing my research project.

Choosing my words carefully, I said, "I'm interested in how these women come to the city, how they work, and what they do when they can't get work from the naka. Most of the women I'm talking to take care of their households on their own. They all have children. And none of them are getting work every day of the week. So, then, part of my research is asking how they get work, and what they do when they can't get work like this."

Both men had been nodding at each new descriptive element in my short speech, recognizing the scenario that I had begun to elaborate. The key theme of the project was being conveyed while it remained unspoken, like so many conversations I had had over the course of conducting ethnographic research for the project. The form of this conversation,

unspokenness of prostitution, had become commonplace,
whom I was describing the project to, be they construction
naka, sex workers in a red-light district, project managers
ernmental organization (NGO), academics, or passengers on
er a considered pause, the man sitting next to my questioner
dressing the unspoken issue. He was also choosing his words
"Yes, you know, *it* must be happening, with women who have
t. I mean, now there's a law that says you can't have a building
construction site in the city that's exposed. You have to put up a temporary wall or something. They just put them up all around the building
site. No one can see in. It's completely closed off." The man sitting directly in front of me nodded vigorously.

"Yes," he added, "*it* must be happening. With contractors there, and if
no one can see in, *it* must be happening. And about those women, who
can say? They have to support their families, yes, but see, they are also
not educated, so really they don't know any better. And the contractors,
they do anything with them."

Our conversation lasted for the rest of the journey to Mumbai, revolv-
ing around the *it* that *must be happening,* that which remained unnamed
throughout, about which we all, nonetheless, were having a detailed discussion. As we approached Mumbai, the man who had initially asked me
"What do *you* do?" told me that he was from Vashi, a suburb of Mumbai.
Then he asked me my "good name." When I paused instead of answer-
ing, he explained, "I am asking because you said you are writing a book
about this, and I wanted to know how to find it. Maybe one day, when I
visit a pavement bookseller in Vashi, I will see your book there, and I'll
get to read it."

The Problem

This book analyzes how women who have migrated to the city from impoverished rural areas within India negotiate selling sexual services as
one of a number of strategies for generating their livelihoods. The book
does this by focusing on the spaces of brothels, streets, and public day
wage labor markets in Mumbai, known as *nakas*, where sexual commerce
is solicited discreetly, or alongside other income-generating activities.
In mobilizing an analysis of sexual commerce as it functions in these
three spaces, *Street Corner Secrets* interrogates the ways in which sexual
commerce and day wage labor are produced as mutually exclusive, and
even incommensurate, categories of analysis in scholarship on prostitution, and in scholarship on informal economies. Rather than reproduc-

ing these incommensurabilities (e.g., people who solicit day wage labor have never done sex work, and vice versa), *Street Corner Secrets* draws on ethnographic fieldwork to argue that legitimized and stigmatized, and legal and criminal, income-generating strategies may be deployed sequentially, or simultaneously, by migrants working in Mumbai's informal sectors. For example, women use nakas in multiple ways, primarily soliciting contracts for construction work there, as well as soliciting clients for sex work or trading sexual services for paid construction work. Women who solicit clients for sexual services from the street also use nakas to solicit paid work, and many women who live and work in red-light districts began their working lives soliciting paid work from a naka or accompanying their parents to a naka as small children. Although each space is used in the same or overlapping ways by people of similar or identical caste and class affiliations (all are economically impoverished and have some kind of official Scheduled Caste or Scheduled Tribe status)[3] having similar origins (all were from rural communities of landless agricultural workers), the spaces of the street, naka, and brothel are discursively produced as being wholly distinct from one another. In exploring the ways in which categorical lines are drawn around nakas, streets, and brothels, the book draws on theories of the dialectics of space in order to argue that the production of public space in Mumbai must be understood in relation to discourses and histories of the urban geographies of sexual commerce.

The idea of urban spaces being defined in relation to one another, one of the key aspects of the dialectics of space I reference here, is particularly helpful in understanding how and why nakas have multiple uses and meanings, while being seen to have only one specific, time-bound purpose. While both men and women use nakas to secure paid work as manual laborers, women are generally paid at a lower day wage rate than men and are rarely defined as skilled labor. The mechanization of construction work in India remains relatively low, and building, like roadwork, is executed through a combination of heavy machinery and manual labor. Women often do much of the heavy lifting on construction sites, unloading trucks or carrying materials manually, including bricks, rocks, and equipment, in batches throughout the day. Work of this nature is desirable, but the glut of day wage labor means that there is never enough paid work to go around. Through the need to fill income gaps in a field of relatively limited options for survival within the lowest rungs of the Indian economy, nakas become sites of regular, intermittent, and irregular solicitation for sexual commerce. While this use of the spaces of nakas was corroborated by many different sources, women at the naka could never acknowledge an engagement with sexual commerce in the first person. This paradox constitutes a core epistemological tension in structuring an analysis of intersecting and mutually constitutive livelihood strategies. In my discussion of these strategies, I discuss how one "knows" what is both universally acknowledged and unsaid, and how the open secret of sexual commerce at the naka reveals what is at stake for underemployed laborers in managing knowledge about naka-based solicitation.

Street-based sex work was organized differently than sex work at the naka, primarily because the street was neither officially nor unofficially sanctioned for individual solicitation of any kind. At the same time, the street was discursively capacious and encompassed numerous forms of solicitation, trade, and, of course, transport. The street that constituted the second research site for this study was located next to a busy local commuter railway station. It was part of a bustling residential and commercial area, where the phenomenon of women publicly soliciting clients for sexual services was still relatively new. As a result, harassment from passersby, local merchants, and the police was frequent, as shopkeepers regularly called on police to remove sex workers from the block. While harassment from shopkeepers and passersby was generally limited to verbal abuse, some police resorted to physical attacks, occasionally clearing the streets of sex workers through beatings and arrests. Like the cycles of demolition and rebuilding that occurred in the slums where most naka workers lived, these arrests were also cyclic, often ending in women having to pay a fine and, less frequently, in a few hours or a day spent in a holding cell at the police station. Afterward, women returned to the street to continue business until the cycle began again. The arrests rarely led to formal legal prosecutions and, according to the police, were conducted in order to remove the women from public view and make the area "safe for families." In an equation in which more open solicitation for sex work meant more access to the income that sex work generates, openly soliciting clients for sexual services also came with greater vulnerability to police harassment and regulation, as well as greater access to advocacy for municipal benefits, such as obtaining ration cards, and to services, such as HIV prevention and, at times, health care.

The book analyzes the third site for this study, one of Mumbai's (and Asia's) most iconic red-light districts, in relation to the other two sites I have described, and in relation to the rest of the city. Most of the women who actively solicited clients for sexual services in Kamathipura had migrated from rural areas in the states of Maharashtra, Karnataka, and, more recently, West Bengal. An older cadre of Nepali women also lived in Kamathipura, although I was told that the era of women from Nepal in the neighborhood had passed. Like the naka- and street-based sex workers I discuss throughout the book, women in Kamathipura had also worked in their villages as landless agricultural laborers, were from similarly lower-caste or tribal communities, and had come to the city with their families in search of better economic opportunities. Like many women at the naka, these women were also heads of their own households, having been widowed or left by their husbands, and were often supporting their own children along with other family members. Significantly, many of the women with whom I spoke in Kamathipura had spent their early years in the city seeking construction work from a naka, like the one I discuss in chapters 1 and 2.

Sexual commerce has been solicited openly in Mumbai's red-light areas since the late nineteenth century, when urban red-light districts became part of a policy of containing prostitution within an unofficially demarcated zone. Over the course of this study, which began in 2002 and ended in 2012, solicitation in Mumbai's red-light districts has waned dramatically. The book tracks these changes in chapter 4 and the conclusion with respect to Kamathipura. Kamathipura is located in the heart of South Mumbai, geographically bounded by some of the city's oldest and most affluent neighborhoods. As public awareness, interest, and funding for AIDS prevention in India grew over the 1990s, red-light areas throughout India, and especially Kamathipura, found themselves at the center of the discourse on HIV/AIDS. By 1992, people in Kamathipura were already subject to a number of research studies and HIV prevention programs. By the late 1990s, concerns about HIV had intersected with concerns about underage prostitution, leading to the heightened frequency of brothel raids. The reasons for the raids, conducted by police, often instigated by local NGOs, at times blurred between rescuing minor girls from prostitution and rescuing women from prostitution. Both public health interventions and brothel raids have continued, with the latter now being more frequent than they had been earlier. While public health programs and interventions like raids were developed with a view toward improving the lives of individual sex workers, their structure and deployment have also had detrimental effects. The detrimental effects of interventions like raids were largely the consequence of the raids indiscriminately targeting people who were being held in brothels against their will, children, and those who were there of their own volition, as if they were one homogeneous group of victims. Taken together, public health interventions and brothel raids, which function quite differently and have aims that are distinct from one another, served to reinscribe the idea of sex workers as being "a thing apart" from workers in other sectors. While this was commensurate with representatives of both governmental agencies and NGOs seeing Kamathipura almost exclusively as a red-light area, many of Kamathipura's residents also saw the area as their best option for stable housing, and availed themselves of services that are accessible because of the visibility of sexual commerce there. The current combination of brothel raids, police harassment, and real estate interests has further entrenched the exceptionalism of the red-light districts in the city, engendering some of the most severe consequences for people who rely on brothel-based prostitution in Mumbai for their livelihoods and housing.

In placing these three forms and spaces for soliciting clients of sexual services within the same analytic frame, the book avails the possibility of crafting an analysis of sexual labor that accounts for the complexities of how poor migrants negotiate different kinds of labor in everyday life. These complexities are elaborated through the book's thesis, that sex work in Mumbai is best understood through the analytics of migration, access to housing and water, and negotiations for work undertaken by people with few formal skills, and little or no formal education. These analytics mobilize an argument that accounts for physical vulnerabilities of all kinds, including the possibility of violence, without reducing all sexual commerce to the tropes of violence and victimization.

Discursive Orientations

The argument that prostitution is a form of violence per se has contributed to blurring the lines between prostitution and human trafficking. The conflation of prostitution and violence was initially driven by abolitionism, which calls for the eradication of prostitution, often articulating its goals in the language of "rescue" and "ending sexual slavery." Because of the slippages between prostitution, violence, and trafficking in discourses on urban sexual commerce in the Global South, it is necessary to clarify the book's orientation toward these debates at the outset. To be sure, the argument I produce here is not "abolitionist," in that it does not call for the eradication of prostitution. At the same time, there are numerous ways in which an "antiabolitionist" orientation to sexual commerce may be produced. Indeed, both these orientations range widely in, for example, how they are used to argue for a given set of policy or legislative outcomes. If this book is not abolitionist in its orientation, it is not an argument for bringing about a specific set of laws or policies on sexual commerce in India, either. Rather, the book demonstrates that a detailed, textured understanding of how sexual commerce operates in a place like Mumbai must also account for the political economy of migration, urban informal economic sectors, state-sponsored regulatory practices, and parameters for material survival, including access to stable housing, water, and basic living expenses, that landless migrants negotiate daily in Mumbai.

Street Corner Secrets shows that sexual commerce is not a totalizing context for everyone who sells sexual services; for many, it is one of numerous livelihood strategies that people engage concurrently, or over the course of their working lives. The idea that sexual commerce is embedded within a complex matrix of economic survival requires an emphasis on the idea of the informal economic sector, a concept that categorizes the vast array of economic activities that lack official oversight and status, and are therefore not taxed. Understanding the informal sector conceptually, as well as understanding why it has grown and changed in importance over the past two decades, lays a foundation for understanding the ways in which prostitution is produced as exceptional, with respect to risks of violence, morbidity, and mortality. At the same time, understanding the idea of the informal sector elucidates the production of urban spaces that are highly variable with respect to the degree of visibility with which clients for sexual services are solicited. Understanding this concept ultimately provides critical context for the book's broader aims, which include repositioning violence with respect to sexual commerce, and arguing against equating sexual commerce and violence, by showing that sexual commerce is properly understood as one of many livelihood strategies that poor migrants engage, where all strategies bear attendant risks that are part of a daily negotiation for survival.

Informal Economies

The research project from which this book is drawn was inspired by numerous concerns, including the growing effects of neoliberal economic policies, deployed under the sign of "globalization," among people living in poverty in India. The "uneven geographies"[4] that have resulted from adopting neoliberal economic reforms have resulted in benefits accruing to a slice of India's urban elites. Poor, working-class people who migrate to cities like Mumbai are members of the legions whom globalization has further dispossessed, as evidenced by the rising rates of farmer suicides and malnutrition in rural areas,[5] where neoliberal economic reforms have reduced or eliminated agricultural subsidies and forced farmers to compete in global markets amid unstable prices for commodities like cotton and sugar. Deepening poverty in rural areas has meant that survival for landless workers there is decreasingly viable, prompting greater numbers of people to migrate for work and contributing to an expanding pool of labor in urban informal economies. The people at the center of this study are these workers, landless migrants from rural areas, who sought work in one of Mumbai's numerous, and multiplying, informal economic sectors.

If the effects of adopting neoliberal reforms have included consolidating the wealth of the rich (India now counts sixty-one billionaires),[6] it has also included the expansion of informal economies. Also known as "unorganized sectors" and "informal sectors," informal economies may be broadly understood as the vast segments of national economies that are bureaucratically invisible; this is the untaxed economy, that part of the economy that does not have official governmental oversight but in which everyone participates as producers, consumers, or workers. The term "informal economy" was coined by anthropologist Keith Hart, in a 1973 article on the economic activities of poor migrants living in Accra's slums.[7] The concept has formed the basis of a significant body of work, including Jan Breman's study *Footloose Labour: Working in India's Informal Economy* (1996),[8] a foundational text for studies of economic informality in India. This body of work shows that informal economies exist everywhere, in rural and urban areas, constituting the economic spaces in which the bulk of the world's landless laborers generate income. Writing on India's informal economies today, Aditya Nigam has pointed out that, as a system designed for global market integration, globalization requires robust formalization of all economic transactions. However, "globalization also requires the cutting down of costs and overheads which lead to what appears paradoxically to be a *reverse process*—the process of casualization and informalisation in the very heart of the organized sector of industry."[9] Informal economic sectors have expanded in part because a rise in India's GDP has been accompanied by extremely low rates of growth in formal sector employment, evidenced in the contraction of formal sector employment opportunities in state enterprises.[10] This is part of a trend across Latin America, Asia, and Sub-Saharan Africa, where trade liberalization, deregulation, and privatization have provided the impetus for further informalization of national economies.[11]

Street Corner Secrets focuses on a subsection of migrants working in

Mumbai's informal sectors: women who were agricultural workers in their villages, and who now survive through Mumbai's day wage labor markets, or who have passed through these markets as construction workers and now earn a living mainly through sexual commerce. The book's emphasis on migrants living in poverty who do construction and/or sex work is not the foundation of an argument that aims to conflate prostitution and poverty, nor is it part of a claim that poverty is an abiding factor for all sex workers. While many sex workers do find that selling sexual services is a way of mitigating or escaping poverty, the experience of poverty is not universal among people who sell sexual services. Rather, the emphasis on impoverished migrants in the book is part of an attempt to analyze sexual commerce as it is instantiated by people who are at the center of juridical debates on how to regulate prostitution. Through this focus, the book produces a critique of sexual commerce as embedded within a complex discursive matrix that includes life and livelihood histories, the production of urban space, the mutually constituted discourses of caste and gender, and the ways in which economically impoverished migrants navigate the idiosyncrasies of state institutions, from the police to systems of health care. Ultimately, an embedded reading of sexual commerce may contribute to a new way of framing and understanding this matrix as a whole.

Human Trafficking, Abolitionism, and Antiabolitionism

Since the late 1990s, human trafficking has emerged as a major discursive framework for understanding prostitution. It therefore becomes necessary to clarify the book's perspective on the trafficking framework at the outset, and specifically why, in discussing sexual commerce and migration in India, this book is not "about trafficking." It would be a simple matter to say that the book is not about trafficking because none of the people whom I discuss in the book, who sold or traded sexual services, were trafficked. While this was true both ethnographically and juridically (no one claimed to be trafficked, and none of the migration histories I recount conform to the legal definition of trafficking), this kind of claim would constitute an uncritical use of the trafficking framework while eliding some of the book's key critiques.

While *Street Corner Secrets* is critical of those antitrafficking frameworks that see prostitution as a form of violence, it is not a critique of those frameworks per se. Rather, I reference critiques of discourses on human trafficking by way of mobilizing an ethnographically grounded argument on the ways in which sexual commerce shapes the political economy of migration and survival in Mumbai's informal economies. Abolitionist perspectives on prostitution conflate prostitution and trafficking by conflating prostitution and violence, arguing that prostitution is equivalent to violence against women and must be completely eradicated. The book's argument builds on extant critiques of abolitionism to argue not only that using violence or trafficking as the primary rubric for understanding prostitution miscategorizes much of sexual commerce as trafficking but that this approach ignores much that is significant about sexual commerce, including the connections between sexual commerce and other economic, political, social, and environmental worlds.

The discourse on trafficking, as distinct from abolitionist discourses on prostitution, is referenced here primarily with respect to the broad network of governments and NGOs that have produced a major international agreement elaborating the definition of trafficking, and the proper response from governments to traffickers and trafficked people. The parameters of a shared international governmental response to trafficking are articulated in the Convention Against Transnational Organized Crime, in the Protocol to Prevent, Suppress and Punish Trafficking in Persons, Especially Women and Children, and in the Interpretative Notes to the Trafficking Protocol,[12] where the interpretative notes have no official status but do explain the meaning of terms, based on the discussions held during Protocol and Convention drafting sessions. "Trafficking" is defined in the Protocol to Prevent, Suppress and Punish Trafficking in Persons, Especially Women and Children, also known as the Palermo Protocol, which was signed in Palermo, Italy, in 2000. The Convention elaborates the obligations of governments on punishing traffickers and protecting the rights of trafficked persons. India ratified the Palermo Protocol in 2011, and adopted the Protocol's definition of trafficking in sweeping reforms of laws relating to sexual assault, passed in 2013. It is worth noting that these agreements do not oblige signatory governments to offer victim assistance or protections that exceed the bounds of law enforcement to people who are identified as victims of trafficking. These are recommended but optional. Hard-and-fast obligations do include the requirement of conforming laws to obligations concerning victims cooperating with the police.

The official definition of human trafficking, as articulated in the Palermo Protocol, reads:

"Trafficking in persons" shall mean the recruitment, transportation, transfer, harbouring or receipt of persons, by means of the threat or use of force or other forms of coercion, of abduction, of fraud, of deception, of the abuse of power or of a position of vulnerability or of the giving or receiving of payments or benefits to achieve the consent of a person having control over another person, for the purpose of exploitation. Exploitation shall include, at a minimum, the exploitation of the prostitution of others or other forms of sexual exploitation, forced labour or services, slavery or practices similar to slavery, servitude or the removal of organs. . . . The consent of a victim of trafficking in persons to the intended exploitation set forth [above] shall be irrelevant where any of the means set forth [above] have been used.[13]

The passage is clear in defining trafficking in relation to a host of labor categories, not limited to prostitution, and allows for victims to be defined across genders, while also claiming that "women and girls" are particularly vulnerable to trafficking. The clause on consent is often interpreted to mean that the consent of people who have been trafficked is always irrelevant. While radical feminists have claimed that consent is irrelevant to prostitution, this reference to consent is not a reiteration of that position. Rather, the reference here precludes the use of the consent of people who have been trafficked in order to prevent traffickers who are being legally prosecuted from mobilizing the consent of their victims in their own defense.

To be sure, there is often a great distance between official juridical discourses and their connectivity with everyday life, and between different versions of official discourses as well. Both of these caveats are exemplified in discourses on trafficking and prostitution when, for example, sexual commerce and human trafficking are disaggregated in the Palermo Protocol but explicitly conflated in some governmental policies. A case in point is to be found in U.S. governmental policy. The U.S. government is a signatory to the Protocol but has had a ban in place since 2003 on offering bilateral aid to organizations receiving support under the President's Emergency Plan for AIDS Relief (PEPFAR) if they "promote or advocate the legalization *or practice* of prostitution or sex trafficking" (e.g., if they work for sex workers' rights, or aim to form collectives of sex workers for the purpose of advocacy). This conditionality, known as the Anti-Prostitution Loyalty Oath, or the "antiprostitution pledge," is presented as a way to curb sex trafficking.[14]

Advocates seeking to eradicate prostitution, as well as antiabolitionists, continue to debate the question of prostitution in relation to trafficking in juridical and policy arenas. For example, Indian abolitionists and sex worker advocates clashed in 2005, when the Ministry of Women and Child Development sponsored an unsuccessful revision of the Immoral Trafficking Prevention Act (ITPA), India's main piece of legislation governing prostitution, such that the ITPA's definition of prostitution would have essentially conflated prostitution and human trafficking. While these kinds of legal and policy debates indelibly shape discourses on sexual commerce and advocacy, the book treats these less as a direct object of critique and more as context for the ways in which abolitionism has increasingly informed the more generalized vernacular of prostitution.

Focusing on the daily life of economic survival and migration in *Street Corner Secrets* entails an emphasis on the idiosyncratic and extremely local (at the scale of neighborhoods) ways in which laws and criminality are interpreted and enforced. This has serious implications for the book's discussions of the connections between sexual commerce and access to water and land, and of issues pertaining to the exercise of state power on the urban street. This emphasis also stages a number of questions that are subsumed, or unasked, when abolitionism serves as the primary interpretive frame for sexual commerce. For example, what would we understand of sexual commerce if we could decenter trafficking as the primary way we understand sex work, especially given that the daily lives of many people selling sexual services do not easily fit within the definitional parameters of trafficking? What could a critical examination of sexual commerce reveal about the politics of day wage labor? What could it reveal about economic survival, in the Indian context, or in any other?

A Note on Language and Gender

My discussion of abolitionism and antiabolitionism draws from international feminist debates on prostitution. Orientations toward the connections between sexual commerce and violence (Are they the same? Is one an example of the other? Are they wholly distinct?) have been marked in these debates through deployments of terminology. This is apparent in the vast differences between using a term like "sexual slavery," for example, and the term "sex work." The question of terminology necessarily leads to questions of history, location, and gender. Here, I begin specifying the book's orientation to these questions by discussing the terms I use to identify sexual commerce and how and why these terms are deployed.

The terminology that initially framed this project was laden with language that conveyed the polarities of international feminist debates on prostitution. As the project began to change over the course of conducting fieldwork, however, it became apparent that the polarities of this debate were far from universal and were often most relevant within the milieus in which they were being produced. Among day wage workers and street- and brothel-based sex workers in Mumbai, where people mainly spoke Hindi and Marathi, the issue of language differed markedly and, unsurprisingly, did not (initially) conform to the polarities of the international debate. Local discourses on sexual commerce did not frame the question of violence, for example, as one of assessing the level of equivalence between violence and prostitution, nor did they eschew the question of the violence either. As we will see, sexual commerce was framed in relation to economic survival and *izzat* (honor) in these spaces, in a context where violence was produced as a subset or consequence of intersections between caste-based affiliations and economic precarity. In this framing, violence could be managed and mitigated but never erased.

Furthermore, descriptively categorical terms like *randi* (Hindi slang for "whore") and *veshya* (a Sanskrit term that references prostitution) were rarely used by the people with whom I spent time. Rather, when people in these spaces did reference sexual commerce, they did so, by and large, allusively. Therefore, in addition to using the terms "sex work," "sexual commerce," and "prostitution" in English, I also became accustomed to discussing sexual commerce using the term *dhandha* (business) and the phrases *dhandha wali* ([female] businessperson) and *bura kam* (bad work). These were used by people in each of the three places in Mumbai I discuss throughout the book, including those who solicited clients for construction work, sex work, or both. Most often, however, no term was used at all, as in the vignette that opens this chapter.

Throughout the book, I use the terms *bura kam* and *dhandha* when relating a conversation or interview that was conducted in Hindi or Marathi. Otherwise, I use the English terms "sex work" and "sexual commerce," in order to mark the project's orientation toward the exchange of sexual services and money. My use of the terms "prostitution" and "sex work" follows on their use in *Global Sex Workers: Rights, Resistance, and Redefinition*, a foundational text in contemporary antiabolitionist scholarship on sexual commerce: "In this book we have chosen the term 'sex worker' to reflect the current use throughout the world, although in many of the essays [in *Global Sex Workers*] 'sex worker' and 'prostitute' are used interchangeably. It is a term that suggests we view prostitution not as an identity—a social or a psychological characteristic of women, often indicated by 'whore'—but as an income-generating activity or form of labor for women and men."[15]

In addition to using the term "sex work" in this vein, I also use "sex work" to evoke a set of debates that have framed selling sexual services as a primary or exclusive mode for generating income. By contrast, "sexual commerce" is an umbrella term that references full-time sex work, sex work that is done episodically, and sexual services that are exchanged for paid work. I have chosen to avoid the term "sex industry," in order to eschew resonances with commercial practices that are highly routine and regulated, and to circumvent a term that implies much more uniformity in inputs and outcomes than that which exists among buyers and sellers of sexual services. The term "industry" evokes Fordist mass production and cannot describe the multiplicity of terms, services, and performativities that agglomerate through terms like "sex work" or "prostitution." I agree that the use of the term "industry," and the labor history which it evokes, may be relevant for the practice of sex work in certain contexts, such as franchised bars and clubs that aim to offer customers the same services in each and every venue. However, the term "industry" was not helpful in the context of this research because the sale and trade of sexual services in the three ethnographic sites was highly irregular and did not produce the same outcomes for the individuals who participated in these transactions. Not using the term "industry" in this way thus became a critique of the production of prostitution as a uniform set of practices, commodifications, and harms that can somehow be apprehended and acted upon with commensurate uniformity.

To be sure, all these terms (sexual commerce, sex worker, sex industry) refer to a form of generating income and not to a particular set of genders or sexual orientations. While I deploy these terms here in this sense, the book is essentially about adult women who sell sexual services. The first reason for this pertains to the fields in which sexual commerce takes place in India. Sex workers of all genders occupy the spaces of the sex workers' rights movement in India—the organizations, national-level meetings, and advocacy campaigns. Spaces used for soliciting clients, however, are fairly segregated with respect to gender. For example, there is a separate brothel where *hijras* (people assigned male sex at birth who live as a "third sex" in the feminine range of the gender spectrum) live and work in Kamathipura. Men, like women, solicit clients from the street, but at times and in areas where women do not, such as in the late-night "strolls" on Marine Drive, the famous seaside highway in affluent South Mumbai. Committing to a detailed, multisited ethnographic exploration of solicitation for sexual commerce meant committing to spaces that were in dialogue with one another in particular ways. It could be said that all spaces in Mumbai are in dialogue with one another—indeed, a central component of theories of the production of cities, and of my argument here, is that urban spaces are relational. I chose a dialogue around gender, and adult femaleness in particular, as a way to engage predominant ideas of prostitution in everyday life, where the linkages between poor women soliciting work in public, abjection,[16] and prostitution are thought to be implicit.

Historiographies of Prostitution

The book's argument hinges on the idea that, by speaking of sex work as embedded in the informal sector, we are able to formulate, and address, questions about sexual commerce that are otherwise foreclosed. Here I formulate some of these questions by elaborating on the ways in which prostitution in India is framed historiographically. The section is divided into three subsections that, taken together, show that the production of the figure of the sex worker in India as always already powerless, and containing an excess of health risk, is based in the production of prostitution as a singular, ahistorical category.

I first discuss deployments of prostitution as an ahistorical category in contemporary discourses on sexual commerce in India that rely upon, and produce, the figure of the powerless sex worker. While these discourses are not the sum of all work on sexual commerce in India, they produce abjected prostitution in ways that are becoming increasingly generalized, and therefore serve as an object of critique. Next, I move to a discussion on scholarly work on HIV/AIDS that uses historically stable concepts of prostitution as indelibly linked with disease. I review scholarship that has shown that this use of the category of prostitution produces sex workers as inherently at risk for seroconversion, and that the idea that people who sell sexual services have indelible and universally shared characteristics (including inherent health risk) is discursively and historically produced. Last, I use a synthetic historiographical critique to show that the production of a unitary notion of prostitution in India begins with the new meanings that red-light districts in Indian cities take on in the nineteenth and twentieth centuries. This unitary notion of prostitution is not totalizing, in that it does not encompass literally every instantiation of transactional sex, such as when sexual services are sold or traded very episodically; however, the forms of transactional sex that are apprehended within the purview of the term "prostitution" are reduced over time to the stigmatized exchange of sexual services and money.

Uses of History

Theoretically, *Street Corner Secrets* begins with the idea that the term "prostitution" is a processual concept, a category that emerges at a specific point in history, that consolidates various, previously disparate practices and social forms in a new iteration, not unlike the category of sexuality itself. I understand prostitution and commensurate terms like "sex work" as categorical agglomerations that include shifting sets of practices, spaces, and attitudes toward transactional sex, and that these agglomerations are mutable with respect to (epochal) time and to systemic political and economic changes. This is a departure from an understanding of prostitution as a naturalized, timeless, a priori category that represents a commoditized relationship between sex and money, where commoditization is also naturalized, timeless, and dehistoricized.

The production of prostitution as an agglomerated term for all non-marital transactional sex occurs over the course of the nineteenth century. In India, the spatialization of prostitution, sharply circumscribed within *lal bazaars* (red-light markets/districts) in the late nineteenth and early twentieth centuries, is a critical parameter for complicating an understanding of how "prostitution" was produced as a universal term, one that flattened many disparate forms of transactional sex into one conceptual frame. Designating specific urban areas for the purpose of prostitution during the period of high colonialism served to render transactional sex as a physically unitary object, even while other forms of non-red-light area, non-brothel-based transactional sex continued to be practiced. This spatialization provided a foundation for the iconicity of contemporary brothel-based prostitution in Indian cities, as evidenced by the spectacularization of brothel-based sex work in media, public health,[17] and, now, abolitionist discourses on prostitution.[18]

The idea that prostitution is timeless and clearly demarcated, always knowable, and therefore actionable, continues to produce knowledge on prostitution in India in a number of ways. These include use of the idea that prostitution in India was historically part of an ancient golden age of high culture, enlightenment, and sexual freedom.[19] The theory of a civilizational golden age posits that sex workers once held high social status, only to decline into contemporary abjection and harm, much like Indian civilization writ large. A countervailing rhetorical strategy has been to present prostitution as having always existed as it does today. The rhetorics of the golden age and of contemporary forms of prostitution being timeless are used differentially, but both are underpinned by an idea of women in India as being essentially powerless objects of nationally endemic sexism and patriarchy, particularly if they originate from impoverished rural areas.

Contemporary writings on human trafficking in South Asia evince some of these problematics, including use of an ahistorical perspective on the category of prostitution. For example, a 2003 report published by UNIFEM, the National Human Rights Commission of India, and the Institute of Social Sciences in New Delhi argues for the need to regulate prostitution as trafficking, along with regulating practices associated with other forms of labor under the ambit of trafficking: "Considering the multi-faceted dimensions and the intricate issues involved in trafficking, *as well as the continued existence of several types of trafficking throughout history*, it may appear almost impossible to prevent trafficking" (emphasis added).[20] Speaking of the regulation of prostitution within Indian law, the report again evokes history: "The Goa Children's Act, 2003 is a state legislation which, *for the first time in the legal history of India*, has defined trafficking" (emphasis added).[21] This latter statement is followed by a rationale for amending the Immoral Trafficking Prevention Act such that prostitution would be understood as a form of trafficking that must be legally abolished, by criminalizing sexual commerce further than it does in its current form.[22] (The ITPA currently criminalizes solicitation in public areas, and living off of the earnings of a sex worker, but it does not criminalize the exchange of money and sexual services per se.)[23] If trafficking has been defined "for the first time in India's legal history" in the Goa Children's Act, it is conceived in the report as having existed in its current form for the entirety of India's legal history.

The unbroken historical thread of prostitution as a category of abjection and violence, and a subset of human trafficking, explicitly shapes contemporary work that conceptualizes prostitution as a form of slavery. The rhetoric of slavery[24] in relation to contemporary forms of transactional sex argues that the commodification of human beings continues to exist in this form, where, if this kind of commodification is an antimodern vestige of the past, then so is prostitution. A radical critique of this position would argue that prostitution is not slavery because the forms, structural contexts, and historical meanings of sex work and chattel slavery are distinct; such a critique would show this to be the case, through careful historical work on the daily conditions of chattel slavery and the uses of sexual assault and rape in that context, those of debt bondage, and those of specific forms of contemporary sexual commerce. However, even if we accept that slavery is a meaningful analogy for describing the daily lives of people who sell sexual services, the degree of prevalence of these conditions, and the reasons for their existence (Is sexual commerce the same as slavery? Or, are exploitative and abusive conditions in sexual commerce produced by its criminalization?), would still be in dispute.

In an interview on his book *Sex Trafficking: Inside the Business of Modern Slavery*, Siddharth Kara offers an emblematic example of how contemporary sexual commerce and slavery are equated:

Q: I thought most countries abolished slavery during the Nineteenth Century. Are there still slaves today?

SK: Yes, there are still slaves today, even though slavery is illegal in every country in the world. By my calculation, there were 28.4 million slaves in the world at the end of 2006. These slaves were in three primary categories: 18.1 million debt bondage/bonded labor slaves, 7.6 million forced labor slaves, and 2.7 million trafficked slaves (slaves who were coerced or deceived then transported into a forced labor or debt bondage situation). Of these trafficked slaves, 1.2 million were sex slaves.[25]

According to this logic, slavery should have been completely abolished but has somehow survived, with prostitution/sex slavery being one example of slavery in our times. For Kara, prostitution is contiguous with human bondage, part of an unbroken and intact history of slavery.

One of the most dramatic uses of slavery to characterize prostitution in India, and to characterize India as a whole, is to be found in the book *Sex Trafficking: A Global Perspective* (2010). The authors bring together several dominant tropes of prostitution in Indian history in the following passage: "Specifically, India was built with slave labor. At one time, young girls were dedicated to serving the priests of the temples both in terms of labor and sex. Debt servitude has also existed for centuries in India along with the caste system of servants and royalty. India is a growing destination for sex tourists from Europe and the United States."[26]

Reliance on both the idea of slavery and the paradigm of timelessness has been evident in the uses of the category of *devadasi* in scholarly work on HIV/AIDS in India,[27] and now in work on human trafficking there. The term *devadasi* is probably the best known of all of the various forms of the dedication of girls (from childhood or birth) to a temple and/or deity in South Asia. Terms, status of the dedicated girl, and attendant practices vary by region, and by deity. To be sure, there is also a growing body of feminist scholarship that complicates the discourse of goddess dedication in South Asia by historicizing and critiquing the term with respect to its various slippages and uses.[28] In the literature on HIV/AIDS, human trafficking, and prostitution, however, devadasis often appear as a trace linking ancient forms of goddess and temple dedications of girls to contemporary forms of vulnerability and harm inhabited by lower-caste women living in poverty. This rhetorical journey of the dehistoricized devadasi often begins in ancient India and ends with the idea that lower-caste families use goddess dedication to callously unburden themselves of financially caring for their daughters. A report by Anti-Slavery International, unambiguously entitled *Women in Ritual Slavery: Devadasi, Jogini and Mathamma in Karnataka, Andhra Pradesh, Southern India* (2007), offers an example of allegorical connections between abjection, violence, and goddess dedication in action:

> During 2006, Anti-Slavery International undertook a research project into the practice of ritual sexual slavery or forced religious "marriage." The custom of "marrying" girls to a deity, thereby depriving them of the right to ordinary marriage and assigning them to sexual exploitation by the deity's priests or devotees, existed in many ancient cultures, including in Europe, the Middle East, West Africa and South Asia. In a few settings, this type of ritual slavery or sexual servitude has continued until the present day, including the practice of *Trokosi* in some parts of West Africa; and various forms of Devadasi (from the Sanskrit words *deva* meaning god or goddess and *dasi* meaning servant) among Hindu populations in southern India and Nepal.[29]

The report goes on to discuss devadasis as victims of sexual exploitation, where trading and selling sexual services exemplify such exploitation. The links between abjection and goddess dedication are clear throughout the passage, most resoundingly via the use of quotation marks around the words "marriage" and "marrying" in reference to goddess dedication. The claim of dedicated women and local people that women and girls are married to the goddess is reinterpreted within this frame as a sign of false consciousness that leads to sexual exploitation, unlike "ordinary marriage."[30] That this "existed in many ancient cultures" is qualified as a perpetual "type of ritual slavery or sexual servitude [that] has continued until the present day."[31]

Within the auspices of scholarly work on HIV/AIDS in India, historical narratives have tended to be deployed as introductory framing devices for articles whose substance is wholly related to HIV treatment, surveillance, or prevention in the present. Examples abound, such as this introductory passage of an article from 2007 entitled "Prostitution in India and Its Role in the Spread of HIV Infection":

> Prostitution as a profession has a long history in India. A whole chapter has been devoted to it in Kautilya's Arthashastra written in *circa* 300 BC and Vatsayana's Kama Sutra written between the first and fourth centuries AD. Vedic texts give account [*sic*] of a mythic empire builder, Bharata, and prove that people were acquainted with prostitution through references to "loose women," female "vagabonds" and sexually active unmarried girls. . . . Devadasi (handmaiden of god) system of dedicating unmarried young girls to gods in Hindu temples, which often made them objects of sexual pleasure to temple priests and pilgrims, was an established custom in India by 300 AD. There are reasonably good records of prostitution in large Indian cities during the 18th and the first-half of the 19th centuries of British rule; prostitution was not considered as a degrading profession in that period as it was from the second-half of the 19th century.[32]

The unbroken line that begins in the golden age of 300 BC ends with a claim about the magnitude of the population of sex workers in contemporary urban India, which is reported to include "estimates of 100,000 in Bombay, 100,000 in Calcutta, 40,000 in Delhi, 40,000 in Pune and 13,000 in Nagpur."[33] These data are qualified by the caveat that the numbers "are considered overestimates by some critics and underestimates by others."[34]

The discourse on goddess dedication has been particularly subject to the narrative of a civilizational golden age and subsequent decline, much like the uses of the figure of the courtesan. Although the textual references themselves, perhaps most famously in the *Arthashastra*,[35] mentioned in the earlier quoted passage, use numerous terms to identify women who did transact sexual services in various ways, these are often consolidated in translation as "courtesan," a term that has come to be understood as essentially equivalent to "concubine" and "prostitute." In the ancient texts, however, women who transacted sexual services are represented as possessing widely divergent social statuses and power (some a great deal, others none at all), and as being categorized in accordance with such variations.

Postcolonial feminist critiques of the golden age narrative have elaborated the ways in which the idea of a downward slide in the historical narrative of devadasis and courtesans has a synecdochal relationship with broader historical narratives of women in India.[36] I have drawn from this critique, as well as from a critique of dehistoricized prostitution, in order to illuminate how both of these rhetorics serve to buttress ideas on contemporary prostitution as harmful. Whether prostitution begins as a sign of high status (courtesanship) and piety (devadasis), or whether it has simply existed for all time as it does today, both of these perspectives end up in the same place—the abject commoditization of women's bodies, that they are powerless to interrupt.

Sex Work in the Era of HIV/AIDS

An ahistorical understanding of prostitution, where prostitution is seen to possess a priori characteristics that, like prostitution itself, are rendered as timeless, immutable, and natural, has been necessary in producing prostitution as a medicalized category, where disease is rendered as being an inherent characteristic of prostitution itself. This is evidenced in contemporary discourses on HIV/AIDS in the Global South, which extend historical renderings of prostitution as disease. To be sure, the medicalization of prostitution has its own history, one that, in India, is traced through the passage of the Contagious Diseases Acts (CD Acts). These acts were passed in the United Kingdom in 1864 and in British India in 1868. They legislated the detention and compulsory gynecological examination of women thought to be prostitutes, examinations that were done without regard to the consent of women so regulated, and helped to govern prostitution in select garrison towns, including Bombay.[37] The CD Acts were a response to high rates of venereal disease among British soldiers,[38] as well as serving as a juridical articulation of stigmatized female sexuality and nonprocreative sex. The compulsory gynecological examinations and "lock hospitals"[39] for sex workers mandated in the CD Acts attracted a well-documented outcry from social reformers, including Josephine Butler and the Ladies National Association for the Repeal of the Contagious Diseases Acts,[40] whose campaign ultimately led to their repeal, in 1886 in Great Britain, and in 1888 in India. However, the repeal of the CD Acts did not mean that lock hospitals, or the idea of diseased prostitute bodies requiring control, vanished. Lock hospitals in India lasted beyond the repeal of the CD Acts; combined with the fact that the CD Acts in India were far more coercive than those in Great Britain,[41] the legacy of the CD Acts in India has been a powerful one.

The CD Acts did not invent red-light districts, but their passage contributed to the consolidation of prostitution within red-light districts in India during the late nineteenth century, contributing to a regulatory regime that prioritized the containment of prostitution, while producing it as a unitary entity along the way. Presaging her historical analysis of the racialization of prostitution in Bombay, Ashwini Tambe synthesizes Michel Foucault's critique of the medicalization of sexuality during this era:

> In the new medicalized discourse on sex, previous categories of debauchery and excess came to be cast as perversions and pathologies. Prostitution can be viewed as one such reconfigured category (although Foucault mentions it only in passing). Whereas prostitution was previously cast as immoral behavior, it took on new dimensions as a pathological activity under modern regimes. It became a "crime" against the species on two counts: it involved heterosexual sex not aimed at correct procreation, and it was associated with venereal disease. Venereal disease assumed a particularly terrifying aspect as an affliction that crippled generations, and the prostitute became a symbol of its spread.[42]

Medicalized, pathologized prostitution serves as the key discursive context in which HIV/AIDS was apprehended when it was initially detected in India. The first few cases of HIV infection in India were identified in 1986, in the southern city of Chennai, among male truck drivers (who were read as migrants) and female sex workers (who were read as nonmigrants).[43] The subsequent trajectory of HIV-related interventions in India followed from the identification of people in both of these categories as constituting risk groups.[44] During this period in the United States, public health research and media representations of HIV tended to characterize gay men as inevitably diseased through the language of risk, by extrapolating demographic characteristics of HIV/AIDS from epidemiological studies. The epidemic in sub-Saharan Africa and South Asia, which epidemiologically emerged several years after HIV was first identified in the United States, was contrasted with the American HIV epidemic in public health literatures and the media along the axis of sexuality, through repeated assertions that, unlike the West, HIV in Asia and Africa was occurring primarily among heterosexuals.

While activists in the United States and Europe struggled to de-link gay male sexuality and HIV, the notion of risk groups in Asia and Africa lent itself to the conflation of sexual commerce with disease, especially with respect to female sex workers. At the same time, official knowledge about HIV excluded the possibility of the existence of homosexuality in the Global South, let alone the possibility of HIV transmission between men. In identifying epidemiological trends, a clear attempt was made by most public health and community-based advocates to emphasize the notion of risk behaviors rather than risk groups, both within and outside of the United States. The identitarian understanding of a risk group, however, continued to shape priorities for targeted HIV prevention for entities like the government of India and UNAIDS.

In an article published in 2001, Niranjan Karnik details how the origin of the notion of HIV risk was applied to female sex workers, and how this notion was transposed onto sex workers in Chennai:

> *Nature* . . . reported the first cases of AIDS in India under the heading "Pool of Infected Women." Based on six cases in the city of Madras [Chennai], the response of health and government officials focused on "female prostitutes aged between 20 and 30," and their clients were estimated to be "10 partners a day, mostly truck drivers; they all denied having foreigners among their customers." This reinforcement of existing categories of lower-class groups becomes underscored by the fact that the screening was done on 102 prostitutes. It should come as no surprise to the investigators that the positive women were prostitutes, since that group forms the only group included in the study.[45]

This gap in the foundational studies on HIV in India would have profound consequences for how the epidemic was tracked throughout the country, and for which populations constituted the highest priorities for HIV/AIDS-related funding. Was the focus on sex work as a primary route for HIV transmission based on a comprehensive study to identify the relationship between risk and HIV, or was it derived from an implicit association between female sex workers and venereal disease that had powerful historical precedents? Karnik tracks the production of sex workers as being at high risk for HIV in India through a critique of an early study in Kenya:

Priscilla Alexander (1996, 1987; Cohen and Alexander 1995), of the North American Task Force on Prostitution, has traced the origins of prostitutes becoming labeled as a high-risk group. Briefly, she concludes that the origins of prostitutes as high risk for HIV/AIDS come from a series of studies in which prostitutes in Kenya acted as subjects for Canadian and U.S. researchers to study sexually transmitted diseases (STDs). She finds that these researchers not only violated international norms of scientific research by labeling their subjects as a "core group of high frequency transmitters" but also conflated the transmission of HIV with other factors by not taking into account the effects of parallel studies of the spermicide nonoxynol-9 they conducted on the same group. Despite its viricidal effects, the chemical compound nonoxynol-9 used without condoms has been found to have a drying effect on human mucosal tissues and could have acted to *increase* the incidence of HIV among these prostitutes.[46]

This leads to what Karnik describes as a "tautological standard" of risk, in that sex workers whose risk was potentially increased (by nonoxynol-9) were then categorized as being at risk by virtue of their sex worker-ness. In other words, "The concept of risk is built on the premise that prostitutes are at high risk as compared with the population as a whole that is under study. Regrettably, the whole population is never defined clearly."[47]

This critique of risk must be placed alongside HIV prevalence data, which are collected from hospitals and antenatal clinics, as well as red-light districts. These data showed that, in 2007, Maharashtra had some of the highest numbers of existing and new HIV infections among all Indian states. Based on the National AIDS Control Organization's reporting of HIV prevalence for that year, while sex workers in Maharashtra had high prevalence rates (17.91 percent of all sex workers tested in the state were HIV positive), the highest prevalence rates were found among injecting drug users (24.4 percent of injecting drug users tested).[48] Although injecting drug users (IDUs) have had the highest rates of HIV infection, IDUs are less visible in popular discourses of HIV/AIDS than are sex workers, who, for a time, literally represented the possibility of disease. This discrepancy is explicable in light of the critique of the risk-group regime. To be sure, HIV poses a real risk of infection that, untreated, leads to real morbidity and mortality. This critique details the ways in which the idea of risk as attached to certain bodies supersedes risk assessed epidemiologically. If sex workers are always already at risk, then we know this notion of risk is based not in data but in the idea that women working in prostitution are inherently at risk of contracting a sexually transmissible disease. Furthermore, the risk of HIV is produced ontologically, rather than being understood as an aspect of working conditions that may preclude access to condoms or the power to negotiate their use. This idea of risk as part of the ontology of prostitution informs a foundational assumption that drives discourses that conflate prostitution and violence:

- Once women begin selling sexual services, they irrevocably inhabit the identity and stigma of prostitution, which is imbricated with extreme HIV risk;[49] life histories prior to the beginning of selling sexual services are subsumed in importance, when compared with the irrevocability of prostitution, where prostitution equals HIV risk.

If HIV reifies the moment when people first sell sexual services, then the frame of prostitution-as-violence takes this reification a step further, constructing a conceptual silo around the livelihood histories of women selling sexual services, who are produced as always already powerless. Therefore, a second foundational assumption that produces prostitution-as-violence references livelihood histories, and may be articulated as follows:

- Women who do sex work do no other income-generating activities at the same time; furthermore, women who primarily do sex work to earn money have always done so and have rarely, if ever, engaged in any other income-generating activity.

These assumptions contribute toward the production of prostitution as an exceptional phenomenon in the lives of women who sell sexual services, one that requires exceptional intervention. The brothel is the point at which these assumptions, and the regulatory regime they inspire, converge.

Red-Light Areas, Cities, and Consolidating Prostitution

In addition to prostitution being produced as exceptional with respect to the risk of HIV infection (and disease more generally), prostitution's exceptionalism has also been produced spatially. Indeed, I suggest that the spatialization of prostitution within red-light districts in cities over the course of the nineteenth and early twentieth centuries is fundamental to the production of prostitution as a unitary category with a fixed set of stigmatized characteristics. Understanding the process of this consolidation, including the importance of how prostitution was defined in relation to the discrete spaces of the red-light district, is critical in formulating an analysis in which prostitution is understood to have been produced, to change over time, and to be embedded within a complex matrix of negotiations for economic survival.

A growing body of work on histories of urbanization in South Asia shows that discourses on the regulation of cities pervaded the British Empire during this period, and that discourses of sexuality were integral to the thinking on what cities were, who they were for, and what dangers were thought to be inherent to urban life, particularly for British soldiers and urban colonial elites. The consolidation of a range of transactional sex practices into a singular concept was both part of and produced through discourses of urbanization. Outlining the beginnings of the consolidation of the category of prostitution in India in relation to discursive shifts in the late eighteenth and early nineteenth centuries, historian Erica Wald writes:

> This process, while relatively gradual, was definitively shaped by a medical and military preoccupation with venereal disease levels among the European soldiery from the late eighteenth century through the 1830s. These groupings extended far beyond the very base "prostitute" classification, and did not easily fit with prevailing British models of sex and morality. Although it is unlikely that women in these categories would have considered themselves to be of "ill repute," British observers, having little to compare their roles to within British society, began to group them all under the misleading title of "prostitute" by around 1813.[50]

Interrupting the paradigm of direct, one-way colonial control, Wald is careful in emphasizing that "the changed view of the Indian women, which had emerged by the mid-nineteenth century, was not wholly imported from Europe."[51] She argues that everyday interactions between local Indian women and European men carrying out the tasks of daily imperial governance were critical in prompting the consolidation of prostitution, while showing that this consolidation was part of a larger shift in how Indian women as a whole were apprehended within official colonial discourses. Others interrupt a unidirectional paradigm of influence, "from metropole to colony," in the consolidation of "prostitution" by pointing to the importance of the declining power of the Mughal aristocracy over the course of the eighteenth and nineteenth centuries.

In an article in *Modern Asian Studies*, Sarah Waheed offers a textured reading of the conflation of the courtesan (specifically, the *tawā'if*) and the "fallen woman" in the late nineteenth and early twentieth centuries, embedded within a larger critique that examines the career of the figure of the tawā'if in the Urdu public sphere.[52] Her reading situates this conflation within the vagaries of British rule, as well as shifting understandings of Mughal cultural elitism where, for some, destroying the high status of the courtesan symbolized the destruction of an old order. Kamran Asdar Ali explains the importance of courtesanship in the city of Lucknow: "Courtesans in Lucknow were recognized as the preservers and performers of high culture of the court. Courtesans held respect within the Nawabi[53] court and young men of noble lineage were sent to their salons to learn etiquette, polite manners, and the art of literary appreciation. Yet they also provided sexual services, albeit to specific patrons, and were, therefore, not entirely considered part of the *ashraf*, the Muslim respectable gentry."[54]

Like several other scholars tracing the loss of social status among courtesans in late nineteenth-century India, Waheed marks the consolidation of direct British governance following the anticolonial uprisings of 1857–58 as a turning point in the high social status of tawā'if, when that category was newly apprehended as being equivalent to that of "common prostitute." After 1858, the demise of the tawā'if signaled the demise of the Mughal aristocracy that had sustained her through its patronage.[55] As Waheed notes, "After the revolt of 1857, the term *tawā'if* was conflated by the *ashrāf* and referred to a wide range of 'disreputable' women: courtesans, female entertainers, and prostitutes."[56]

The conflation of the category of tawā'if and that of prostitute was concomitantly conceptual and spatial. The spatialization of the transition to a unitary notion of prostitute as a highly stigmatized category for women has perhaps been written about most extensively with respect to the city of Lucknow. Lucknow served as a seat of Mughal power from the mid-fourteenth century until the nineteenth century and was the artistic capital of the Mughal Empire. In an early, widely cited piece on the courtesans of Lucknow, Veena Oldenburg traced the demise of their status there during the same period discussed by Wald and Waheed.[57] Charu Gupta builds on the body of work on courtesanship in nineteenth-century India, detailing the spatialization of the "common prostitute" in Lucknow. She links the regulation of sex work in Indian cities following 1857 to the establishment of red-light districts several decades later, where anyone transacting sexual services would be expected to live and work, although compliance with this expectation was highly contested:[58]

> The position of the prostitute became increasingly precarious after 1857. . . . A large number of prostitutes operated outside the cantonment areas, were largely unregistered, and posed a threat to British order. A detailed system was therefore worked out for registering prostitutes, inspecting them, and detaining them in hospitals if they contracted venereal disease. For this purpose *lal bazaars* (red light districts, literally meaning "red markets") were established as brothel areas in regimented cantonments, Contagious Diseases Acts passed, and lock hospitals set up. The shifting terrain of old courtesans in post-Mutiny nawabi Lucknow has been linked to British policies and legislation concerned with regulating, sanitizing and cleaning the city. . . . Courtesans now found themselves mostly inhabiting the same public space and bazaar as regular prostitutes. . . . Stripped of all emotional and intellectual functions, they now had the exclusive role of specialists in sexual entertainment.[59]

Legal and health regulations, as well as spatial reorganization within cities, consolidated a unitary notion of prostitution that emerged across and within the spaces of the colony and metropole. In *Codes of Misconduct*, Ashwini Tambe notes that the first reference to prostitution in law was in 1812, in listing "brothels as one of the several sources of disturbance to neighborhood peace. . . . Along with public bars, opium and gambling houses, brothels were to be issued licenses that could be revoked if owners did not maintain order on their premises."[60] By the late nineteenth century, brothels themselves had been harnessed for their regulatory potential.

Framed by global economic transitions that were catalyzed by industrialization,[61] the discursive shift to a more consolidated, unitary notion of prostitution was shaped by the symbolic power of the figure of the courtesan for Mughal imperial power, and by the changing physical and economic landscapes of cities like London and Bombay. Brothels were in existence in cities like Bombay long before the reorganization of colonial power spurred by the 1857 uprisings. However, when colonial power was consolidated, brothels became the spaces into which courtesans and others deemed to be "common prostitutes," within late nineteenth-century discourses of sexuality, were shunted. To be sure, this was a gradual process, one that was facilitated by the ways in which the Contagious Diseases Acts, among other pieces of legislation governing the policing of cities and the regulation of cantonments, were enforced. The CD Acts institutionalized the registration and surveillance of sex workers, while also identifying sex workers with the spaces of the lock hospital and the brothel.

One theme that emerges from this brief historiographical critique is that, over time, sexual commerce in India was made to encompass a geographically fixed and locatable set of practices, contributing to the idea that prostitution always has an address. The iconicity of the brothel in legal and policy work dealing with sexual commerce is the product of this long-standing ideal, where the concept of iconicity references the ways in which the brothel signifies prostitution qua prostitution, where the brothel, in effect, *is* prostitution. In India, the brothel not only is equivalent to prostitution but also has become equivalent to all of the harms with which prostitution has come to be associated. Within prevailing abolitionist frameworks, the brothel now inhabits a space of abject violence, and of social and physical death. By contrast, in the not too distant past, brothels were popularly figured as spaces of licentiousness that evinced ambivalence to the law, but also as places that were generative of income and pleasure. The changing meanings vested in the brothel are evidenced in the slow but steady physical erasure of brothel-based prostitution in India, which I discuss in the final two chapters of the book. Given the continued transitions in the meanings, and locations, of sexual commerce over the course of the twentieth and early twenty-first centuries, as well as the ongoing massive postindustrial economic and political changes that "produce" this historical moment, we may surmise that now, as earlier, the constitutive questions of prostitution are far from being settled.

Migration, Space, and Temporality

The paradigmatic notion of prostitution as a singular activity that exists autonomously, that overshadows the possibility of any other income-generating activities, is concomitant with the premise that prostitution is equivalent to violence, and that the significance of the moment at which one begins selling sexual services surpasses all others. The reification of the point at which a person begins to sell sexual services is relational, de-emphasizing, and even erasing, the importance of every subsequent life event and survival strategy, let alone routine events in everyday life. This moment is produced as that which demands redress and repair for anyone engaged in sexual commerce. Interventions such as brothel raids and rescues are effectively structured around redressing this moment, removing women from brothels often with little regard for how long they may have been working there, or for the conditions and circumstances of their daily lives. This perspective on sexual commerce has numerous consequences, including that of materializing an ahistorical, naturalized understanding of the brothel itself.

The idea that prostitution is experientially exceptional precludes all that comes before and after the moment when someone begins to sell sexual services. This idea renders migration and livelihood histories, and survival strategies, irrelevant to an understanding of sexual commerce. In *Street Corner Secrets*, I use the rubric of migration as a way of countermanding the idea of singular or exceptional prostitution, because an account of the contexts and constraints attached to mobility provides critical information for analyzing and theorizing an individual's current livelihood strategies. However, at a time when the slippages between prostitution, violence, and trafficking are pronounced, what does it mean to use migration to understand the ways in which landless agricultural workers come to Mumbai to work in some combination of construction and/or sex work?[62] In some corners of the discourse on prostitution, the use of migration as an organizing rubric for understanding urban sex work is produced as an assertion that sex workers have made a rational, unencumbered choice to migrate, flush with information and consent. When prostitution is deemed to be equivalent with violence, and conflated with trafficking, the invocation of migration is seen as trafficking's opposite; if being trafficked is having no choice, in the popular imaginary of human trafficking, then migrating is produced as a free, unencumbered choice; migration becomes trafficking's Other. This renders a dichotomized notion of choice and force as the limit of what can be asked about the experience of selling sexual services. Rather than reiterating these dichotomies through the use of migration, *Street Corner Secrets* deploys migration in a literal sense, to indicate movement, and the condition of having moved, from one place to another. This movement is understood to have taken place within a complex matrix of decisions, and of power and powerlessness, in which people aim to negotiate their best option for economic survival. In other words, rather than claiming that migration equals unmediated choice, I use migration to indicate movement where, in the cases that I describe throughout the book, migration and sex work are options for survival in a highly constrained field of possibilities.

Although none of the people with whom I spoke for this study said that they had been trafficked or forced to sell sexual services, noncon-

sensual induction into sex work in India has been well documented, as
has violence from clients, pimps, brothel owners, and the police. By em-
ploying migration to understand how people came to use sexual commerce as an income-generating activity, I do not mean to suggest that
people do not experience violence in the course of selling sexual services.
I do mean to suggest that, rather than excluding violence from its purview, the framework of migration allows for a discussion of the nuances
of consent, force, compulsion, power, and powerlessness, the sum of
which is the granular negotiations that include all of these in the lives of
people who sell sexual services.

In addition to describing the ways in which people move from the
village to the city, I deploy the framework of migration with the understanding that migration serves as an integral component of village life
in India. Villages throughout the country have significant populations
of out-migrants, and the survival of people in villages through remittances from elsewhere, or through wages that were earned elsewhere,
is routine. This potentially undermines the bucolic ideal of the village
as a place to which, for example, rescued sex workers must be "repatri-
ated," or from which people are torn for the profit of others. Villages are
neither this ideal nor its opposite; rather, the places from which people
migrate, and the places they go, are part of a web of material parameters
that landless people from rural areas navigate in order to support themselves, and others.

Rather than simply exchanging terms (e.g., "migration" for "trafficking"), my use of migration in *Street Corner Secrets* is imbricated with the
rubrics of space and time. Unlike the uses of trafficking I have discussed
so far, where trafficking is deployed atemporally and aspatially (because
it is a state of being), I understand migration to indicate a spatiotemporal process, where space accrues meaning through migrant workers' con-
ditional and limited access to spaces within the city and, thus, through
the specific temporalities governing these spaces. The regulation and
demarcation of how migrants may use urban space includes the ways in
which solicitation from nakas and streets is allowed at certain times and
not others, or the ways in which red-light districts have different times
of work, rest, completing household chores, and so forth.

A theoretical matrix that accounts for migration, space, and time
allows for a critique of sexual commerce that is otherwise foreclosed.
Within this matrix we may consider the temporalities of sex work, for
example, where sexual commerce is neither a constant activity nor

one populated by people who have only just arrived in the city, and are therefore figured as particularly vulnerable to violence. The ethnographic work for this project showed that, for landless rural migrants in Mumbai, migration retains acute relevance as a category of analysis for understanding the vagaries of daily life. This counters the notion of migration as a linear journey with a finite moment of completion. Following on this idea, and on scholarship on migration that engages questions of temporality,[63] I understand the migrants in this study as continuing to inhabit the category of migrant, of "being migrated," despite the long tenure of some in the city. Some of the people I discuss in the book had been in Mumbai for twenty years; others had been there just a few months. For yet other groups of workers, Mumbai was part of a circular itinerary, in which people came and went seasonally. And yet, while living conditions were contingent on the duration that people had been in the city, all lived in conditions of precarity with respect to basic municipal services, including access to water, stable housing, and steady income. This precarity informed negotiations for economic survival that included sexual commerce, while also constituting an orientation to the future. Precarity was something to be managed, in part through the use of multiple income-generating strategies in the city. Engaging diverse strategies for generating income may be seen as a sign of futurity itself, of precarity never fully banished but attenuated in the service of attempting to ensure a future for oneself and others, where none may otherwise exist.

To be sure, the future is neither a space nor a place, but futurity marks a type of temporality in the spaces that migrants used for solicitation throughout Mumbai. The ethnographic descriptions and conversations I relate throughout the book were drawn from the times I spent with people while they were waiting to solicit contractors or clients, literally waiting for the future, when paid work would allow for their meeting as many daily financial obligations as possible. In this sense, the spaces of solicitation were spaces of endeavor and expectation, defined in relation to the future, and monetized in the present. That present times had different monetary values was evident in the temporal rhythms of fieldwork. Occasions when it was possible to spend significant periods of time with workers were also times in the day with the least monetary value; they were times of waiting, of inhabiting spaces, when it was still possible, but not likely, to earn some money for the day.

The Production of Space

If, indeed, "(social) space is a (social) product,"[64] then it is not a thing that exists outside of sociality, history, or temporality. It is not purely or even primarily "natural," but, rather, it is assembled, enunciated, negotiated, and reassembled in an ongoing process. A critique of sexual commerce in urban zones that accounts for space in this way necessarily centers the valences of power rendered visible in the course of the production of space(s). Lefèbvre shows that space is a social product, and that it is also a means of production: "The space thus produced also serves as a tool of thought and of action; that in addition to being a means of production it is also a means of control, and hence of domination, of power; yet that, as such, it escapes in part from those who would make use of it. The social and (political) state forces which engendered this space now seek, but fail, to master it completely; the very agency that has forced spatial reality towards a sort of uncontrollable autonomy now strives to run it into the ground, then shackle and enslave it."[65] The idea that space as a means of production also renders it as a means of power would be simple enough to imagine in the context of migrant labor; we need only travel a short distance further to say that migrant spaces, and brothels in particular, are produced through the valences of structural domination, be it the domination of the state, of capital, or of gendered hierarchies.[66] However, Lefèbvre's qualification, that space "escapes in part from those who would make use of it," precludes the possibility of a simple overlay of powerlessness onto spaces where migrants work and live. Space is produced through a process that is never unidirectional, but one that is also shaped by a potentially endless host of agents, events, laws, and practices. The spaces that I discuss throughout the book did not only provide a backdrop for the production of certain subjectivities (migrant worker or sex worker); the people who used these spaces also shaped the discourses about them, or used the prevailing discourses of these spaces in order to extract more from them than was officially sanctioned. Women's use of nakas to solicit clients for sexual services, while maintaining that these spaces were only used to solicit construction work, is a case in point.

In her book *The Promise of Metropolis*, Janaki Nair uses a Lefèbvrian framework to elaborate the ways in which the city of Bangalore comes to be in the twentieth century. She writes, "The space of the city is eventually produced by far more than the plans and drawings of the technocrat, and extends beyond the physical-material to include the mental-imaginative aspects of the production of and claim on city space. One may thus consider the distinctions made by Lefèbvre, between the conceived city, the perceived city and spatial practice, as three possible levels of analysis."[67]

Nair's is a study about the city of Bangalore, writ large, a much broader remit than that of *Street Corner Secrets*. While the task at hand is decidedly narrower, her theorization is useful for drawing out the valences of urban space in this discursive context, as accommodating multiple uses, encodings, and narratives. This multifarious analysis is mobilized by mapping the distinctions, and imbrications, between the "conceived" and "perceived" city, and spatial practices (or, as Nair says later on, between "lived space," "systems of verbal and worked out signs," and "systems of non-verbal symbols and signs").[68]

In *Street Corner Secrets*, the conceived city is the official discourse of what the city's spaces should be used for, and how far local authorities will go to regulate that use. The perceived city is assembled through local discourses on the city's spaces, in stories, rumor, gossip, and secrets, in the ways in which people in each space define it and represent their relationship to it, in media and public health discourses, and in nongovernmental public policy debates. There is no unitary perception or set of discourses on the city's spaces—the perceived city contains many cities, many spaces, and myriad perceptions of the same space. The perceived city and the conceived city are operational in spatial practices, which I use to frame an ethnographic critique of the naka, the street, and Kamathipura.

The complexities of the naka, like those of the street and the brothel, recall Michel Foucault's meditation on space that became the piece "Of Other Spaces."[69] Foucault's schematic framing of space is built around heterotopias, those "certain [sites] that have the curious property of being in relation with all the other sites, but in such a way as to suspect, neutralize, or invent the set of relations that they happen to designate, mirror, or reflect."[70] This concept seems almost designed for an analysis on sex work in Mumbai, not least because the piece ends with a tantalizing gesture toward "brothels and colonies" as "two extreme types of heterotopia."[71] Nakas and brothels, and, of course, streets, are heterotopic because they are places "outside of all places, even though it may be possible to indicate their location in reality."[72] Beyond noting the ways in which the sites I discuss conceptually align with this particular framing, one insight in particular is helpful in conceiving the relationalities that operate between all of the city's nakas and those at which

I spent the most time, between and among streets and brothels, and between and among nakas, brothels, and streets. As Foucault observes, "The present epoch will perhaps be above all the epoch of space. We are in the epoch of simultaneity: we are in the epoch of juxtaposition, the epoch of the near and far, of the side-by-side, of the dispersed. We are at a moment, I believe, when our experience of the world is less that of a long life developing through time than that of a network that connects points and intersects with its own skein."[73] Nakas, brothels, and streets do not simply evoke one another. To enter a naka in Mumbai, such that an open-air market has formal points of entry, is to enter an echo of every other naka in the city, as brothels and streets echo one another as well, within a variable auditory range. The analytic task at hand requires assembling this melee of evocations and resonances in a critical narrative, one in which distinct spaces contribute insights that, in turn, also resonate with "the near and far," while maintaining the irreducibility of each location.

Methodology

The primary modes of inquiry for the study from which this book emerges were those of critical ethnography, archival research, and discourse analysis. Much of the internationalized policy response to sexual commerce that figures prostitution as violence relies on the assertion that there are vast numbers of women and girls who suffer abuse resulting from the commoditization of sex. The ways in which these data are produced draw their own critique, as these numerical assertions often rely on the use of agglomerated figures, guesstimates, and nonstandardized definitional parameters of the phenomena being measured. This numbers game notwithstanding,[74] there is comparatively less qualitative research on sexual commerce, and even less research that considers the everyday life of places where people sell and buy sexual services. My analytic methodology accounts for this by resisting the conflation of prostitution and violence (especially where this conflation results in equating prostitution and trafficking), and by accounting for local parameters for struggles over livelihood, housing, and access to water. This ethnography enters the discursive fray by addressing gaps and elisions in discussions of sex work as a strategy for daily survival, joining a growing flurry of recent and forthcoming ethnographic work on sexual commerce in India and elsewhere in the Global South.[75]

Ethnography itself is a broad methodological category, one now used by researchers in numerous disciplines, and perhaps especially by those pursuing cross-disciplinary and interdisciplinary social science research. My use of ethnography in this project was shaped by the growth of urban anthropology and multisited ethnography and was deployed in the service of showing the nuances and complexities of life-as-lived, where that life includes the use of sexual commerce as a livelihood strategy. Regarding the former, the title of this book, *Street Corner Secrets*, is a methodological homage to William Foote Whyte's *Street Corner Society*,[76] published in 1943, a book in which the street provided a lens and a metric for understanding immigration, class, and racialization in the United States. Whyte's pioneering methodology, and the work that it inspired, provided a template and methodological context for my own engagements with the street in the course of this study.

Multisited ethnography and urban ethnography, with an emphasis on street-based ethnography, were interwoven in the research for this book, affording a comparative perspective on the various modes of sexual commerce in Mumbai, and on the city itself. My core methodology was participant observation, in that I spent time with women while they were soliciting clients for sexual services in each of the three research sites that I discuss in this book. This does not mean that I participated in sexual commerce, nor that I did construction work. Rather, I inhabited the places that people used to generate their incomes, places that were largely out of doors, on the streets and in the lanes that people both traversed and used to solicit paid work. To be sure, every urban street is unique. At the same time, the street is a site that has "the curious property of being in relation with all the other sites."[77] The street is held in this relation throughout the book, as a site that produces sexual commerce with respect to normative ideals of the city, within the auspices of the licit and illicit dyads of the city's publics.

In identifying "the street" as my main locus of research, I am also identifying my residence as having been elsewhere. Having never lived in Mumbai for more than three months prior to the beginning of my longest sustained period of fieldwork of eighteen months, I arrived in Mumbai in early February 2002. My aims for the period of field study exceeded the aims of the study itself. I wanted to know and, somehow, to belong to the city, as did the overlapping circles of people who would eventually become my informants, friends, colleagues, and comrades. This entailed not only engaging with the project's field sites but also engaging with the political discourses circulating within Mumbai at the time. I became part of these discourses as they were being produced in the spaces of the autonomous feminist movement and the then-burgeoning queer and trans movements. The cataclysmic events in the state of Gujarat in late February 2002, when the deaths of 58 people, of whom some were Hindu pilgrims, was used to justify the state-sponsored massacre of some 2,000 Muslims and the displacement of 100,000 more, served to galvanize the discourses of nation and resistance of that moment. My engagement with these discourses offered indelible insights into the ways in which power is manifested and resisted in the age of the NGO sector. These lessons continued to present themselves, as I continued to return to my three primary field sites after the initial eighteen-month research period, during shorter research trips taken each year from 2004 until 2007.

The initial phase of the ethnography included meeting representatives of organizations doing AIDS education, training, and service programs who had any interaction with migrant sex workers. It soon became clear that, while there were many organizations working with sex workers, most of these had the primary agenda of preventing new cases of HIV, as well as conducting surveillance to identify the incidence and prevalence of infection. None were framing their understanding of sex workers as migrants, a framing that would have had necessitated prioritizing consideration of issues like remittances and rural economic contexts. On the other hand, although migrant workers' organizations often included sex workers as constituents, sex work was never named as part of their mandate. Most of these organizations defined male migrants as workers in their constituencies, but not women. Organizations working with construction workers seemed to have a broader definition of a "worker," given that construction labor in India includes both men and women. I had initially met with various NGOs in an attempt to connect with a local group that might already be operating at the intersections of migrancy and sex work, and would perhaps serve as a partner in this research. I had reasoned that partnering with a local organization might both facilitate my own access to local communities of sex workers and provide a vehicle through which the results of the research might be put to use immediately.

After three months of meeting with NGOs throughout the city, it became clear that the lack of organizations working with migrant sex workers required that I take a new approach. I searched instead for organizations that worked discretely either with migrants, or with sex workers. In the end, three different organizations facilitated access to each of the three research sites discussed in the book. These organizations worked, respectively, as advocates and trainers for migrant construction workers, as providers of HIV prevention services to street-based sex workers, and as providers of free health services for sex workers in red-light areas throughout the city, including in Kamathipura. Each organization's field staff provided initial introductions to people at each site, after which I was left to pursue further contact on my own. The idea that the research would somehow be put to immediate use by these organizations faded quickly, replaced by a steep learning curve and a complex and long-term set of engagements with individuals and organizations.

I have chosen to follow many of the conventions of ethnography here, including changing all names of the people with whom I spoke, locating myself within the interactions that I report, refracting my critique through interactions with recurring key informants throughout these chapters and, ultimately, using my field notes and jottings as sources for categories, language, and theoretical insights, rather than mapping a priori frames onto my own archive. At the same time, writing through the critiques of ethnography and representation of the 1980s, and critiques of feminist ethnography in the 1990s, I have aimed to use my interactions with people in the three sites in this study as signposts along a discursive path. In other words, I do not treat these interactions as indicators of an authentic or indigenous set of truths about prostitution, migration, construction work, or urbanization. Rather, they are instantiations of the kind of conversation about prostitution that is possible, given the vast divides of class and privilege that marked some of the many differences between my interlocutors and myself, differences that are emblematic of almost all institutionally supported research on sexual commerce.[78] As Sharad Chari and Vinay Gidwani write, "Critical ethnography has always to engage with its grounds of knowledge: on the one hand, the conditions of possibility that make things intelligible in particular ways; on the other, the material and cultural elements of the rapidly changing social, spatial and natural world which it is hoped to represent."[79]

In foregrounding what can be known about sexual commerce in the particular discursive field(s) in which it is currently being produced, I aim to show that the discourse on sexual commerce is highly varied, overdetermined, and contingent, rather than claiming to reveal definitive truths. With this aim, I have chosen to relay certain conversations without reiterating or reinterpreting them in their entirety, as some ethnographic conventions require. Instead, I present these conversations alongside my critiques; taken together, they constitute the contours of the book's argument.

Conclusion

This chapter lays the foundation for an analysis that aims to reposition violence with respect to sexual commerce, by showing that sexual commerce is properly understood as one of many livelihood strategies that landless migrants engage, where all strategies bear attendant risks that are part of a negotiation for daily survival. Beginning with a criticism of conflating sexual commerce and violence, I have elaborated three key elements of the book's overall argument in this introduction. First, in elaborating the book's orientation with respect to abolitionist and antiabolitionist perspectives on sexual commerce, I have identified the informal sector as a major conceptual frame for analyzing each of the three spaces in Mumbai that constitute the book's focus. Second, I have offered a historiographical critique of prostitution in India, showing that histories of sexual commerce have relied on the idea of prostitution as a stable, ahistorical, ontological concept, one that is produced in relation to the idea of prostitution as occurring in urban spaces that are visibly demarcated for this purpose. Third, I have discussed the ways in which the book uses migration, space, and temporality to understand how sexual commerce is constituted in the city, and how the different spaces where sexual commerce is solicited are produced in relation to one another. These analytic frames underpin the idea that migrants who sell sexual services do so by actively negotiating urban spaces that are variably coded with respect to sexuality and legality, while accounting for structural power and the politics of poverty in everyday life. Ultimately, the book calls the totalizing idea of the knowability of urban sexual commerce into question, arguing that local epistemologies of sex work are produced through speech and silence, through elisions and secrets as much as they are produced through verbal claims. Understanding sexual commerce as an assemblage of highly mediated forms of knowledge, where survival is often predicated on secrets and silences, disrupts unitary notions of prostitution while allowing for an analysis that accounts for the ways in which prostitution is produced spatially, especially when it is something other than discursively legible and brothel-based.

CHAPTER 1

DAY WAGE LABOR AND MIGRATION

Making Ends Meet

This chapter offers a frame for migration, as well as navigations of Mumbai's infrastructure and municipal services, that are shared by day wage laborers, street-based sex workers, and brothel-based sex workers. The focus on migration to Mumbai and daily survival aims to countermand the idea that sex workers and day wage laborers are worlds apart. Along with *naka*-based construction workers, women who worked as street- and brothel-based sex workers had also migrated from rural areas, where they did not own land, were often from Scheduled Castes (SCs) and Scheduled Tribes (STs) and had worked as agricultural laborers.[1] Many street- and brothel-based sex workers had solicited paid work from a naka in the past. Some street-based sex workers also sought work from a naka from time to time or returned to their villages during seasons when agricultural labor was especially in demand. Constrained access to paid work and potable water in villages where workers originated was of particular importance, as both of these are in sharp decline for landless workers. In the city, they ran a gauntlet of negotiations for access to water, housing, and paid work, which each person negotiated in his or her own fashion.

What Makes a Naka a Naka (and Not a Stroll or a Brothel)?

Nakas are often the first and last resort for securing paid work among groups of migrated people in Mumbai, and serve as a barometer for the city's ability to absorb ostensibly "unskilled" workers into its paid workforce. People who seek paid work at nakas are landless lower-caste and tribal migrants from rural areas seeking a sustainable livelihood, something that, according to naka-based workers, was lacking in their villages. The migrated workers who used the particular naka I discuss later in this chapter came to Mumbai in the 1980s and 1990s. Most were from rural areas in Maharashtra, Andhra Pradesh, and Karnataka. Virtually all were from Scheduled Castes and Scheduled Tribes. In their villages, they had worked as agricultural wage laborers who did not own the land they farmed. They came to the city with the expectation of earning a better livelihood, of having access to an infrastructure (the public distribution system, schools, roads, water that did not have to be purchased exclusively from the "[water] tanker mafia") that did not exist to the same degree, or at all, in their villages, and to leave behind at least some aspects of a system of caste-based violence that also entailed severe economic privations.[2]

The narrative of the city as a place where money can be made has animated the formation of the city historically and serves as a foundational trope of contemporary Mumbai. Money and the city were intertwined for naka-based workers; everyone had had networks of friends or family in the city before they arrived, and everyone who worked at the naka sent remittances to their relatives in the village. During the 1980s and 1990s, the narrative of access to the possibility of a more stable sustainable livelihood in the city was contextualized by the boom in the building construction industry, which began near the end of the decline in textile manufacturing. By the mid-1990s, Mumbai's industrial sector had stalled, leaving even fewer formal sector jobs than there had been previously. Rural migrants who had hoped to work in the textile mills, as well as those who had been laid off, responded by trying to secure livelihoods through the far more insecure day wage labor market. Day wage labor markets form at nakas throughout Mumbai and constitute the most visible aspect of the city's vast informal economic sectors.[3] This phenomenon has been more pronounced during employment crises in the city, as during the textile mill closures in the 1980s and early 1990s.[4] Many workers at the naka I discuss here recalled this as a time when nakas throughout the city were "flooded" with textile workers who had lost their jobs and were trying to make ends meet.

The term *naka* itself has a variety of vernacular meanings and is formally defined as (1) a crossroads, corner, or intersection where traffic and people meet and are regulated; (2) a toll station, a place to collect or pay money for passage or service; or (3) a police station.[5] The term *naka* in this research context adheres most closely to the first meaning, but its sense extends beyond that of a space that is simply a crossroads or a street corner and follows the usage by the workers who utilized nakas to solicit day wage labor contracts. A naka in this sense should be understood to mean a day wage labor market that forms for a specific period of time in an outdoor space where people solicit contracts for providing manual labor, primarily for construction work. This kind of naka occurs at a crossroads, street corner, sidewalk or pavement, intersection, or commuter railway station and, beyond its use in soliciting day wage labor contracts, has several elements that distinguish it from other kinds of nakas in the city. First, this kind of naka includes people who use the space to sell their labor episodically, meaning that labor is sold in discrete units by day; this paid work is not salaried or necessarily ongoing, although some jobs continue for a number of days. Most workers defined the naka as a place of last resort, a stopgap strategy that had to be used because other, more stable forms of generating income were not available. Second, the space of the naka is not designated through any official zoning or legislated use of public space, as police stations, toll plazas, shops, and produce markets might be. Rather, the labor market naka is formed through spoken or informally purchased agreements with local police and/or shopkeepers. Third, unlike other kinds of nakas, which are bounded spatially, labor market nakas are bounded by space and by time. The space of a street corner or intersection functions as a labor market naka only as long as workers and contractors use the space to buy and sell services; this usage is sanctioned for a fixed period each day, often by local shopkeepers who share the same pavements and storefronts as the workers. Shopkeepers and local police enforce this time-bound use of the space. The presence of the naka is signaled by the presence of workers in numbers. It is visually marked by throngs of people standing around or sitting on their haunches, smoking, chatting, or drinking tea, waiting for someone to offer work for the day. Fourth, these kinds of nakas are populated by both men and women, often soliciting work while sitting in gendered clusters, with groups of men sitting

FIG. 1.1. Waiting for work in sight of Sri Sri Ravi Shankar

together in greater numbers than women. Inflected by the stigma of prostitution that marks almost any economically impoverished woman standing on the street seeking paid work, the gendered geographies of these urban spaces become implicitly characterized by notions of solicitation, work, and sexuality.

Introducing the Naka

There are dozens of day wage laborers' nakas throughout the city. Estimates of the total number of people who sought paid work from a naka in Mumbai over the course of this project varied, with one political party estimating that some 300,000 people sat on a naka in the city each morning. The sizes of nakas varied, with some, located in farther-flung suburbs, attracting 50 to 100 people each morning, while those closer to the commercial districts of the city, where the demand for labor was higher, claimed 500 people or more. The demand for naka-based workers was largely formed by the need for labor required for small-scale repair jobs by private contractors and for infrastructural development and maintenance projects by the municipality. This kind of work was secured through verbal agreements, negotiated in the absence of enforceable regulations of pay and working hours.

According to construction workers, NGOs, and union organizers, the market rate for day wage labor available from Mumbai's nakas should be in the range of 100 rupees per day for women and 125 to 150 rupees for men. The provisional reason for the discrepancy between men's and women's pay scales, given by workers and contractors alike, is that "skilled" labor earns higher wages than "unskilled" labor. Over the course of fieldwork it became clear that, as far as everyone was concerned, a woman could never be a skilled worker, no matter how long she had been working in the construction industry. Instead, women were almost always identified with what they termed *begari kam*, which they explained as "helpers'" work, although it is also translated as "unpaid labor," and which includes doing much of the heavy lifting and transport of materials on a construction site. The difference between men's and women's wages and the differential classification of women as unskilled by virtue of their gender indicate a problem of gender-based labor discrimination that is consistent with national trends, in which women's participation in the workforce is obscured and minimized by definitions of work that do not include unpaid and self-employed workers,[6] and where the level of participation by women workers in informal sectors has been underestimated.

Because of the sheer numbers of unemployed and underemployed people who use a naka to find work each day, the competition for jobs is a tangible, everyday reality. Workers are necessarily hired on the basis of a number of factors beyond their skills, physical strength, or willingness to undertake a job. Transactions at the naka also require prior knowledge of the kind of work that is available there, which contractors will be willing and able to hire workers for the day, rapport and personal relationships with contractors and other workers, and a certain level of access to mobility, both to reach the naka and, in some instances, to reach any day job that it may yield. Only a fraction of the workers who use nakas are ultimately hired, leaving open the question of what other livelihood strategies are undertaken when soliciting construction work from the naka fails. The constant refrain at each naka was one of needing paid work and of there not seeming to be enough work to meet everyone's economic needs.

At the Naka with Meeta

The naka that formed one of the primary ethnographic sites for this project was in a suburb located near the northern edge of the city, a twenty-minute autorickshaw ride from a major commuter railway station. Most of the workers at this naka were from Marathwada, an arid region in eastern Maharashtra. In their villages, most had been agricultural laborers,[7] working in sugarcane fields and cane-processing facilities. According to watershed development activists in Marathwada, the state's intensification of sugar production over the 1990s depleted water tables, while reducing the possibility for landless laborers to continue to survive through a combination of day wage work and subsistence farming, as every inch of arable, irrigated land came to be used for growing and processing sugarcane by agribusinesses and small-scale farmers alike. The story of migration from Marathwada is one of infrastructural underdevelopment, a crisis of water and watershed management, and years of out-migration of poor laborers from SC and ST communities. This story continued in Mumbai, as even workers who had lived in Mumbai for more than twenty years struggled to maintain access to stable housing and potable water.

I went to the naka with Meeta, a woman whom I had met through a local autonomous women's organization.[8] She had taken me to Marathwada and introduced me to watershed development activists who worked in the same area where most of the workers at this naka had originated. We spoke with two workers whom I knew well, Kanna and Giri, as well as another older woman sitting near them; by the time these introductions were done, a number of women had gathered around us. One woman began her story, saying to Meeta, "Tai,[9] we're not getting any work." Each woman said she had worked twice, at most, in the past six weeks. It was almost eleven in the morning, and the women, having sat there from seven or eight, had decided that no work was to be had for the day. They rose and invited us to have tea across the street instead, at a tea stall that had been a store for household items the week before. Meeta, three women from the naka, a man who said he worked as a plasterer (*mistry*), and I walked over together.

"Look," I said, "they'll open a tea shop in every little nook on this street." I used the slang *galla* for "shop," a loose term that did not imply a refined place of business.

The bearded proprietor, looking slightly offended at my description of his new shop, asked, "Where do you see a galla?"

The mistry had also not had work in a long time but insisted on handing over a ten-rupee note for everyone's tea. When I protested, he said, "This [Meeta] is our guest. She is our *gaon-wallah* [from the same village]." I understood this to mean the subject was closed, his having asserted his right to host his fellow villager and, subsequently, the rest of us, by paying for our order.

The most expensive tea shop on the street was boarded up for renovations. It was the most expensive because, unlike the other tea stalls, which consisted of only one or two benches under a makeshift roof, a kerosene stove, and a rack for tea glasses, this shop was in a building, with an entrance, booths with tables and veneered benches, and snacks. It looked as though the owners were adding another floor to this shop, and the older woman with us complained that no one from the naka was hired for that job. The women started speculating about who was hired instead, saying it was probably the waiters who worked there full-time. One of them commented, "It's either the waiters, or they hired someone else they knew well."

As we sat longer, the owner of the newer tea stall launched into a diatribe about the existence of this naka in the neighborhood and, according to him, the negative effect the naka had had on the economic well-being of the area. "You think we can all spend 8,000 rupees to build a toilet for all of you every few feet down the street?"

The older woman retorted, "We've been sitting at this naka since before you were born! I knew your mother!" She started describing in detail his mother and where his family used to live in the neighborhood. In an aside to me, Giri added, "Our old age has happened in this place."

The proprietor relented, saying, "Well, why didn't you say you knew my mother in the first place?," and then began making our tea.

Like nakas throughout the city, this one, located in a city suburb, offered a unique point of intersection for people of many different castes and economic classes who passed through the space. At the same time, social interactions were segregated by caste and class such that, despite having grown up down the road from the naka, the lower-middle-class tea stall owner had never spoken with the women at the naka until my presence had provided a reason for them to have tea there. This was also evidenced by local market responses around each naka in the city, which included the proliferation of inexpensive tea and snack stalls that sprouted nearby to cater specifically to laborers waiting for jobs for the day. For workers, circulating between the naka and cups of tea at a local stall was a way to pass the hours while they waited for paid work. At one of the city's largest nakas in South Mumbai, close to the city's main red-light districts and to some of its most expensive commercial areas, the naka had stimulated other market responses as well. The surrounding sari and clothing shops there also carried replacement circular saw blades for the bulky marble cutters that many of the women at that naka rented out to male workers on a daily basis. Some stores incorporated the building equipment in their window displays, placing saris and blouse pieces artfully alongside the saw blades and other replacement parts for construction tools.

Public Space and Abjection

The naka is a publicly accessible, visible space that is produced in part through socially shared parameters that distinguish solicitation from the naka as something other than solicitation from a brothel or the street. At the same time, the naka has rules about entry that conform to Foucault's fifth principle of heterotopic spaces. As Foucault observes, "Heterotopias always presuppose a system of opening and closing that both isolates them and makes them penetrable. In general, the heterotopic site is not freely accessible like a public place. Either the entry is compulsory, as in the case of entering a barracks or a prison, or else the individual has to submit to rites and purifications. To get in one must have a certain permission and make certain gestures."[10]

Although the examples Foucault gives for this kind of heterotopia are saunas and hammams, this descriptive parameter applies to a host of other kinds of spaces as well, including the one at hand. The operative word here is "permission." Without permission, an outsider who approaches a naka is ignored, approached by the police, or immediately surrounded by a throng of workers asking for an explanation for the outsider's presence, hoping that it is for the purpose of recruiting workers. Each of these possibilities precludes nonworkers spending time and interacting with people there and constitutes a closed point of entry. Solicitation is subject to these rules of approach and entry as well. Solicitation from the naka is, by definition, for the sole purpose of securing paid construction work, to the exclusion of all other forms of income generation, including sex work. Ostensibly, this means that, were the naka to be seen as a place for soliciting sex work, this would close its points of access immediately. This reading of the naka emphasizes the tropes and politics of respectability and honor in the production of this space, while also highlighting the extremely regulated, highly mediated enterprise of poor migrants accessing public space in Mumbai in the course of soliciting paid work.

Defining solicitation from the naka in relation to legitimated paid work ensures access to the space for workers who use it to generate income. Outside of the spaces of the nakas, laborers are rarely visible en masse in the more moneyed, middle- and upper-class areas of the city, namely, in South Mumbai and in areas on the city's western edge, facing the Arabian Sea. Laborers are much more likely to find paid work in these areas than they are in the relatively more economically depressed eastern and northern areas of the city, where many naka-based workers live. In addition to the times that they are present in numbers at the nakas, poor migrants are visible in the more affluent areas of Mumbai during the annual festival commemorating the birth anniversary of Dr. B. R. Ambedkar, whom I discuss more at length later in this chapter, or during the occasional protest marches and rallies called by trade unions or new left organizations, such as the National Alliance of People's Movements or the Ghar Banao Ghar Bachao Andolan (Build and Save Homes Movement), to protest the displacement of poor people from urban slums or from rural villages.

With the intensification of high-end real estate development, and lifting government regulations on individuals and corporations accumulating and converting large swaths of urban land for commercial purposes, the class divisions that have historically structured the economic geographies of Mumbai have intensified. Poverty has been visibly embodied in the public spaces of Bombay/Mumbai throughout the city's history, as slums scattered in almost every neighborhood, or as people living on pavements, begging for money and food on the street. However, the municipality's removals of street hawkers, increasing since the late 1990s, and its demolitions of slums throughout the city (both in keeping with similar moves in Pune, New Delhi, Bangalore, and Ahmedabad) are signs of the intensification of the city's economic segregation. The deepening spatialization of social divisions between people of different economic classes and castes has meant that, for the city's middle and upper classes, poverty recedes from the banalities of daily life. Differences in class and caste markers that were seen, heard, touched, or felt all over the city are increasingly sequestered to the context of employment being given or received. This membrane-like division, maintained from every direction, finds a certain respite at the naka and in red-light areas, where unemployed and economically marginalized social groups become a sizable pool of workers to be accessed by contractors needing a job to be done or by clients seeking to pay for a service.

In a sense, "public" is both an apt and a dissonant nomination for the naka. The term "public" necessarily carries the baggage of the "public sphere," a term that describes a space for rational discourse, theorized and historicized most famously by Jürgen Habermas. For Habermas, the public sphere was the space by which freedom would be achieved, through unity in a discourse that would render material differences between people irrelevant, even if only momentarily. Contemporary, vernacular uses of "public" are laden with this baggage, the baggage of who or what constitutes "the public." Habermas's treatise on the public sphere continues to serve as a touchstone for theorizing public space in the city, where public space is a space inhabited by *the* public. For Hannah Arendt, on the other hand, "The term 'public' signifies two closely inter-related but not altogether identical phenomena: It means, first, that everything that appears in public can be seen and heard by everybody and has the widest possible publicity. . . . Second, the term 'public' signifies the world itself, in so far as it is common to all of us and distinguished from our privately owned place in it."[11] Arendt's reference to the rela-tionality of public and private, and the genealogy and critiques of this dichotomy in liberal philosophy and feminist theory notwithstanding,[12] here I evoke a sense of the naka as public in the first, sensorial mode that Arendt describes, a place that is seen, felt, heard, while also drawing on the problematics of "the public" as a group of people.

Habermas argued that the public sphere's brief career in eighteenth-century Europe embodied the values of inclusivity, a disregard for social status, and a space for crafting common concerns within a broad social body. These concerns could be brought to bear on the state, having been churned through the machinations of public discourse. Feminist and queer critiques of Habermas's formulation notwithstanding,[13] this ideal of the public sphere has formed the basis of structuring an ideal for the "world-class" cosmopolitan Indian city. However,

> [World-class city] is a slogan, as if devised by a marketing agency, to sell the latest fashions in cosmetic urbanism—an alluring ready-to-wear one-size vision that promises to fit all. It is a visual narra-tive made up of bits and pieces taken from distant places that exist primarily as urban fantasies in our imaginations. Now Dubai, now Singapore, sometimes with a hint of the Manhattan skyline. . . . At the end of the day, all that remains behind is physical space designed to accommodate an idea of the public that has been stripped of its fundamental property: inclusiveness.[14]

In this passage, urban studies scholars Matias Echanove and Rahul Sri-vastava draw on a critique of inclusion that shadows the notion of the city as a place that produces secular public space almost from the be-ginning of the idea that the city belongs to residents who are defined as *the* public. Architectural historian Will Glover reminds us that the con-cept of public accrued meaning over a long historical period, and that "Widespread use of the term 'public' to describe a type of urban space,

one accessible to all of a town's residents and owned by none in particular, probably began in medieval Northern Europe."[15] Situating this usage
of the term "public" in South Asia, Glover connects the European discourse of public-ness with that of South Asian urban centers during the
period of high colonialism: "The association of urban public space with
municipal order and the protection of propertied interests has been du-
rable. It remains meaningful in Western cities today. It has also become
meaningful beyond its original context, in areas colonized by European
powers. . . . Public space became a new object of discourse in Indian cities during the late nineteenth century." Before this period, "Indian cities had physical spaces that were shared in common, accessible to all or
most of the city's residents, and in many ways physically identical to
what the colonial government would later call 'public' urban space. . . .
By naming certain urban properties and spaces 'public'" and drafting and
enforcing rules governing activities there, "the colonial government created both a concept and a coporeal substance—'public space'—that had
no prior history in the Indian city."[16] The late nineteenth century was
the era of transition from Company Raj, the rule of the East India Company, to that of direct administrative governance by the British state.[17]
The first task of direct governance was to craft a legal system for colonial
India through the codification of India's criminal code (which defined
acts deemed to cause "public" moral harm, and was to be applied equally
to everyone) and Personal Law (which mainly pertained to family law,
governing marriage, divorce, inheritance, adoption, and the like, and established different legal codes and arbiters respective to distinct religious
communities and customs). While Personal Law did govern sexuality, in-
sofar as it governed aspects of daily life such as marriage and the rights
that devolve from marriage, it governed sexuality that was seen to reside
"in private." Prostitution (and sodomy) did not fall within the ambit of
Personal Law, defined instead as being within the purview of public harm.
Prostitution was addressed in the Indian Penal Code through several laws
that, together, outlawed all aspects of buying and selling people for the
purpose of prostitution.[18] Legally categorizing prostitution as falling
within the purview of "the public" and establishing red-light districts in
urban areas helped to define the lack of prostitution as a parameter of
municipal order, while linking the regulation of sexuality with the notion of public morality. Apprehended as being shared by all members of
the public, where parameters of membership are clearly marked by caste
and classed comportment, this morality takes on a spatial valence when
read through laws and policies that regulate nakas and red-light districts.

Public morality is therefore, in this context, morality *in public*, in the open spaces of the city, and most importantly, on the commercial street.

The inauguration of the red-light district simultaneously marked the inauguration of the rest of the city as a "non-red-light district," as a set of spaces where sex work was explicitly, or ostensibly, absent.[19] As in other cities, red-light districts in Bombay would come to be defined as areas where sex work could be solicited, but also where rules of public morality and public decency could be bent, such that soliciting clients for prostitution would be regulated, rather than banned, as it had been in other city spaces. Given the interpolation of public space within the late nineteenth-century juridical discourse of the British Raj, public space was itself produced as a category that outlined where public decency and public morality could appropriately reside. This suggests that public space was produced in Indian cities through narrowing definitions of prostitution, as well as the discursive emergence of the family as a kind of privatized fortress of nationalist morality.[20] Together, these produced an idea of legitimated commerce, defined against illegal and illicit forms of trade that, over time, have come to include a number of forms of transactional sex.

In the contemporary moment, the production of public space in Mumbai continues to be iterated through a complex set of exclusions from that space. These include prohibitions of solicitation for the purpose of sexual commerce from space defined as public, and the aggressive regulation of poor migrants and slum dwellers in public spaces. Consequently, large gatherings of poor migrants in the city's commercial areas are only truly permitted in certain contexts, most notably in the time-bound formation of the naka.

The inclusions and exclusions that are constitutive of public space may be analyzed through abjection and its charged relationship to public space and migration. On migration and abjection, anthropologist Nicholas De Genova writes,

> As the objects of an unprecedented and escalating climate of securitization, migrants have been increasingly depicted over the last several years as possessing a dubious agency that is unsavoury at best, if not plainly dangerous. . . . Abjection is an especially apt interpretive frame through which to appreciate the complexities of the migrant condition, precisely because migrants are always-already within the space of the state and can never really be entirely expelled. Julia Kristeva has memorably depicted the specificity of the concept of the abject

as "something rejected from which one does not part." Although she depicts it in terms of "the jettisoned object," the abject is not in fact a properly external object. It becomes difficult to fully differentiate the self from the abject which it seeks to expunge.[21]

This notion of the abject as something that is "jettisoned" but not a properly external object elucidates the texture of migrant exclusions from public space in Mumbai, while also problematizing the notion of abjection, which is often applied to sex workers. Although naka-based workers are abject-ed in that they occupy a lower socioeconomic status, live in unstable housing, if they live in "housing" at all, and exemplify the precarity of poor migrants' existence in urban space, De Genova's evocation of Kristeva's abject-as-self, rather than the abject-as-object, offers a way to understand naka-based workers' strangely liminal subjectivation. Migrants who seek work from nakas exist both within and outside of a sense of belonging to the city. Within, because migrants provide a set of services that are crucial for the city's daily functioning, while generating transactions that attempt to ensure a measure of economic survival. Outside, because migrants' exclusion from and regulation within the public spaces of the city are essential to maintaining the status quo of differential access to public spaces, especially for those numerous migrants who do not successfully procure paid work on any given day, and remain in waiting until the appointed hour, when the naka (temporarily) disintegrates.

Migrating from Marathwada

The naka that constitutes the main point of interest and analysis for this chapter was located in a northern suburb of Mumbai that abuts Sanjay Gandhi National Park, also known as Borivali National Park. With a stable population of roughly 150 to 200 workers who used the space each day, this naka was much smaller than the larger nakas in South Mumbai, some of which saw 800 to 1,000 people daily. This naka was also distinct from those nakas because it was located a short distance from where most naka-based workers lived, in slums and low-income housing of various forms nearby. People walked down the hill from their homes to this naka, as opposed to paying to take a local commuter train for an hour or more. The area near the naka was at an edge of the city that is rapidly expanding into the national park, where some of the largest tracts of slum developments in Mumbai were located and, therefore, where, some of the fiercest battles over landownership and use were being waged.

The naka itself and the slums where naka-based workers lived were steeped in the discourse of the anticaste movement. Most workers at the naka identified themselves as belonging to the Nav Buddho community, where Nav Buddho literally means "New Buddhist," a moniker adopted by Mahar communities that, following Dr. B. R. Ambedkar, chose to opt out of the Hindu caste system by converting, as he advocated, to Buddhism. Ambedkar was born into the "untouchable" Mahar caste and was both a founder of the dalit rights movement and author of the Indian constitution.[22] People at the naka who were members of his caste referred to themselves as "Nav Buddho" belonging to the "Ambedkar jāt" (Ambedkar caste). They invoked the histories of Dr. Ambedkar and the dalit rights movement frequently. The slums where they lived on the nearby hillsides of the national park were organized into neighborhoods with names like Ambedkar Nagar, Kranti (Independence) Nagar, and Bhim Nagar, where Bhim is a reference to Dr. Ambedkar, whose full name was Bhimrao Ramji Ambedkar.

Workers claimed that the numbers of people at the naka varied between the "off-season," which started at the beginning of the monsoon in July until mid-October, and the "season," which began after the rains had stopped, when temperatures were milder. During the season, some 2,000 people were said to use this naka to find work, although the space could scarcely accommodate the 150 who used it regularly throughout the year. Most of the people at this naka were from Maharashtra and spoke Marathi; some were from northern Karnataka and Andhra Pradesh. The Marathi-speaking people at the naka were from near Aurangabad, to the northeast of Mumbai, or from Latur, to the southeast, near Andhra Pradesh. Like many nakas, this one included seasonal, or "circular," migrants, as well as a larger population of workers who had migrated to Mumbai years before and lived in the city year-round. The latter group's living conditions were, in general, more stable than those of the former.

The naka formed around a street corner in front of a Gujarati-run pharmacy from roughly eight in the morning until noon each day. Most nakas in the city form at seven or eight and continue until eleven or noon, by which time the majority of the workers have been hired or have given up finding work for the day. Workers both adhered to and seemed to adhere to these timings, running the risk of losing the privilege of using the naka, or even of jeopardizing the very existence of the naka, if they were seen to flout the time-bound parameters of the space. Overtly, the labor market naka was produced less as a place of lingering than as a place where transactions occurred, where people were meant to arrive, wait, find work, and leave for a construction site, a makeshift factory, or a replacement shift for a municipal service worker. If people did not find work, they were expected to leave after the timing of the naka had ended. However, the naka was also a space with a relatively flexible sense of sociality, where interactions occurred that might not otherwise have taken place, such as between men and women who were not defined as kin, or between local upper-caste shopkeepers and dalit workers.

The apparent chaos of traffic, pedestrians, shops, and naka workers rested on an underlying spatial order where social groups, demarcated by caste and gender, sat together in distinct clusters. This social geography of the naka was organized less by formal design than it was by virtue of people sitting with their own kin groups and friends, these groupings reflecting the vagaries of caste and gender. The spatial order was nominally hierarchical, such that more and less dominant groups vied for position at the naka based on the "best" (most comfortable, most visible) places to sit during a potentially long wait for a contractor with a job to offer. Members of the same social group advocated for one another's right to sit or stand in a given space, to the exclusion of members of other groups at the naka. For example, Maharashtrian Nav Buddho women sat on planks that had been placed over the large wastewater drainage ditch at the street corner itself, around which the naka congregated. These women were thus able to take advantage of one of the most visible and comfortable positions in the space, where it was possible to both be seen by contractors and sit on level ground, rather than squat or stand, for the full three to four hours that one might spend waiting for that day's job. Farther along the street stood the Maharashtrian Nav Buddho men, who outnumbered the women at the naka by roughly three to one. Throngs of men also vied for positions to rest and were generally standing and waiting for contractors alongside a group of Marathi-speaking Banjara tribal women. In the middle of the men's space sat a group of Lambadi tribal women from northern Karnataka.

For all of the women there, the space of the naka served a number of functions. It was an important potential income-generating space, to be sure, but it was also a space for socializing and exchanging information. According to the household rules by which most women lived, the most appropriate space for a woman was the home or else public spaces that facilitated the smooth operation of the home, such as the fruit and vegetable market. For women workers, sanctioned social spaces were limited to their own homes, the naka, and nearby homes of friends in the area, unless they were hired for a day job, with restrictions being considerably stricter for young and unmarried women.

Unlike other nakas, which solely consisted of an outdoor area on the street, this particular one also had the auxiliary space of an office, which constituted a unique extension of the naka's spaces, and was used as both an organizing space and a social space for Maharashtrian Nav Buddho men. The office was a long, narrow room, with the entrance looking out onto the main road; it was one of a row of offices and storefronts, sandwiched between the pharmacy at the intersection where the naka formed to its left and a small warehouse that stored building materials to its right. The office had been established in May 2002 by the NGO that had attempted to organize workers at this and several other nakas, the same NGO that had initially introduced me to workers here. Eventually, several men informed me that this was the second office that the NGO had rented for its work at the naka, work that included organizing skills training in the building trades and providing advocacy for workers on issues of pay and obtaining steady employment. The first office had been nearby as well, on the second floor of a building in the neighborhood, with its entrance far from the main road. According to men who used the office, because the previous space had not been visible from the main road, women had been barred from going there, "because people would think that they [the women] are doing some 'bad work' [bura kam] there. Now that the office is on the street and everyone can see, they [the women from the naka] can come and go from there freely." This was the first instance, but not the last, in which the phrase bura kam was used in relation to the practice and perception of selling sexual services. The concept of bura kam was applicable to all women, as women embodied either the presence of bura kam or the lack of it. Bura kam was produced relationally through the bodies and practices of women at the naka; the discourse of prostitution—often understood implicitly, usually unstated—served as a means for producing ideas about how women did or did not inhabit the naka. While heavily coded, "bad work" referenced women in private spaces, engaging in morally suspect, paid or traded sexual services that could only take place away from the visible spaces of the public street. The repeated use of the phrase "bad work" in relation to women was linked with both actual and perceived practices of sex work and sex trade negotiated from the spaces of the naka's labor mar-

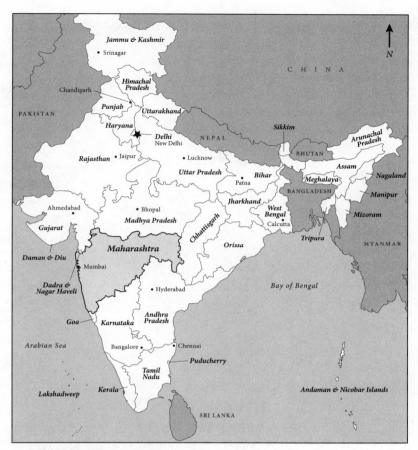

MAP 1. Map of India. © Daniel Dalet, d-maps.com

ket, through statements such as, "Those contractors, sometimes they take young girls and *go* with them, have them do some bura kam." These discourses were structured by the valences of power attached to migration, housing, and water, as well as the ways in which caste was produced through a discourse of gender that is linked with the political economy of debt and dowry. To explore each of these components in some detail, we must first address the conditions for naka-based workers' migration to Mumbai.

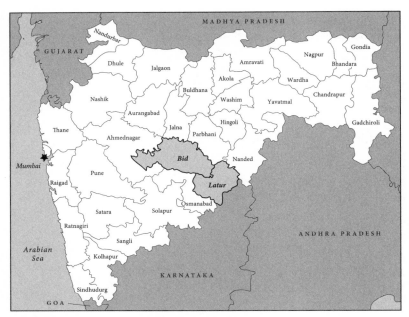

MAP 2. Map of Maharashtra. © Daniel Dalet, d-maps.com

In the Village

Marathwada is composed of the eight districts that extend east from the center of the state of Maharashtra, two of which border the states of Andhra Pradesh and Karnataka to the south. As of the 2001 census, Marathwada (comprising the districts of Aurangabad, Nanded, Latur, Jalna, Beed, Parbhani, Osmanabad, and Hingoli) "account[s] for 16.84% of the state's population and is home to nearly 30% of the state's Below Poverty Line families. Its per capita gross domestic product [GDP] is Rs. 10,373—a good 40 per cent below the state's per capita GDP of Rs. 17,029—and contributes just 8% of the state's industrial output. Its literacy rate is the lowest in the state (51.23%, Census 2001). All eight districts figure in the list of the 100 poorest districts in the country."[23]

The Maharashtra State Development Report, which calculates the Human Development Index (HDI) as a combined indicator for mortality, literacy, and income, calculated Marathwada's HDI for 2002 as 0.58, a little more than half of Mumbai's HDI of 1.00 (on a scale of 0 to 1). Of the 35 districts in the state, Latur ranked 25th for its literacy rates, Bid 30th, and Osmanabad 28th.[24] In addition to having low development indicators with respect to education, health, and income, Marathwada is also known for having a high population (roughly one-fifth of all Marathwada's residents) of people belonging to SC and ST communities.[25] Historically, Marathwada has been an understudied region of Maharashtra.[26] Until 1956, it was administrated as part of the Hyderabad region, first as a Marathi-speaking region within the Hyderabad Princely State and, later, from 1948 until 1956, as part of Hyderabad State. In 1956, the Marathi-speaking districts of Hyderabad State, which constitute Marathwada, became part of Bombay State. In 1960, Marathwada became part of the new linguistic state of Maharashtra. This complex history has had a number of consequences for the region, including, perhaps, its marked lack of infrastructural development, thanks to having been a far-flung area in Hyderabad Princely State and, later, the newest addition to Maharashtra in post-Independence India. The political economy of development in Marathwada is linked with historical problematics of dacoity and a tenuous relationship with formal structures of governance.[27]

In the contemporary context, Marathwada seems to garner press and policy attention primarily during disasters, such as the severe drought in 1972, upper-caste attacks against dalit and tribal people in 1978,[28] and the 1993 earthquake, which measured 6.3 on the Richter scale and led to the out-migration of thousands, including a number of families who were trying to find work from the naka I discuss in this chapter.[29] At the same time, Marathwada has been the site of a network of grassroots activists and organizations attempting to address watershed development and other infrastructural problems, including the lack of roads, largely in the face of what some activists described as a lack of political will to invest in any infrastructural development in the region. Despite these efforts, Marathwada remains an economically impoverished, largely rural, and drought-prone region. It was described by watershed development activists working there as a "supplier" of cheap migrant labor to the state's agricultural industries, particularly to the sugar and cotton plantations in the western regions of the state, and to urban labor markets. The region remains relatively remote, due in part to the lack of a rail line. While Latur and Bid are accessible by road, a bus journey from Mumbai to Latur takes approximately twelve hours, although Aurangabad, the largest town in the region, is only 400 kilometers (about 250 miles) from Mumbai and should be accessible in less than half that time. *Frontline Magazine* took the release of the first Maharashtra State Development Report in 2002 as an opportunity to report on the resource disparities between Marathwada and the rest of the state:

The uneven contribution to the State Domestic Product (SDP) from the [Marathwada] districts is further indicative of the role that unequal resource distribution plays. Parts of the State other than Mumbai and the western districts do not have a reliable infrastructure. . . . The western belt of the State is so rich because of sugarcane. One-third of the sugar produced in India comes from western Maharashtra. About 60 per cent of the irrigated water is given to this region when the total area under sugarcane cultivation is a mere 4 per cent. In a state which is drought-prone, is it wise to grow a crop like sugarcane which is so water-intensive? And is it fair to the rest of the State?" asks Seetha Prabhu [area head of the UNDP's Human Development Resource Center].[30]

Meeta, who was herself from Osmanabad, one of the larger towns in Marathwada, articulated these insights succinctly. "It's totally political," she said. "There are some very powerful politicians in Maharashtra state who are from there. It's not as if they don't know what is going on there, or as if they couldn't do something for the people there." She added, "The sugarcane plantations, which a lot of those guys own, are in the western part of the state, like near Solapur and Sangli, and they need cheap labor, which comes from the eastern part of the state, from Marathwada."

Water

The difficulty in obtaining water in Marathwada was a constant theme in naka-based workers' renditions of their stories of migration to Mumbai. Water was "both a real crisis and a trope through which communities imagine themselves as marked by the lack of development."[31] In other words, "There's nothing there, absolutely nothing," said Mukhu, a naka-based worker who had migrated from Marathwada some twenty years earlier. He began to talk of the earthquake there in 1993 and the drought before that, in 1972. "There was no food anywhere," he said. "People ate grass. They ate what the animals eat. The land there is so dry."

"Why is it so dry?" I asked.

"No water in the sky, so there is no water in the ground. No water in the ground, so there is no water in the sky. And when it does rain, the rain just slips off the ground, it doesn't soak in. So why would we ever go back there to live?"

Meeta brought the discussion of water closer to home, as she spoke about one of Mumbai's newer suburbs, built in an area known as Navi

Mumbai (New Mumbai), where new districts for sex work are emerging, partially as a result of the confluence of real estate interests and anti-trafficking interventions in the South Mumbai red-light areas, which are discussed further in chapter 4. Navi Mumbai is being built to the south and east of Mumbai proper, on land that is semiarid. In Navi Mumbai, Meeta was able to purchase her own flat for 4 *lakh* rupees (US$9,090) in 2001,[32] a much more affordable rate than what was available even one or two neighborhoods closer to the main commercial areas of the city (a similar-size flat in South Mumbai at the time could easily have cost several hundred thousand dollars). Although she lives in a middle-income apartment complex with running water in each flat, water flows through the taps for only one designated hour each day. During that hour, the household's water for twenty-four hours must be stored. Of her hometown in Marathwada, she said, "It's gotten as bad as water coming [through the tap] once in five days, or once in eight days. Imagine having to store enough water for eight days! There are water tankers, of course, for people with money." She said that they had dug yet another borewell on the farm in Marathwada that her family has owned for three generations. They expected it to run dry in three or four months.

Watershed development activists working in Marathwada argued that the cycle of drought, water scarcity, and poor irrigation is not a problem of inadequate rainfall but, rather, of the consolidation of control over natural resources and the rising amount of land used for cash-cropping water-intensive plants. In this regard, one activist commented, "Look, the average difference in rainfall in this area in the last one hundred years is only 10 percent reduced, so the difference [in the availability of water] isn't that there is less rain. The difference is that before, there weren't electric pumps or cash crops—people are using more water, and water is more expensive than it was before—before, there were fewer people using less water." He went on to describe how local political parties regularly promise water access as part of their election campaigns. When asked why more wasn't done to resolve the water issue, Meeta gave another example from Navi Mumbai, where she said the head of a private water tanker business is now actively attempting to block the municipality's water services. Private water tankers, in urban high-rises and on rural farms alike, have blossomed into a formidable profit-making venture.[33]

Workers in the City

Upon arrival in the city, naka-based workers from Marathwada were dependent upon existing networks of friends and relatives in Mumbai for assistance with housing, money, and employment. Despite their relatively long tenure in the city, most of the people at this naka retained the material contexts of newer migrants to Mumbai, having extremely tentative access to secure housing, potable water, and steady employment. The liminality that these migrants experience with respect to their access to municipal services has been documented among groups of poor and working-class migrants in other cities, often through the rubric of citizenship. Even though much of the work on the problematics of citizenship and migration has been done in relation to transnational migrants and globalization, ideas of citizenship and precarity are helpful as overarching rubrics for mobilizing a critique of naka-based workers' daily lives, while providing a link to similarly positioned migrants in other cities and regions.[34]

Shubha, who had come to Mumbai from Bid some fifteen years earlier, and who sought work from the naka, often alluded to the problems of urban citizenship and precarity in discussing the contours of her days and weeks. After I had visited the naka almost daily for a month, during which time Shubha became my primary contact there, she invited me to her home for lunch. Whereas most of the other people who came to the naka lived in the slums on the nearby hillsides of Sanjay Gandhi National Park, Shubha, her son, daughter, daughter-in-law, and infant grandson lived in a solid-built room located in a *basti* (settlement, low-income neighborhood) at the edge of the national park.[35] Slum demolitions were a constant theme in my conversations at the naka, as was the case in my conversations with Shubha as well.

The basti was a ten-minute walk up the road from the naka. An old arching blue metal sign formed a kind of doorless gate that led to the basti's outer compound. The sign had been standing long enough to be rusted in places; written in Hindi, it phonetically spelled out the words "Republican Party of India," representing one of several national parties that seek to represent dalit voters, and to consolidate a dalit vote bank. Of the Republican Party of India, feminist scholar Sharmila Rege writes, the "Republican Party of India (1956) and the Dalit Panthers (1974) were the major political formations which attempted in varying ways and with varying successes to construct political groupings of dalits, irrespective of internal jati distinctions."[36] Rege goes on to critique the idea that the

FIG. 1.2. Posing for a portrait, in front of the pharmacy at the naka

anticaste movement actually succeeded in rendering "internal jāti distinctions" less relevant to political groupings of dalits, a critique that becomes critical for understanding how the mutual imbrications of caste and gender produce women as sex workers or non–sex workers at the naka.

A row of taps stood just behind the Republican Party of India sign in the outer compound. Shubha said that water flowed for two hours each afternoon. As I left her house later that day, I saw rows of women standing in a queue near the taps with buckets and other plastic and metal containers; they were walking back and forth between their rooms and the taps in order to fill up the giant, sixty-gallon plastic containers sitting outside each doorway that would store the family's washing and drinking water for twenty-four hours.

Everyday Life in the Basti

Shubha's home was a partitioned room in a row of other solid-built, attached one-room homes. The room in which Shubha's family lived was divided into front and back areas by a sheet of corrugated aluminum serving as a wall that they had erected themselves. Another sheet of corrugated aluminum covered the wooden beams overhead. The front section of the room contained a narrow, iron-framed double bed, with space for storage underneath. Shelving in the corner above the bed held the twelve-inch rented TV, which was generally tuned to cricket matches or Hindi films. One wall held painted framed pictures of Dr. Ambedkar posed with his wife, and of Shirdi Sai Baba, a popular saint, who, like Kabir, has been held up as an exemplar of combining elements of Hinduism and Islam in his teachings and philosophy. Like Kabir, Shirdi Sai Baba is apprehended as an "ecumenical" religious figure. These two images—Ambedkar and Shirdi Sai Baba—were commonly displayed together in the homes of dalit naka-based workers.

The floor next to the bed was the main living space in the house; it was used for watching television, working, and preparing food that was then cooked in the adjoining space behind the partition. The second space, which was less than half the size of the first, contained a short counter on which stood the single-ring kerosene stove. This stove was in better condition than most, though it had been well used. This smaller area also held a single bed on an iron frame, which Shubha said was for her recently married son and daughter-in-law. One corner of the room served as a bathing and washing area, with a built-in drain and a concrete barrier between it and the counter space.

Shubha asked her son to go out and buy mutton in honor of me, her guest. She prepared a spicy mutton curry and also made wheat chapatis, which I later realized were especially for me. Shubha herself ate tougher millet (*jawar*) rotis and urged me to eat the soft chapatis, marking the difference in our economic class by explaining that the millet would be "too difficult" for me to digest. Wheat was more expensive than millet and was kept aside for guests and special occasions, as was rice. Shubha's lunch consisted mostly of the thin gravy of the curry, in which she soaked pieces of the thick rotis, as she placed pieces of cooked meat and fat on my plate throughout the meal. After lunch, she pulled out her son's wedding album. As we flipped through the pages, she explained that she had changed her daughter-in-law's first name when they were married. The daughter-in-law's name had been Sheila. "But," Shubha said, "that's my daughter's name, and they couldn't live in the same house and be called the same name, could they?" In the photos, her son and daughter-in-law were both wearing nail polish and henna (*mehendi*) on their hands, as well as generous layers of a "fairness cream."[37] In the photos from the end of the wedding day, the cream had formed a white sheen over the deep browns of their faces.

Over the course of the afternoon, the conversation eventually turned to the subject of the NGO that was trying to advocate for people at the naka. Many people there remembered when this organization had previously tried to establish a trade union among the workers, an effort that had been aborted in favor of the organization continuing to do social work and advocacy. Shubha complained that the organization was focusing its efforts on the men at the naka, thereby leaving out the female-headed households. "Those people [the men], they get work as a right. They just got 2 lakh rupees worth of work from the BMC [Brihan-Mumbai Municipal Corporation, the municipality]. We have four adults and a baby living here. Between marriages, deaths, and the fifty rupees a day it takes to run the household, how can we live?"

For workers who went to the naka, the question of how to survive was framed by a host of issues that ranged from access to education to access to paid work, but the question of survival seemed to hover perpetually around having regular access to potable water. As my visits to Shubha's home became more regular, it became clearer that access to drinking water was critical for any decisions that naka workers would make about negotiating their own basic needs. On a later visit to Shubha's home, I walked under the Republican Party of India sign to find a group of women looking angrily at the dry taps in the outer compound. I had had to walk on the edge of the road leading up to the basti because the municipality had commenced retarring it. This had prompted complaints from residents in the area such as "We haven't gotten water [from the communal taps] for three days and here they are paving the road!" Later, when Shubha and I were sitting in her front room, a woman came in abruptly and said, "Let's go." She was assembling the women in the basti for a protest march on the municipality's offices, in order to have the water restored. Shubha declined and instead sat enumerating her monthly budget aloud for me. Her water bill alone was fifty to sixty rupees per month. Had she or her daughter-in-law been away when the taps were flowing, they would also have had to pay someone, most likely a neighbor, to fill their household vessels for them. This service could cost as much as twenty rupees per day, or six hundred rupees per month.

As I returned to the local train station from Shubha's home later that day, the shared autorickshaw I had decided to take hit a traffic jam. Taking advantage of the jam, a woman darted out between the stalled rows of vehicles to a metal plate in the middle of the road. The plate covered the opening to an underground wastewater pipe, the same pipe that eventually opened into the ditch over which women sat at the naka. The woman lifted the plate and dipped the plastic jug she carried into the hole to fill it with the water. As the autorickshaw rounded another corner, I saw her carefully carry the jug back to a doorway by the side of the road.

Slum Demolitions

Unlike Shubha's house, where the communal tap was located a few steps away from her doorway, residents of the hutments in the hillside slums nearby walked a kilometer or more for water. Some paid one rupee per vessel to the "tap woman," who controlled access to this tap by sitting in front of it; failure to pay her would result in violence and a permanent lack of access to this water source. The free tap was a much farther walk. The temple located amid the hutments was closer than either of these and had its own tap. Children from SC and ST families in the area made a game of approaching and, sometimes, drinking out of the tap and running away, playing with injunctions against dalits entering the temple and using the same water source as upper-caste people.

The hillside slums were in Sanjay Gandhi National Park, named for the deceased younger son of the late prime minister Indira Gandhi. The park usually made the news only when a panther emerged from its dwindling forested habitat to attack a young child in the settlements, or when slum demolitions were being conducted there by the municipality. The settlements technically fell within the borders of the park, sitting on areas that were designated as protected forestlands. However, the hills that housed the settlements were barren of trees or any vegetation, save the short scrub grass and packed earth trails defined by years of pedestrian traffic.

Over the years, this area has become a flash point in struggles over land use and economic development in Mumbai. These struggles have involved a host of actors, including the municipality, building developers, environmentalists, housing rights advocates, political parties, and slum dwellers. Due to its location, the park contains land that could be profitably developed and expanded to accommodate the rapidly growing suburbs. Because the settlements are located within the confines of the park, its inhabitants are officially marked by the state, via the municipality, as "encroachers" on the land. This official designation has meant that residents of the settlements have been subject to repeated evictions and demolitions of their homes although, legally, the municipality is barred from displacing people who can prove that their residency in the area precedes January 1, 1995. The area has been at the center of highly publicized legal disputes over whether and how the thousands of encroachers should be displaced from the park.

By 2002, calls to evict slum dwellers from Sanjay Gandhi National Park had been undertaken under the rubrics of both environmentalism and real estate development. By 2010, slum demolitions in the city of Mumbai, like Delhi and many other major metropolitan centers, had become the hallmark of a strategy that has prioritized the capitalization of land by national and multinational investors. The concomitant ejection of slums and street hawkers from older neighborhoods and streets throughout Mumbai is part of an effort to move Mumbai toward "world-class city" status, while erasing poor and working-class people from the evolving notion of public space within the city.[38]

Narrating Slum Demolitions

Suma's *jopdi* (hut) had been destroyed by the forestry department three years prior to our acquaintance at the naka. I was told that, before the demolitions, the settlements on the hillsides had consisted of solid built houses, latrines, a school, and a health clinic. All of this had been wiped out. The residents came back and rebuilt, but, she said, the homes and other facilities were probably destroyed in the first place because the structures were beginning to seem too permanent. Giri recounted in detail the slum demolitions of 1999, when her locality of Jamrushi Nagar had been flattened.

"How did they do it?" I asked. "Did they use machines?"

"Arey!" she said, "They brought bull dozers!" (*Dozer le-ke-aya-tha!*) First, she said, the police had come and emptied everyone's belongings from their homes. When she and her son came to collect their belongings, a police officer was standing there. He grabbed her by the front of her blouse. She recounted this by grabbing the front of my shirt forcefully and, looking into my eyes, reenacting the police officer's taunts about why her things were so important that she had to retrieve them. "Is it your inheritance from your father or something?" he had asked. Anti-demolition activists had had to obtain a court order just to make sure that evictees could leave with their possessions. When Giri had gone to a second policeman for help, he addressed her with the respectful Marathi suffix of "aunt," using the term that means "mother's sister." "What is it, Aunt?" (*Kai ahe, Maushi?*) She had looked at him incredulously, as she looked at me in the midst of her dramatic retelling, and said "*Maushi*???"

as if she couldn't believe she was being addressed by this police officer in such an intimate tone, after having been assaulted by one of his own. Upon hearing her complaint, the second policeman promised that Bal Thackeray himself, then head of the Hindu nationalist Shiv Sena Party, would come and see what had happened. In her reenactment, Giri's response to the police officer rang, "Bal Thackeray!," followed by a string of expletives. Many people, including Suma and Giri, believed that Thackeray himself had ordered these demolitions. Giri related her opinion of Thackeray in no uncertain terms several times more during the telling of this story.

The demolitions that occurred in the late 1990s in Sanjay Gandhi National Park were the first significant wave of slum clearances in Mumbai, and were an effect of neoliberal economic reforms.[39] These focused on reducing tariffs, encouraging foreign direct investment (FDI), and reducing or eliminating state-sponsored economic protections for poor and middle-class people. One example of these protections, the Urban Land Ceiling Act, passed in 1978, was designed to limit the amount of urban land acquired by a single entity; the limit was intended to regulate the pace and amount of building construction in India's cities. In a sign of the ongoing pursuit of neoliberal reform in economic policy, the Urban Land Ceiling Act was repealed in Maharashtra in 2007 as a precondition of receiving funds under the Jawaharlal Nehru Urban Renewal Mission (JNURM),[40] a scheme that was partially funded by the Asian Development Bank (ADB).[41] The ADB could therefore set this as a precondition for releasing funds. The repeal of the Urban Land Ceiling Act in Maharashtra, alongside mounting pressure on slum dwellers to vacate their homes, also reveals the ways in which ideas of urban citizenship are changing. As Aditya Nigam writes, "The transformation to bourgeois private property involves, and has always involved, a violent decimation of all forms of common property and even non-capitalist private property."[42]

In addition to defining whom the city serves, the demolitions have also helped to define a strategy for evictions, one that relies on a high degree of day-to-day regulation in slum areas. Police regularly patrolled the entrances and exits of the areas of the park that led to the settlements. I was able to enter these areas only during the day, and only when accompanied by a local resident; I never entered or exited unobserved by a policeman. The slum demolition policy also instantiated a legal hierarchy among slum dwellers by restricting access to the hillside slum areas for newer migrants, through the January 1, 1995, cutoff date for making claims for resettlement and compensation for evicted slum dwellers. The legal battle over Sanjay Gandhi National Park was, then, less a battle about returning the area to some pristine, uninhabited state; rather, it was about which individuals, institutions, or government bodies could obtain development rights to the land.

Beyond the legal battles about landownership and use, these slum clearances are tied to rural economic policies and growing numbers of rural agricultural workers migrating to cities as life becomes harsher and more economically untenable in their villages. In some instances, this migration is the result of outright displacement, such as that associated with the Bargi Dam project. The Bargi Dam was the first dam built on the Narmada River; its reservoir, filled in 1990, submerged a wide swath of land that was dotted with villages and forests, leading to the mass migration of displaced tribal villagers to the slums of Jabalpur in the state of Madhya Pradesh. This was one of a cascade of instances in which villages were displaced due to the damming of the Narmada River.[43] The more common impetus for urban migration throughout India, however, conforms to the narrative of the villagers from Marathwada who, finding it increasingly difficult to maintain access to basic necessities, including water, found it necessary to migrate to the city, where sustainable access to both work and water might be more readily available. For slum dwellers in the city, the looming threat of state violence, particularly with respect to housing, maintained a degree of economic instability and, more fundamentally, of political marginality among these communities. A woman at one of the larger central Mumbai nakas characterized her life in the city by simply saying, "No rain, no work." (*Barisht nahi, kam nahi.*) She spoke of the jopdi demolitions and demands of bribes from other slum dwellers in her area to prevent further demolitions from taking place. "What does the government do about this?" I asked, referring to the underground economy of protection money that the threat of demolition seemed to inspire. She replied sharply, "They beat up poor people. What else would they do?" (*Garib lok ko marte hai. Aur kya?*) Wondering if these conditions would inspire a return to the village, I asked whether she preferred the village to the city. "I prefer anywhere I can fill my stomach," she replied.

In chapter 4, I discuss the politics of slum demolitions as they impact red-light districts. People living in red-light districts in Goa, New Delhi, and Mumbai, all classifiable as slums and low-income housing, have become subject to pressure to vacate that is similar to what people have been experiencing in urban slums throughout India. In some cases, as in Goa, this has led to sex workers going "underground," soliciting clients from the street and via networks that operate as invisibly as possible. In other cases, as in Mumbai, red-light districts are coming under increasing pressure to vacate, and sex workers are either going underground or shifting to other, more far-flung areas of the city, like New Mumbai. However, unlike slum demolitions in Sanjay Gandhi National Park, the demolitions and displacements occurring in red-light districts are also imbricated within the rhetoric of stopping prostitution and, because prostitution and trafficking are increasingly conflated, of preventing human trafficking.

Money: Remittances, Dowry, and the Village in the City

Activists in Marathwada working on issues of water management and sustainable farming had many theories for why migration from these areas had increased so significantly over the years. In addition to the theory that survival in rural areas was simply less tenable than it once had been, another idea was also emerging. "Before, there was migration for economic need, like for food; now, there is migration for weddings, for dowry, for paying off land, for new house construction." This analysis is consistent with the problems associated with the expansion of cash-dependent economies in rural areas, places where survival had previously been negotiated through a combination of bartering and subsistence farming, as well as earning money. For example, whereas wealth exchanged between families to consolidate marriage alliances might previously have been negotiated in terms of goods as well as cash, cash now holds primacy. Although paying a dowry in the amount of 1 or 2 lakh (100,000 to 200,000) rupees for the marriage of one child is the equivalent of three to five years of earnings as a day wage laborer in the city, this was not an uncommon expectation among naka-based workers. Because it is impossible to raise 100,000 or 200,000 rupees through day wage construction work, people often resort to taking loans from local moneylenders, who may also function as contractors for day wage labor. With interest rates as high as 100 percent or even 500 percent—sometimes calculated as compounded interest per month, sometimes as a simple percentage, and sometimes calculated arbitrarily—it is likely that such loans may never be fully repaid.

Discussions about economic survival with naka workers inevitably returned to questions of how unmarried family members would be "married off," and how much this would cost. The vast sums required to find suitable marriage partners for workers' children constituted a system of monetary exchange that was incorporated within a system of

exchange that included sending remittances back to family and other social networks in the village. Most naka workers, like street- and brothel-
based sex workers, sent money and/or gifts back to their villages regularly through friends and acquaintances traveling there. The amounts of
these cash remittances ranged widely, from 2,000 to 30,000 rupees per
year. The considerably larger sums associated with dowry carried the
added symbolism of kin alliances forged and maintained between members of the same caste and class, and contributed to the web of connections between these villages and the settlements in Mumbai. Giri's story
illustrated this point in some detail. Originally from Gulbarga district, in
northern Karnataka, she was widowed with five children, two of whom
were unmarried. Her working life was structured to facilitate their day-
to-day economic survival and to finance the impending marriage costs
for her unmarried son.

Giri

Giri had told me that we could go back to her house to do the interview
I had requested. I was waiting at the appointed time in the naka office
with Mukhu and Chotubhai when she arrived to report that she had to
go collect some money that was owed to her for a job. "You should come
back tomorrow," she said. "We can speak then." Giri's errand prompted
the men in the office to comment on there being no work, less work, and
underpaid work, and how often they had to spend time chasing contractors for the money they were owed for work they had already done. Giri's
situation was slightly better than that of most women who were heads
of their own households, ever since her son Manas began earning 2,500
rupees a month working in a biscuit factory. Giri's main goal now was to
save up for his marriage, for which they "had to pay 1 lakh." This would
be accomplished through Giri's own day wage labor and Manas's salary.

"One lakh for what?" I asked.

"For the girl's family," she replied.

"But isn't it usually the girl's family who has to pay the groom's?" I
asked, thinking of the dowry system with which I was more familiar,
known as *dahej*, in which the bride's family sends her to her marital
home with what is ostensibly considered to be her own personal wealth.
I had not encountered *mul* before this, the system in which the groom's
family pays a set amount to the bride's natal family.[44]

"No, not for us" she replied, referring to her tribal community in Karnataka. "For us, the boy has to pay."

I asked Shubha later if Giri belonged to the Banjara tribal community, to which, through a mouthful of mutton and *jawar ki roti*, she replied "No" and said the name of another tribe in the region where Giri's home village was located. Although Shubha had never been to Gulbarga, people from districts all over western and central India had lived here side by side for so long that it seemed as if people at the naka were as expert on the places they had never visited as they were about their own places of origin. The stories of drought, caste-based discrimination, and lack of infrastructure in the Maharashtrian and Karnatic districts were extremely congruent, if not, at times, identical. The fact that almost anyone at the naka could reliably identify the caste and subcaste to which individual workers belonged was a powerful lesson in the identifiably differentiated nature of rural communities in the city. This was emphasized by the gloss that these communities applied to middle- and upper-class and upper-caste people, understanding anyone who was not poor as Brahmin, wealthy, and somehow powerful, myself included.

Giri said, "God-willing, Manas's salary will add up to a lakh by next year, and he can marry. He's seventeen. The girl has already been chosen. She's ten."

When I asked Giri about the age at which girls can marry, she said cautiously, "Now, seventeen-, eighteen-year-old girls they want." I wondered if I had misunderstood her, or if Manas would be marrying an eleven-year-old girl in a year. She changed the subject, saying, "Now, I'm thinking about leaving Mumbai."

"Why?"

"No work."

"And you get work in the village?" I asked.

"Yes, ten, twelve rupees a day you get."

"Cutting sugarcane?" I asked.

"Yes, yes, sugarcane."

I asked if her son spoke Kannada, thinking of his young bride from the village who probably spoke the mixture of Kannada and Marathi that was typical of border districts like Gulbarga. She smiled and replied that he did not, preferring Mumbai-style Marathi instead. One of her four married daughters sat in the doorway of the hut, nursing her newborn daughter. One daughter lived in the village with her marital family; the other three were in Mumbai with Giri. The daughter who was living here was with her own two young daughters and the newborn. She had come to her mother's house to give birth; seeing that the child was a girl, her husband had decided not to return for her. Where he was now, no one could say.

Giri's family situation showed that the need to procure money for dowry was a structuring context for day wage labor, and that marriages are often sought by parents for their children when they are still minors. At the same time, Giri's married daughters' presence in her home showed that paying or receiving dowry has little relationship with the afterlife of weddings, which, in the case of Giri's daughter, included staying in her maternal home because she had failed to produce a son. Some workers linked these kinds of phenomena with the changing terrain of money and marriage. Kanna and her family lived next door to Giri in the hillside settlement, in an area known as Bhim Nagar. Kanna had two sons, both of whom were working for a small business that specialized in selling naturally forming granite crystals; I was told that these came in purple, white, and black. Kanna said that each son earned 2,000 rupees per month cleaning and weighing each piece of granite. If she and her husband could also earn during the month, she reasoned, then her sons' income could go toward saving for their marriage costs, which would be substantial, even though they would be receiving dahej from the brides' families. As it was, they were primarily living on their sons' steady, salaried earnings, as she and her husband's earnings were reliant on the amount of work they could secure from the naka. "How much can you make in day wage work [hazari] anyway?" she said. She went on in rapid Marathi describing how much things cost today, and what expenses lay ahead. "It cost my parents 15 rupees to marry me off. Now, what could you do for 15 rupees? You would spend 15,000, at least. My parents' wedding cost 5 rupees. My father paid 3 rupees and my mother 2. How could you even think of doing that now?"

These exchanges illustrate some of the ways in which questions of capital and monetization are embedded within local discourses on dowry, questions that are elaborated to some degree in the classical literature on dowry. This literature includes certain touchstones, such as the politics underlying legal prohibition of dowry in 1961, as well as discourses and instantiations of dowry-related violence. My focus here is less on these aspects of dowry than it is on how the problematic of dowry specifically impacts naka-based workers' financial negotiations, which include maintaining caste-based affiliations through endogamous marriage rules, which in turn have their own sets of histories and politics. Of the monetization of dowry, M. N. Srinivas wrote, "modern dowry is entirely the product of the forces let loose by British rule such as mon-

etization, education and the introduction of the 'organized sector.' The
attempt to equate the huge sums of cash, jewellery, clothing, furniture
and gadgetry demanded of the bride's kin by the groom's to *dakshina*
is only an attempt to legitimize a modern monstrosity by linking it up
with an ancient and respected custom, a common enough and hoary
Indian device. What is surprising is that the imposture has had so much
success."[45]

Srinivas's invocation of the history of dakshina was fascinating,
but his appeal to the idea that an "ancient and respected custom" had
been sullied by British rule smacks of the idea that there was an indigenous, untainted culture within India, and that the exchange of bride-
wealth under the sign of dakshina, a Vedic concept for a donation or
payment to a guru or priest, was an instantiation of this unmediated
indigeneity. Uma Chakravarti, V. Geetha, Veena Oldenburg, Srimati
Basu, Bina Agarwal, and Sharmila Rege have all shaped the body of feminist work on dowry that, much like earlier work by Lata Mani on *sati*,
disputes this notion of culture as born of an ancient and good tradition
that was suddenly and detrimentally disrupted by British rule.[46] At the
same time, Srinivas's linkage of changes in dowry systems with the introduction of a difference between informal and formal economic sectors is helpful in mapping the profound impact that dowry has on the
daily lives of rural, landless agricultural workers, including those who
migrate to Mumbai seeking work in one of a range of informal sectors.
This impact is most severe with respect to cost; the profound escala-
tion of dowry- and marriage-related costs among naka-based workers
may be understood from three directions. First, from the direction that
Srinivas suggests, dowry is linked with the increased demand for goods
like electronics, vehicles, and furniture that can only be purchased with
cash. Second, dowry is linked with rising costs of living, including food
and transportation, as well as rising costs of medicine and health care.
These are all costs that a dowry, which amounts to an unparalleled and
rare windfall, is expected to attenuate. Third, dowry is embedded within
an economic matrix for landless migrants in the city that includes daily
negotiations of economic precarity. Injuries, deaths, births, and the lack
of access to steady and sufficient income all require an economic solution; incurring debt or receiving dowry are two prime means of meeting
these financial challenges, leading, in turn, to a heavy reliance on earning in the informal economic sectors to which poor urban migrants have
access as workers.

Conclusion

In discussing the politics of migration for rural agricultural workers negotiating livelihood strategies in Mumbai, I have suggested that understanding the economic contexts driving the intranational migration of landless agricultural workers in India offers an overarching frame for understanding the three primary ethnographic research sites for this study—the day wage construction workers' naka, the street from which women identified as street-based sex workers solicited clients, and Kamathipura, one of Mumbai's iconic red-light districts. This shared frame includes commonly held struggles for access to housing and potable water, and the collective experience of a permanent migration to the city, or seasonal migration between the city and rural areas when agricultural work was available there. The most striking set of connections among these sites was conveyed by sex workers in Kamathipura, who said that they had started to work from ages as young as five, that they had always had financial dependents, and that their histories of trying to generate income included a time when they "stood on a naka" to solicit day wage construction work.

If caste, class, migration, and livelihood histories are shared between people in all three sites, they also share a relationship with the informal economy. The informal economy, defined as the economic sector that is not officially regulated or taxed by the state, is estimated to constitute more than half of all economic activity in the Global South, with the proportion of informal economic activity in some countries, including India, being much higher. In the following chapter, I discuss the vagaries of the informal sector with respect to sex work. My discussion of caste instantiations in relation to these questions should not be taken as an argument for the impossibility of class solidarity in the informal sector, an idea that is in keeping with the argument that the informal sector is hopelessly fragmented and can never be a site of class-based solidarity. Rather than deploying caste as a means of sustaining this framing of economic informality, my discussion of caste divisions further complicates the ways in which caste is produced as an axis of difference, through the lens of sexuality. The context for the instantiations of caste-based differences here is not the reification of essentialized differences based on caste or tribe among *naka*-based workers but, rather, animates the competition for paid work and the necessity of distinguishing one group of people among many others, when all are vying for a finite number of economic options.

Ultimately, this chapter illustrates an analytic methodology for examining sexual commerce, by placing prostitution alongside a discussion of migration, housing, water, remittances, and solicitation. Here, soliciting clients for sexual commerce and soliciting contractors for construction work are figured as being neither fundamentally distinct nor as essentially the same. Instead, the differences between these two modes of solicitation are produced through a careful interplay between the production of some urban spaces as respectable and others as necessarily lacking respectability. Workers at the naka, as elsewhere, inevitably deploy these differences as they navigate the space.

While only a fraction of women working from the naka solicited clients for sexual services, the idea of sexual commerce permeated the naka, where women understood that, by being poor, not upper caste, and sitting on the street to solicit work, they were apprehended as being potentially available for sex work. This idea structured many of the interactions at the naka, obliging women there either to distinguish themselves as people who did not participate in sexual commerce or to signal that they were selling sexual services. This was framed by the need to maintain rules of propriety at the naka, which mandated that no one could openly solicit clients for sexual services, lest the concomitant disrepute of the naka lead to its being shut down.

CHAPTER 2

SEX, WORK, AND SILENCE FROM THE
CONSTRUCTION WORKERS' *NAKA*

In this chapter, I elaborate upon the ways in which women at the *naka* were always already subject to a "normalizing gaze." Since they were visually marked as lower-caste or tribal, and as experiencing a degree of poverty that required them to seek work in a public place, this gaze, refracted through the registers of class and caste, mapped the possibility of prostitution onto women as they sought paid work there. This was a twofold gaze, deployed implicitly by the middle-class public that surrounded the naka, and deployed explicitly by workers at the naka against one another. This middle-class public that contextualized and, in many ways, allowed the naka to exist included passersby, shopkeepers, commuters, contractors, and the police. The gaze as deployed by workers at the naka toward one another was constituted within a conjoined discourse of honor and respectability that instantiated caste differences as part of the competition for paid work.

I use the notion of a normalizing gaze as that which "makes it possible to qualify, to classify and to punish. It establishes over individuals a visibility through which one differentiates and judges them."[1] The process by which naka-based women workers were subject to this form of "public looking" may be understood as a set of perceptual practices that deployed economic abjection and (female) gender as a single, conjoined signifier for prostitution. The naka's perceptual practices were dialogic, in that women at the naka were never simply the objects of these perceptions; rather, women at the naka both deployed and were subject to them, evincing a system and discourse of gender and sexuality in public that have no singular locus of control.

This chapter examines the dynamics of these social codes at work vis-à-vis the *visibility* of sexual commerce in Mumbai by considering both women's solicitation of clients for sexual services from nakas and forms of knowledge, including rumor and gossip, which circulated about that solicitation. Building on the previous chapter's discussion of migration, day wage labor, and the production of the naka as a time-bound space for soliciting paid work, I specify my analysis of the relationalities between the naka and the idea of sexual commerce there, arguing that the discourse on sexual commerce at the naka is simultaneously pervasive and denied, and rarely self-referential. Everyone at the naka spoke of widespread sexual commerce there, but almost never in relation to themselves. Contextualized by the politics of housing and slum demolitions, access to potable water, and Mumbai's erratic market for cheap manual labor, this chapter explores the euphemisms, secrets, and rumors of sexual commerce that swirl around the naka, as well as the instantiations of solicitation for sexual commerce that took place there. Taken together, the discourse and practice of sexual commerce at the naka both mark and produce gender and caste. This discourse is powered by the force of the stigma of prostitution, articulated against enmeshed notions of honor (*izzat*) and respectability.

Instantiations of sexual commerce at the naka manifested in women using their access to the space in order to solicit clients for sexual commerce—which included both paid sexual services and sex for work—without the fear of arrest or legal reprisals to which sex workers all over Mumbai are subject. (I discuss this phenomenon in some detail in chapters 3 and 4.) However, this use of the naka was much less prevalent than was a practice that I term "sex for work," where women traded sexual services for paid day wage construction work. Both iterations of sexual commerce were engendered by the intense competition for wages from the naka and beg the question of how people survive when paid work is scant, at best.

The perceptions and practices of sexual commerce from the naka call into question the knowability of prostitution, by locating sexual commerce in a space that is produced through the perceived absence of prostitution. I draw an epistemological critique from this exploration of knowledge production of sexual commerce at the naka that calls into question the ways in which the discourse of sexual commerce is built on the foundational assumption that prostitution is knowable, and that, in this knowability, it is constituted by a discrete and fixed set of practices. The contemporary biopolitical regulation of prostitution is pursued largely through the rubrics of knowability and transparency, and the presumption that prostitution is a stable category that can be enumerated, for example, through widespread urban anti-HIV/AIDS mapping projects that aim to show where sex work is specifically located in almost every major city in the world. The presumed fixity of prostitution in efforts like these exists in tension with the secrecy and lack of fixity that describe much of the daily life of sexual commerce, a situation that can only intensify as the criminalization of prostitution works to erase the possibility of selling or trading sexual services in any way that is scrutable, visible, and easily perceived.

The visibility of the naka is a given—even more so than the visibility of the brothel, which is a space that must be accessed in a way that nakas do not demand. Brothels require intimation, prior knowledge, getting directions. As we will see in the next chapter, even street-based sex work does not command the naka's visibility. When soliciting from the street that constituted the second major site for this study, sex workers walked as discreetly as possible, alone or in pairs, signaling that they were soliciting clients without drawing attention from shopkeepers, passersby, and police. By contrast, nakas are positioned for visibility in heavily trafficked areas, a visibility that is rich in meaning. A throng of laborers gathered together is part of the visual grammar of the city, of the discourse of the city's uneven economic geographies, and indicative of the expansion, or lack, of formal employment. In light of this apparent scrutability, what does it mean to pursue multiple il/legitimate activities within a space that renders impoverished laborers visible en masse, within a rubric that requires the invisibility of anything other than one mode of legal, licit solicitation? Furthermore, what does it mean to suggest that the spaces of nakas, brothels, and streets are produced relationally, and that this relationality includes a dialectic between the licit and the illicit, between legality and illegality, which, in this case, references sexual commerce? These questions, and the broader question of visibility at the naka, must be apprehended within the context of the discursive history that has produced them. This history is situated within scholarly debates on day wage labor and the informal economy.

Problematics of the "Informal Sector"

Anthropologist Keith Hart coined the term "informal sector" in a 1973 article, drawn from his ethnography of people who lived in Accra's slums and earned their livelihoods through a range of income-generating strategies, including day wage labor.[2] For Hart, the informal sector served as "a label for economic activities which take place outside the framework of corporate public and private sector establishments . . . the 'hidden,' 'underground,' 'black' economy, and so on."[3] In his ethnography of textile workers in Chennai, Geert de Neve follows on the work of Barbara Harriss-White in defining the informal economy as "the economic activity of firms and individuals that is not registered for the purpose of taxation and/or regulation by the State."[4] As denoted in scholarship on India's informal economy, being "outside the framework of corporate public and private sector establishments" does not mean that informal sector economies are invisible or superfluous to those establishments.

The informal economy (where the singular form is an umbrella term for a range of informal economic sectors) is where the largest number of people are employed in the Global South, and yet it remains a less researched zone of economic activity. Informal economies have expanded under neoliberalism,[5] calling into question not only how the informal sector is defined, but also the descriptive power of a term that, in practice, describes an extremely diverse array of economic activities that, globally, are being conducted on a mass scale. The category of informal sector, like the categories of political society and public space, has traditionally drawn the question of parameters, of what should properly be included and excluded from its purview, as we aim to account for those who would otherwise be marginalized or elided in normative critiques of poverty and migration. These critiques have tended to focus on the dialectics between formal and informal economies, with scholars of economic informality arguing that the distinctions between these are blurred, while the terms themselves imply clear demarcations between the formal and informal that do not describe these sectors as they are instantiated in everyday life.[6]

Ethnography of what Hart called "the economy of the streets"[7] raises these questions because economic and legal categories are regularly upended in daily life. For example, women who solicited clients for sexual services as well as manual labor were negotiating options for survival with respect to a very local set of parameters, to pragmatic choices that revolved around relationships with family and friends, as well as relationships with local police. Scholars who have addressed economic informality in India have marked the problem of the wide swath of economic strategies that the rubric is meant to describe. The vastness of the informal sector in India, and therefore the need for specification within it, is demonstrated by its sheer size. In its January 2012 report on the informal sector, the National Sample Survey of India reported that more than 93 percent of all workers in rural and urban areas worked in informal sectors, including construction work.[8] This equals approximately 370 million workers, out of a total workforce of 458 million, of which roughly 34 percent (155 million) are women.[9] Writing on the need to disaggregate the "unorganised/informal sector" with respect to "traditional vocations, mainly artisanal," "enclaves of casualization and sub-contracting within the 'modern' sector of the economy," and "artisans-turned-proletarians, working as wage labour,"[10] Aditya Nigam writes, "We, therefore, need to look beyond the current usages of such catch-all phrases as the 'unorganised sector' in order to unravel the different entities concealed within these terms. The very act of such a categorization that lumps all these 'unviable,' 'low productivity' activities, into a single class, I suggest is an act of power."[11] Writing some fifteen years later, Nigam points to the problematic of illegality within the massive, unspecified category of the informal sector: "The poor who come to cities in search of livelihoods come most often without any asset and have to initially make do by squatting on government land in some unauthorized settlement. From that initial 'illegality' to various aspects of daily life—hawking, vending, pulling a cycle-rickshaw—everything involves being caught up more and more into a web of illegal existence."[12] If lumping a whole swath of work into the categorization of "economic informality" is an act of power, then classifying a whole swath of people, or their work, as illegal is a component of that power. People who live in slums and work in informal sectors are always already illegal in a sense. This chapter argues that day wage workers, well aware of their positionality in the spectrum of il/legality with respect to the state, use the tensions between il/licit and il/legal activities in order to negotiate daily existence.

If the first problematic of the informal sector is that of a reified distinction between the formal and the informal, the second is the problematic of specifying the informal sector itself. Here, I understand the term "informal sector" as a rubric rather than a specific sector, in light of the scale and diversity of activities that take place within it. The book's main concern with respect to this rubric is the dialectical relationship between the licit and illicit, and the legal and illegal, within the category of the informal. Particularly if the number of workers in the informal sector is set to multiply, how are we to understand the dialectic between licit and legal income-generating activities, and those deemed to be illicit, or categorized as criminal? Is illicit and illegal work an exception to legal work? Is it indicative of weaknesses in the rule of law? Or does the coexistence of these under the sign of economic informality point to the necessity of reevaluating the parameters of informality itself?

Hart has noted that "the informal economy does not exist in any empirical sense: it is a way of contrasting some phenomena with what we imagine constitutes the orthodox core of our economy."[13] Rather than using the concept of the informal economy, as Michael Denning has argued in the *New Left Review*, to reify the space of the informal or "fetishize" the wage and the contract, I understand the concept of the informal economy almost as a kind of method.[14] It is, as Hart has claimed, "a way of contrasting some phenomena with what we imagine constitutes the orthodox core of our economy."[15] If the rhetoric of economic informality is that which fails to reproduce whatever passes for the formal and the regular, perhaps we may think of the informal sector itself as having formal and informal aspects. If the informal sector is layered, with respect to dialectics between legal/licit and illegal/illicit income-generating strategies, sexual commerce becomes an instantiation of the underground aspect of the informal sector—the informal of the informal sector, so to speak. This informality is not necessarily rendered through the regulatory power of the law, but through that of visuality and speech.

Speaking of Sex Work at the Naka

Around ten women were left at the naka at eleven in the morning, the majority having either found jobs for the day or gone home an hour earlier. There were still around thirty men, sitting a little farther down the street. For the most part, women sat separately from the men, the gender segregation of the space going as far as most male and female workers rarely interacting with each other at the naka. However, regardless of gender, all of the interactions here conveyed familiarity, a close-knit feeling shared by people who had seen each other regularly for years. I walked over to sit with Shubha. Shubha was one of the only women there who seemed to ignore the gender segregation of the space, interacting with both the men and the women at the naka. Her slightly advanced age partially explained this relative freedom, which younger women did not enjoy. However, few older women availed themselves of this social latitude as she did. While everyone knew someone at the naka, everyone knew Shubha. Over the course of my visits to the naka, Shubha had been extremely generous to me with her conversation and her time. She would say with pride, "No one will even look at you wrongly, because they know I'm here right behind you. They're all afraid of me." When I would ask why they were afraid, she would smile and say, "They just are." After I had been going to the naka for a few weeks, various men had begun to ask me, "So, has Shubha told you yet that she's a prostitute?"

I had been talking that day with Shubha about other areas in the city where women use public spaces, usually the block of a busy street, to find clients for sex. Almost all of those women reported looking for construction work from their local manual laborers' naka in the morning. "If we don't find work there, we come here," they said, adding, "it has to be done for the stomach." (*Pet ki liye karna pad ta hai.*) I asked Shubha what she thought about this "for the stomach" argument for doing sex work. She replied, "Yes, for honor, a person could sit inside their house, but . . ." (*Hahn, izzat le kar ghar ka undar bayt sakte hai, laykin . . .*) She trailed off and would not speak about it further.

This extremely rich moment offers up insights on how solicitation can be understood in this context, given that, for some workers at the naka, Shubha's identification as a sex worker was a foregone conclusion, one that she both maintained and denied by her refusal to discuss it further. To be sure, all women at the construction workers' naka were not identified as sex workers all of the time. On the other hand, having proximity to large groups of men, being unchaperoned by a family member in public areas, and visibly using public space to seek out paid work are all necessary to be hired for a day job by a contractor for women soliciting work at the naka. These are also signs of transgressing gendered norms of propriety (such as the idea that women belong at home, in private, not seeking work in public from strangers) and overlap with some of the strategies used by women working as street-based sex workers in the course of soliciting male clients.

The similar modes through which a variety of paid work was solicited coincided with the fact that, in conversations at the naka, almost any mention of the category of "women" working on the naka implied an actual or perceived availability for selling or trading sexual services. An example of these perceptual categories in action included the attitude toward women accessing the office space of the NGO that worked at the naka, the organization whose outreach workers had initially introduced me to workers there. The first office space of the NGO at the naka was off-limits to the women there because it had been visible from the main road. Men who worked from the naka said that the women had been banned from that space to guard against a generalized perception that women could be doing some "bad work" (*bura kam*) in the privacy of the office space. Being sheltered from public view automatically targeted the office with suspicion about the activities that could take place there, especially with respect to female laborers.

In addition to managing these kinds of perceptions, men and women repeatedly asserted that a major problem at the naka was that of "contractors taking young-young girls and driving around with them" and contractors "wanting to get girls for jobs." Never, ever, I was told, would younger unmarried women be sent to wait at the naka for work. Thus the perceived or actual availability for engaging in sexual commerce was indicated through informational gaps and insinuations. These allusions were linked to the unspoken strategies women might use to fill the monthly income gaps produced by insufficient construction day jobs, especially for those who were the primary wage earners in their homes.

Women at the naka regularly accused one another of selling sexual services to male contractors and other clients, while they themselves were subject to such accusations as well. These allegations were filtered through the notion of izzat. Honor was key in the local regime of caste differentiation, in which the lower the caste, the less honor women were said to possess. At the construction workers' naka, lower-caste women deployed such rhetoric against tribal women whom, they argued, had rampant sexual proclivities, conferred by their tribal status. Alongside contentions that they engaged in paid and traded sex with contractors, tribal women were also accused of undercutting the standard day wage rate in order to secure paid work for themselves more often. We may understand these kinds of accusations as residing within a relational matrix of social propriety. For women belonging to the Nav Buddho, Mahar (Scheduled Caste, SC) community at the naka, izzat resided in their community because it did not reside in others. Izzat was asserted through the refusal to engage in, or the refusal to corroborate engaging in, sexual commerce of any kind.

Early in our acquaintance, Shubha told me how she had come to be widowed years earlier while her children were quite small, the youngest still a nursing infant. Her elder daughter and son were now married, and the youngest child, her daughter Sheila, was around fifteen years old. When I asked if she had ever thought about remarrying, Shubha told me about a married Muslim man with eight children who had taken a liking to her long ago. She said, "You should have seen me, Shotti,[16] when I was younger, how I sparkled! The naka lit up when I would go there, really. Every man wanted to talk with me. But if I'd *done* anything, who would marry my kids? How would I survive?" She said that, in the end, "it's the Banjara [tribal] women who let men do that to them," adding, "No one gives work for free" (*Koi phukat mein kam nahi dete hain*).

Shubha explained that because the man who had liked her was married and a member of another religious community, it was outside the realm of consideration to have a relationship with him. These concerns went beyond the basic taboo against widowed women in Shubha's community remarrying. The man whom Shubha described had died some years ago. He would give her gifts, she said, including a pair of gold earrings that she showed me proudly. They were small studs that she wore above her dangling earrings. Shubha told me, "I cry sometimes when I think of him, but it's for the best that nothing more happened between us, for the sake of honor." This statement resonated when, months later, she described the situation of women at the naka by saying, "What do we have, really? Our honor, house, water, and food. [*Hamari izzat, ghar, khana peena.*] And one woman's honor is every woman's honor."

When I asked whether she thought it might not just be the Banjaras who were engaging in sex work or trading sex for work with contractors, she answered with an analogy: "Women have become like that shoe [*chappal*], something to use and, when it's torn and used up, to throw away and get a new one. *That's* what women have become worth."

We may read this exchange both as Shubha's denial of doing sex work herself and as an elaboration of the stakes involved in doing sex work openly from the naka. Shubha's assertion that "no one gives work for free" alludes to all women soliciting work from the naka and especially indicates those trading sex for work with contractors. While the use of the term "contractor" generally implied a masculine subject, a male contractor passing time at the local tea shop pointed out that, like "worker," and "naka," "contractor" cannot be thought of as a uniform category. "What is a contractor?" he asked rhetorically. "It's anyone with a *relationship*, with the government, police, builders, it could be *anyone*." In other words, just as women at the naka were subject to layered perceptual categories (female, lower caste, worker, impoverished, whore), male contractors were also subject to layered perceptions of their roles at the naka (contractors, clients for sex, passersby, men engaged in "timepass"). While most people at the naka flowed between the permutations of these layers in the social and economic matrices of the space, a few women were fixed in their generalized categorization as prostitutes. Prema, another naka-based worker, was seen first and foremost as a sex worker there; her situation was widely discussed and acutely felt by the people at the naka who had had a long association with her.

Mukhu's Explanation

I arrived at the naka around ten in the morning, worried that I had missed everyone. The day before, Prema had said that she would be there at eight thirty to meet with me, and I'd felt badly that I hadn't been able to call to say that I'd be late. I was sure I'd miss her now, especially given my impression that she was no longer part of the regular crowd at the naka. A handful of women were still sitting there and waiting. Their recounting of the number of days since they last worked was starting to sound like a greeting. Seeing me, they began. "We don't get work." (*Kam nahi milta hai.*) "Now it's been ten days [since I last worked]." (*Abhi das din hogaya.*) "Now it's been two months." (*Abhi do mahina hogaya.*)

Shubha was not there because, like the day before, she was somewhere else making sweets for the festival of Sankranti. Sankranti was on January 14, and Shubha was earning fifty rupees per day for the work, for a whole month. One of the women remarked cheerfully about Shubha's employment, saying, "It's good, no?" (*Accha hai, na?*) After finding neither Shubha nor Prema, I was preparing to leave when I saw Mukhu. He was walking over to the small tea stall with the naka's *tekhyadar,* the middleman who sometimes procured work for people at the naka. I fell in step with Mukhu as he said, "Will you have tea?" We squeezed into the stall, which was more like a small closet off the main road, displacing a few people along the bench in the process. Mukhu was eventually settled on the bench inside the stall, with me in the middle and the tekhyadar on the other side of me, reading that day's *Lok Satta,* the Marathi paper that they passed around in the office, sometimes with one person reading the stories aloud to a small group.

"Yes, so yesterday . . . ," I began, wanting to ask him about his negative reaction to my having spoken with Prema the day before, which I had detected through his unmistakable glower.

"Yes, yes," he replied, "I was going to ask you, why were you talking with her?" Not expecting such a direct question about my interaction with Prema, I found myself explaining that I wanted to talk with her because I wanted to talk with everyone who was part of the naka and because I'd heard a lot about her already. I left out the part about being told that she was a sex worker and an alcoholic. He heard my explanation judiciously, with his eyes half closed. The more I spoke, the more I felt as though I was giving my uncle an explanation for why I had been seen with a disreputable person. After I had finished, we all sat in silence for a moment. The tekhyadar seemed to continue studying the paper.

Mukhu finally took a deep breath and said, "What all you are saying is right and good, but I am there, Shubha, Minee, we are all there, we all have worked with the organizations here for so many years, you could just talk with us." He added, "Some people you keep close contact with, others you don't."

"I don't understand," I said.

He closed his eyes and nodded. "I'll explain."

On the other side of me, the tekhyadar rose to leave, saying to Mukhu as he walked into the street, "You can explain it to her, but she won't listen." (*Tum samjaho, leykin voh nahi manegi*.)

"Who, me?" I asked

"Hahn," he said definitively as he walked away.

Mukhu continued. "You should keep friendships, talk with everyone, without prejudice, but this person . . ." His voice had dropped to just above a whisper, and he started hesitating in his speech, looking for the right clauses and phrases. I knew that the conversation would not be happening if it were anywhere more public, like the office, or the naka itself. His entire tone and bearing indicated that what he was talking about was not public at all, that it was shameful, wrong, and bad. He took on the air of an elder male relative explaining, giving a lesson.

"See, how you come, you sit with men, you talk with them *frankly*, she does that too, but for her, it's because she has a habit of drinking." I noted his use of the English word "frankly" here, much as people at the naka often used the word "tension."

Mukhu explained that Prema drank and then "went around" with strange men. "She needs a quarter of Haywards whiskey a day," he said, putting up his hand and miming the size of a small bottle of liquor. "Haywards, you know Haywards? She drinks that. And she drinks with men."

"She drinks?" I said. "But I saw her yesterday morning. She said she was taking someone to the hospital. She looked fine."

"Yes, she looked fine, but you haven't seen her after five. After five, she'll start drinking."

He said that everyone at the naka used to be friends, and they had all tried to help Prema. Once, there had been an occasion when she couldn't provide for herself and her four children. They had pooled their resources and bought her a month's rations. He recited the items, like a shopping list: ten kilograms of wheat flour, ten kilograms of rice, *jawar*, vegetables, oil, spices, kerosene. At the end of it, when they had given it all, she had asked for fifty rupees. "We asked her, 'Why do you need fifty rupees? We've gotten everything for you that you could need,' and she didn't say anything." Fifty rupees, Mukhu said, is what a quarter bottle of Haywards costs. "And how do you think we felt, after getting all of that for her, and then being asked for fifty rupees?" he asked.

I replied with a question. "So, does she take money from these men who she drinks with?"

He shook his head and tried a different tack. "You know Jaya? Jay-abai? She and her husband live in [the hillside slums]," he said. "She is like that, too. Once, something was happening, and we all went up there to meet them, and, usually, when you go there, the doors and windows are open, you can see inside, but this time, we went, and the door was shut, all the windows were shut, so I went to the door, and I pushed it in a little, to look inside, and I saw her there, with her clothes off and thrown around everywhere, and there was a man, close to where she was, and you could see that they both had been drinking."

"So, Jayabai, Prema," I asked, "they drink, and they go with men?"

He nodded solemnly. "Now, with Shubha, I've never seen it with my own eyes, but . . ."

"But then," I asked, "you still keep social relations [*samband*] with Shubha? And you don't with Prema?"

He nodded. "Yes, there is some relationship. Like with Shubha, I say hello, I sit, that's all. I don't go to her house, ever. And you shouldn't either."

I thought for a moment, and said, "Yes, but, what I think you are talking about, what they call 'business' [*dhandha*], or 'bad work' [*bura kam*], you know what I mean?" He nodded firmly. "Some people say that they do this just to fill their bellies [*pet ki liye*]."

Mukhu's eyes widened, and his tone intensified. "Yes, they say that, but is this why you were born? To sell one's body? [*Jism bechne ki liye?*] Yes, to fill their bellies, that's what they say, but *is this* why God has given them birth? [*Hahn, pet ki liye karte hai, esa bolte hai, lekin isliye Bhagwan ne paidya diya hai?*] To sell their bodies?? [*Jism bechne ki liye??*]" He said the words even more softly, projecting intense disgust and moral outrage. He went on to list all the various members of his household; most were women, and they included a couple of young girls who were not his daughters, but whom he had taken the responsibility of caring for. All of them were contributing to the household in some way, he said, including making jewelry or doing other home-based piecework. The juxtaposition of this example with his outrage against bura kam produced a clear message: all these women were paying their own way, and none were "selling their bodies" to make ends meet. "You see these young, young girls [*jawan jawan ladkiyan*] here?" he asked. "The women who come to this naka looking for work? I would say, of one hundred women who come here, seventy are into this bura kam. You see the young girls [*jawan ladkiyan*] here, and the old women? The old women are there figuring out who will go with whom, and for how long—they get paid for that. Minee could tell you more, but it's a racket [*chal hai*]."

At the mention of Minee's name, there was another pause. Mukhu's wife was living in the village, and Mukhu and Minee shared a house in one of the solid-built rooms near the naka. "Now, Minee's and my relationship has been going on for eighteen years," he said. Minee was also married, and her husband also lived in the village, while she lived and worked in Mumbai. "No one would dare say to either of us that what we are into is wrong. Why? Because everyone knows that we share the same values."

Someone else came along whom Mukhu knew. While they chatted, I watched the boy in the tea stall strain a fresh pot of sweet, milky chai through a cloth and into a brass vessel. Trying to make small talk as our conversation ended, I said, "Of all the tea shops around here, this one makes the best tea." Mukhu nodded as if I were speaking gibberish. I gave him a half-sideways nod and stood to leave, but then he decided he needed to go to the office. As we walked there together, I noticed Prema going by with a man I had not seen before. She stopped to greet me, saying that she was on her way home. She was carrying a bag of vegetables she had just purchased. The man stood behind her, shifting his weight from one leg to the other, looking at me as if he wished he could disappear. Prema didn't seem as steady on her feet as she had the day before, and she smelled faintly of chewing tobacco and alcohol. "I gave you the wrong phone number yesterday," she said brightly. "That was one relative's number, I meant to give you another friend's number. Tomorrow, tomorrow I'll give you the right number." I nodded, aware of being observed speaking with her in front of the office, after being given a firm warning from Mukhu to avoid her entirely. I said good-bye, and Prema left, the man walking after her.

Beyond Mukhu's assertion that Prema sells sex, what was also significant in Mukhu's warning was his assertion that Prema should not be the subject of any study, and that I should keep my distance from her. This attitude, expressed many times about this particular woman, served to make an example of Prema at the naka. Prema was subject to the stigma of prostitution as someone who once held a respectable social position, and the community support that it came with, which she was thought to have squandered through alcoholism and sex work. Other exemplars like Prema were constantly circulated as subjects of gossip, though none were spoken about as vigorously as she was. All of these narratives taken together delineated the negative space of illicit activity conducted from the naka, a space that was juxtaposed against the positive space of legitimate work, such as the piecework done by the women in Mukhu's home. Ironically, Mukhu offered his own long-term extramarital relationship with Minee as an example of respectability, because everyone "knew" that they adhered to "the same values." Everyone having the same values in this context indicated that Mukhu, his wife, and Minee were all perceived as being respectable because none of them were implicated in sexual commerce. At the same time, Mukhu's relationship, and others like it among people who used the naka, pointed to a degree of complexity in romantic relationships among this community of workers that was outside the purview of conventional biological and marital kinship ties.

Mukhu's presumptive motivations in telling his own story and the story of Prema—to protect the naka as a space for "legitimate" business, and to protect me—were often repeated by others. On an initial visit to the naka, Shubha had said, "They [the contractors] take young girls like you, who look nice, and they take them around." When I had asked, "What do they do with them?" Shubha had looked away, embarrassed, and then replied, "Look at them, have fun [*maza*, an allusion to sex] with them. If I was ready to do that, I would be getting so much work, yes!"

Suma and Jaya were more direct than Shubha on this issue. In one interview near her home in Kranti Nagar, in the hillside slums, Suma said she could earn 1,000 rupees per month doing basic housecleaning in two or three households. From the construction workers' naka, she could earn the same amount in ten days, provided she could find a contractor to hire her. "Last week," she said, "I got five days doing repair work on a new building. Taking sand up. But I know the contractors want a nice woman, beautiful, she becomes desired, she's surrendered to someone [*hawala de diya*], the big boss [*sheth*] doesn't come to know, but the male skilled worker [*mistry*] takes her in hand, and he slips up into the Banjara [tribal] women's skirts [*Banjara ka gagra mein ghoos ta hai*]."

Giri, who was also Suma's neighbor, had been sitting nearby and interjected. "Yes! Put red [makeup] here!" she said, pointing to her cheeks. "Put it here!" gesturing to her lips. "Here, here! Put earrings, yes, you'll get work all right!" By this last comment, several people had gathered round, laughing.

At a larger suburban naka nearby, located in front of a massive commuter railway station, women declared that, after eleven in the morning, only women "who want to do bad work" come to the naka. When I asked about the nature of this work, one woman replied, "All right, you want to speak openly, I'll speak openly. They take these young girls, and steal love from them." (*Jawan ladkiyan le kar pyar loot-te hain.*) When eleven o'clock approached, I made it clear that I intended to stay to talk with other women who may be left at that naka. The three women I was standing with, who had been there since eight o'clock and were preparing to leave, encircled me and said, "You, stay, now? No, that's not possible. It's a matter of honor. A young girl like you, what will people think?" When I had spoken with them for a few more minutes, it was apparent that I would not be speaking with anyone else at that naka that day. After taking their leave, I noticed the three of them waiting quietly but firmly until I was well on my way back to the station.

Some months later, I went to meet representatives of the migrant workers' organization at yet another naka at ten o'clock in the morning. This naka was also located directly in front of a local commuter train station, closer to the commercial hub of South Mumbai. Thousands of people were lining the front of the station and the streets that radiated in front, to the left, and to the right. Directly in front of the station sat the women, some of whom, from their style of dress, looked to be tribal people (ST) from Karnataka. The people I was scheduled to meet were not there, so I tried to find a place to sit where I would not be in anyone's way, from which I could see what was happening. During the fifteen minutes that I waited, three different men came and stood in front of me, looking expectantly. When I rose to walk around, each followed me, until a glare in their direction sent them away. Eventually, the people from the organization arrived, and we stood across the street from the naka discussing their HIV prevention program there with women and men.

"Are you doing this program because there is sex work going on from here?" I asked.

"That's not the only reason," the woman replied, and she went on to explain how women did solicit clients for sex from this naka, going with them to lodges and guest houses in the area that rent rooms by the hour. "It took a long time for the guest house owners to agree to distribute condoms for us. At first they just said that nothing is going on there." She also explained that the workers who came here lived all over the city, and most were originally migrants from Maharashtra, Andhra Pradesh, and Karnataka. At eleven o'clock, there was a clear thinning of the crowd, especially among the women. Twenty minutes later, the social worker stopped her description of her organization's work in the area and gestured toward the women's space. It had filled up again, with around twenty women who had not been there before. "What do you think they're doing there?" she asked. "All the contractors for construction work have been and gone, they're not going to come here looking for workers now. And why do you think they're dressed like that?" Unlike the women who had been sitting there earlier in the morning, these women were dressed in more expensive-looking saris, carrying handbags on their arms, and wearing earrings and makeup. I looked at my watch and recalled the injunction against my standing at the naka after eleven in the morning.

Although these conversations with women and men, NGO workers, and other observers at the nakas confirmed that many kinds of commerce, including sexual commerce, were negotiated from these spaces, there is as much to be said of the politics of speech regarding those moments when an illicit activity is indicated without ever being named. With respect to sexual commerce solicited from the naka, phrases like *yeh bura kam* (this bad work) and *jawan jawan ladkiyan* (young young girls), or *faltu baat* (bad/foolish/offensive language) signified women's transgression of space (e.g., women occupying public or private spaces alone with men not of their own kin network), of propriety (e.g., driving in a car with a stranger), of boundaries of verbal intimacy, of boundaries of familiarity with strangers, or of age (e.g., young girls being out alone or with unfamiliar older men in a public space) and, taken together, the practice of soliciting clients for sexual services. Both the silences in conversations like the one with Shubha and the nuanced usage of phrases like "bad work" pointed toward a kind of double language that was needed for discussing any form of paid sex or sex trade at the naka. In this double language, the solicitation of paid sex or sex traded for paid work from this space was simultaneously affirmed and denied.

There are several ways we may read this doubling. For example, the negations may have functioned as a shield against the potential loss of social standing in a relatively interdependent community and even, possibly, to protect against police harassment and arrest for engaging in illegal solicitation, defined in the Immoral Trafficking Protection Act

FIG. 2.1. Policeman at the naka

as solicitation that is "for the purpose of prostitution." In an economic context in which survival is contingent upon maintaining community goodwill and social acceptance, in which the honor of one indicates the honor of all, and in which honor and respectability for women are defined in opposition to prostitution, the consequences of being perceived as engaging in sexual commerce in any way whatsoever must be avoided at all costs.

The silences and the denials and confirmations of sexual commerce from the naka—of both paid sex and sex for work—may also be read in relation to the social, legal, and economic parameters of soliciting work from this space. These parameters were in play as I attempted to discern sexual commerce from a space where it was both illegal and socially taboo, the official discovery of which would have led to the naka being shut down, at worst, or even more highly regulated, at best. Within the context of the research sites I discuss in this book, I was read as an extremely elite person, someone who eventually became familiar and friendly with people who used the naka to find paid work, but who was always read as coming from a separate material universe. This was relevant to the conversations around sexual commerce I attempted to have because my eliteness took shape specifically in relation to the income-generating activities that people at the naka engaged. I was elite because I did not sit on the street corner to look for paid work. I did not do piecework in my home. I was seen as a potential employer of domestic workers, not as someone who would work as a domestic worker. Regarding the question of sexual commerce, that I was someone who had never sold sexual services, and that I would never have the economic necessity of doing so, was a foregone conclusion for everyone I encountered at the nakas.

When I asked Shubha what she thought my caste was, she answered "brahmin" without hesitation. That my family is not of a brahmin caste was immaterial in this interaction. That Shubha placed me at the very top of the caste hierarchy is pertinent because she, like everyone else at the naka, interpellated my perceived class and caste privilege as an understanding of myself as someone who would never need to use the livelihood strategies that I was aiming to discuss with workers there. The difference between selling sexual services and not doing so is already highly overdetermined, through the production of sex work within the matrices of stigma, taboo, and respectability. I was respectable by virtue of my perceived caste and class, because class is always already coded through a long-standing, relational matrix of respectability.

Since the inauguration of the ideas of charity, social reform, and urban space, bourgeois individuals and entities have entered working-class and impoverished spaces in cities the world over specifically to assist people there. This phenomenon has produced much in the way of real help, while also reinstantiating and reproducing a class-based social hierarchy. This hierarchy has been mediated through the discourse of respectability, the performance and habitation of which render all actors in these cross-class interactions as equivalently human, if not rendering them equal. If a mutual sense of honor and respectability facilitated my interactions with people at the naka, wherein we treated one another as honorable and respectable, then this sense also precluded an explicit discussion about people selling or trading sexual services from the naka, especially one in which people implicated themselves in that equation.

I elaborate these dynamics here to suggest that the discourse of sexual commerce produced within my interactions with people at the naka may be understood as somehow emblematic of research on sex work. Even when researchers of sexual commerce have had the experience of selling sexual services themselves, they have generally not engaged in sexual commerce in their field sites, with a few notable exceptions where this has been a component of the research. The bulk of research on sexual commerce, then, is produced through a mitigation of the stigma of selling sexual services on the part of sex workers interacting with researchers who, at least in that moment and in that place, are not selling sexual services themselves. At the naka, these dynamics far exceeded my discrete interactions with workers there. While these dynamics were disrupted to a degree by the relative transparency of my own views on sexual commerce and manual labor, the force of the stigma could never be completely dissipated. The totalizing effects of prostitution as a social category precluded avowing even episodic or occasional engagement with sexual commerce from the naka. Acknowledging even a partial identification with prostitution was impossible. Women at the naka were able to negotiate the public deployments of stigma through consistent disavowals from the practice of prostitution, and by performing the embodiment of izzat itself.

The Molars of the Naka

I discussed the problems of visibility and euphemistic references to sexual commerce at the naka at length with Rajbhai, a contractor from Marathwada who frequented the naka near the national park. On one occasion, Rajbhai took me to the more expensive tea stall across the street, which had recently had an additional floor built. As we sat in the booth with cups of chai, he told me that he was doing work for someone at Film City, the oldest-running Bollywood movie set, which is still used for producing a wide range of Hindi films. Rajbhai invited me to see his work there, an offer I accepted because it was also an opportunity to speak with him uninterrupted, and away from the naka. As we walked through various temporary housing clusters and back alleys to the bus stop that would take us there, Rajbhai spoke of the hillside slum demolitions again, and how the municipality had come and razed everything. "It was illegal," he said, "the government was just trying to get in with the builders. They wouldn't have done it if everything there hadn't been so good." He spoke of the rows of taps near the entrance to the area, of the permanent structures that had housed stores and a clinic that had been built farther inside. He spoke of the settlement as having become "too established," and therefore targeted for demolition.

A long walk and two bus rides later, it seemed fitting to be discussing increasingly ephemeral housing as we approached a long-standing movie set. Film City, I discovered, was as unreal as a permanent movie set can be. Manicured lawns and new buildings stood next to older sets that consisted of buildings with several exterior façades. The most prominent of these had the columns and Greco-Roman accents of a courthouse on one side and the brick silhouette of a Catholic church on another, and probably at least two more façades on the sides we could not see. We walked for a bit before settling next to a stone wall laced with bougainvillea, set on the hill below the building with multiple façades.

Rajbhai began chatting about his own family back in the village and about his legal work here in the city. Since the demolitions, he said, much of his work involved doing legal advocacy for people who had been displaced. His conversation was interspersed with trivia about Film City, including what kind of food is served in the canteen, and personal information about himself, including how much money he had spent on gifts for his family for Diwali, how much work he had done with advocacy organizations at the naka in the past, and personal information about others at the naka, including who had been involved in romantic affairs with whom, and for how long. Eventually, the conversation turned to the economic situation of the workers there and the fact that numerous people reported often waiting for days, if not weeks, between jobs.

"Look," he said, pointing to one of the newer buildings that was being constructed for the set in front of us. "Do you know why I brought you here? Because I wanted you to see what it's really like. I wanted you to see that there really is work if people want it." He explained that, in the construction industry, a contractor generally comes looking for a pair (*jodi*), a man and a woman, or a number of jodis, for a certain job. The structure of the industry, he said, is such that, "It's 150 rupees per jodi. These people who look for work from this naka, they charge too much, they want to take rickshaws everywhere, and in the end they don't even work." He said that the two communities most represented at the naka were of the Mang caste, like himself, who were Hindus, and Mahars, who were converted Buddhists. "It's these Mahars who are into all this *faltu* business," he said. He pulled out a notepad from his shirt pocket. Cards with elaborate illustrations of different Hindu gods had been inserted between the pages. He listed all the images in the notepad ("Here is what *we* believe in, see? Sai Baba, Shiva, Parvati, Ganesh, my parents . . ."), then carefully put it back in his shirt pocket.

Hoping to clarify what he meant, I spoke about street-based sex work in another locality, where women were more openly soliciting clients for sex, and asked him if this also happened at the naka we both knew, if women were selling or trading sex from there as well. He replied, "How can I explain? . . . You look at someone's face and see their front teeth, but really it's the back ones they eat with."

I thought about the image for a moment and asked, "So, people are coming to look for work from this naka, but it's not the work they seem to be looking for?"

He nodded vigorously. "Yes! Now you understand!"

Rajbhai's poetic assertion corroborated the idea that women soliciting day wage labor from the naka were selling and trading sex, and were also constantly negotiating their own relationship to prostitution as a perceptual, stigmatized category. His metaphor described the discursive result—the spectrality of paid sex and sex traded for work from the naka. The naka had a public, visible symbolism that was both related to and distinct from the ways in which it actually operated as an income-generating space for its workers. As critical as molars are to nourishment, that which was unseen sustained that which was seen.

Producing Caste through the Idea of Sexual Commerce

Caste as a mode of self-narration was ubiquitous at the naka, especially in the stories that workers told of their own migrations to the city. Caste as linked with regional affiliations was constantly deployed in competition for work from the naka. The strong rhetoric of anticaste struggle at the naka necessitated presenting a united front based on class affiliations and mobilizing the idea of solidarity among broadly defined categories of caste. However, the intensity of competition for work from the naka was manifest in the production and maintenance of caste- and subcaste-based hierarchies. These hierarchies were often articulated through the ascription of stigma attached to selling or trading sexual services. The accusation of doing sex work was often deployed as an epithet linked with a caste or, more often, tribal affiliation. This use of the idea of sexual commerce reiterated social and economic hierarchies at the naka, while communicating a great deal about the imbrications of caste and gender.

The first instantiation of caste-based hierarchies was the nomination of caste and tribal affiliations. These affiliations were most often acknowledged spatially among workers and contractors. People sat in distinct, caste- and gender-affiliated clusters at the naka and competed for work accordingly. Caste-based distinctions were also maintained verbally, through the accusations that members of different groups hurled at one another. These accusations ranged from the assertion that one group was undercutting the standard day wage rate in order to secure work, to the charge that women of a particular community were either selling sex from the naka or trading sex for work with contractors, to the detriment of those who did not. The latter accusation often reiterated a specific hierarchy at this particular naka, where the Maharashtrian Nav Buddho workers were dominant. Female members of this group, like Shubha and Minee, minced few words in conveying that, for them, the Banjara and Lambadi tribals were "basically untouchable," and that the characteristic sexual impropriety of tribal women was a major reason for this. The assertion that the other group was engaged in sexual commerce constituted caste by constituting sexual impropriety, as women who were accused of this practice were immediately labeled as lacking honor, trustworthiness, and shame. And yet, modes of sociality at the naka were relatively fluid, with people of different groups eating together, knowing details about each other's lives, and, at times, providing financial or other material support to one another.

While the production of a hierarchy based on caste within a social milieu that seemed to decenter caste in favor of class may seem deeply incongruous or incommensurate, a feminist reading of caste and gender renders the coproduction of these features of the naka more legible. Offering one such reading, Sharmila Rege argues that a critique of gender, and specifically of women, in relation to caste challenges a singular notion of a dalit mono-community.[17] Uma Chakravarti calls codes of conduct among women an important "index in fixing rank within the caste-hierarchy," an argument that troubles the anticaste ideal of a single *dalit* voice, mobilized across Scheduled Caste (SC) and Scheduled Tribe (ST) communitarianism.[18] Of the ways in which this ideal of dalit unity operates for women, Rege writes, "The upper caste status of the feminist modern is thus signified as absence of caste in claiming to represent the ideal subject of feminist politics," that is, dalit women.[19]

If the ideal Indian modern is constituted through the absence of caste, then the instantiations of caste at the naka are produced as a sign of the antimodern. This constitutes an oppositionality between the old endogamous rules of marriage that produce notions of purity and pollution, and a secular ideal in which caste is disrupted, for example, by hypergamy. Of marriage and caste, Rege writes:

> In his review of the different definitions of caste put forth by Nesfield, Risley, Ketkar and others, Ambedkar points to the inadequacy of languages that speak of caste in other terms, namely the "idea of pollution." He argues that the absence of intermarriage or endogamy is the one characteristic that can be called the essence of castes (Ambedkar 1992). Thus, it is the superimposition of endogamy on exogamy and the means used for the same that hold the key to understanding the

caste system. . . . He underlines the fact that the caste system can be maintained only through the controls on women's sexuality and in this sense women's subordination is located in their being the gateways to the caste system.[20]

If the discourses that produce idealized female sexuality are key to understanding the politics of the naka (and of prostitution), then Ambedkar, read through Rege, goes a step further, arguing that understanding the ways in which women's sexuality has been at the center of discourses on Indian nationalism is key to understanding how caste itself is produced and maintained. According to Rege, dalits are laboring under a regime of caste that has continuities between the nationalist period (1920s through 1950s) and anti-Mandal violence (1990),[21] which deployed the rhetoric of citizenship, meritocracy, *and* endogamy in the service of preventing reservations for SC and ST students in higher education. It is within this political context that SC and ST migrants to the city, who are variously classified as *dalit*, must ensure their own survival. Ultimately, Rege writes, "the nationalist project mobilized modernity and nation to make the public expression of caste illegitimate."[22] Caste, in other words, became the "other" of "neobrahmanist" modernity, which was also, ironically, overtly marked by its upper casteness, while producing a dyad in which modernism was opposed with caste-based communitarianism. The project of interlacing modernity with the discourse of caste begins during the colonial period, when the "'fractured modernity' . . . of the dominant public sphere . . . was . . . a site of formation of the middle classes in colonial India."[23] Referencing the critique of the public sphere and public space in chapter 1, this sense of fractured modernity may be understood in relation to economically impoverished SC and ST urban migrants being rendered as antimodern through a "public expression of caste" that became conceptually fused with people understood as belonging to SC and ST categories.

Caste, Honor, and Competing for Paid Work

In many naka-based workers' homes, portraits of the Buddha and Dr. Ambedkar hung prominently side by side, sometimes next to portraits of Shivaji, Sai Baba, and Indira Gandhi. The reason for the Indira Gandhi portraits became clearer when Kanna, a dalit Maharashtrian woman who came regularly to the naka, said, "No one has been for the poor since Rajiv and Indira Gandhi, because Indira was so good, she would say, 'Remove poverty! [*Garibi hatao!*].'"[24] Sonia [Gandhi] is good, but the dynasty is over now [*gharana abhi khatam ho gaya hai*]."[25] The Maharashtrian Nav Buddho community, of which Kanna was a member, was composed of people who identified themselves as belonging to the Mahar caste, the same caste as Dr. Ambedkar's. People who identified themselves as belonging to the Maharashtrian Nav Buddho community would officially be classified as Mahars, and as SC, though people at the naka who were Nav Buddho rarely used the term "Mahar" to identify their caste. In addition to calling themselves Nav Buddho, they also used the term "Ambedkar *jāt*."

Mukhu on Ambedkarite History

When I asked whether he preferred the word *dalit* in reference to himself or his community, Mukhu answered by explaining Dr. Ambedkar's role in Indian history to me. "'Nav Buddho' is better to say than 'dalit.' Do you know that today is a day of pain and sorrow? It is the anniversary of Babasaheb Ambedkar's death. Today we prepare a feast, like food you would make for a wedding. Not any bad [*faltu*] food. Really good, amazing food, and we all go down to that place at the beach."

"How many go down there?" I asked.

"How many? Ten or fifteen. *Lakh*," he replied. (One lakh is 100,000.)

"Not ten or fifteen thousand?" I asked, genuinely amazed.

Mukhu grinned and then continued:

Lakhs. They hire trucks, and people come from all over, Thane, Malad [two Mumbai suburbs], everywhere, and all gather in that place and eat, and if you go there, you won't leave without your stomach being full. And why do we do this? This is a question of history, which we know. We're able to tell people like you, talk with people like you, because we've studied it ourselves, so we know. See, first there was this term *harijan*. *Hari* means *dev* [god], and *jan* means *janata* [people]. Gandhi had come up with this term, but Ambedkar said, no way, nothing doing. So then there was *dalit*, but that wasn't good either, because it included four different castes [*jātis*]—*chamaar*, *dhogra*, *mang*, and *mahar*. All these jātis were there to do the dirty work. In the village, someone from this *jāt* had to wear a vessel [*lota*] on their front, with a broom [*jhadu*] hanging behind.[26] There was no question of even saying the word "school." They had to walk down the street banging a bell, so that the upper-caste people would know that a dirty person was coming, and they should avert their eyes so that they wouldn't get polluted just by looking at them.

"So what word do you use?" I asked again.

"Nav Buddho . . . see, when Gandhi was in, where? Africa."

"South Africa," I offered. Mukhu nodded, and elaborated.

Yes. And what was the struggle [*ladhai*] there? "You're black, I'm white." [*Tu kala, mein gora.*] If you were black, they would push you off the bus, saying no, you can't come here because you're black. Gandhi was pushed off the bus for this reason. Now, when Ambedkar was in London, the queen from there and her son wanted to know about where Ambedkar came from, and he offered to take them, along with Gandhi. He said come and I'll show you about my people, come and see how they live. Without Ambedkar, we wouldn't have these clothes to wear, we wouldn't have this naka to come and stand on every day. And Ambedkar said, I'll show you my people, and they will welcome me. So he came with them, and they got off at Santa Cruz station, and there were all these people of his caste sitting there, poor, with torn clothes, women who had split one sari into four and were wearing each piece, and they saw all of this, and there was an old *chamaar* woman there, with her husband. And they were eating bread made from millet [*jawar ki roti*] that was four days old. Do you know how dry four-day-old millet bread is? They were eating it dry, with a little bit of salt, and some ground up chilies, because they were in the habit of eating very hot food, because they were poor. I have that habit, anyone has that habit who was born into a poor household. So then Ambedkar came, and there were so many people to greet him and welcome him, and he went to this couple, and he sat with them, and he started to eat [*Mukhu pantomimed eating a hard roti*], but he didn't have this habit, and it was so hot, tears started to flow from his eyes. And Gandhi came as well, but then, these were not his people, and so who was there to welcome him? No one. And Jinnah, when Jinnah said that they wanted a separate Muslim state, what happened? Instead of doing what Ambedkar said, sending all of the Muslims there to Pakistan, Gandhi said let whoever wants to go, go, and whoever wants to stay, stay. And that's why we're having all this violence [*mara mari*] today. If we had done what Ambedkar suggested, we wouldn't be having these problems.

I thought for a moment, trying to assemble the pieces of this narrative, and especially attempting to place Mukhu's ascription of anti-Muslim sentiment to Dr. Ambedkar. Disagreeing about the ascription and the sentiment, but not wanting to engage a debate on communalism with him at that moment, I said, "I see, so, is that what you think/feel?" (*Aacha, aap ko esey lagta hai?*)

"It's not what I *feel*, it's what I *know*." (*Lagta nahi—esey malum hai.*)

At that, our conversation ended rather abruptly, as Shubha came over and grabbed my hand. I stumbled up and walked with her to the autorickshaw stand, where they charged three rupees per customer for a shared ride to the commuter train station. The walk to the stand, which was located at some distance from the naka, afforded us some privacy. Along the way, as we passed a restaurant on our left, she looked over almost coyly at a shopkeeper in a cloth store who was filling the shop's doorway with his bulky frame. He smiled at her discreetly; she raised her hand and made a circle with her thumb and forefinger to indicate "A-OK" and waved it at him.

"Is that your friend [*dost*]?" I asked, smiling. She vaguely nodded, and said, "Yes."

I thought of my conversation with Shubha earlier that day, when I had spoken with her about women who worked as sex workers in other parts of the city. In response to their reasoning, that they sold sex "for the stomach" (*pet ki liye*), Shubha had said, "Yes, you could take your honor and sit inside your house, but . . ." (*Hahn, izzat le kar ghar ja undar bayt sakte hai, laykin . . .*) before trailing off into silence. Brimming with thoughts on Mukhu's lecture, I also thought of the conversation with Shubha as I watched her unspoken exchange with the shopkeeper on the road.

Relationships (*Rishtey*)

The most striking aspect of Mukhu's story was in his linking the anticaste movement, and the person of Dr. Ambedkar, with his own access to the naka. For Mukhu, the existence of the naka was a sign of progress for the anticaste movement, a space of liberation. Mukhu's history of anticaste struggle, as well as observing interactions with men on the street like the ones with Shubha and Prema, further complicated my understanding of the relationalities between caste, sexuality, gender, and sex work at the naka.

The repeated instantiation of caste through the lens of sexuality— literally through women of different caste-based communities accusing one another of selling or trading sexual services—could be read as a sign of the hopeless fragmentation of a group of people who otherwise would and should identify as part of the same economic class. However, the assertion of caste carried an added valence when inflected by the oft-repeated phrase "Without relationships [*rishtey*], no one gets work." (*Rishtey beena kam nahi milta hai.*) *Rishtey* literally means "relationships" or "relations" and is a term often used in reference to marriage, such as when a family is seeking a marriage "alliance" or *rishta* for one of their kin. It can also simply indicate a familiar relationship. The romantic and sexual undertones of rishtey resonated with the economic context of the naka, in which workers used any competitive edge available to them in order to secure as much paid work as possible.

These kinds of rishtey resonated with other forms of sociality, and particularly with kinship, but it was not kinship per se. The term itself— *rishta* (a relation), as opposed to *rishtedar* (a relative)—conveyed that, at the very least, a distinction was being made between kin and people with whom one has a rishta (singular). If this was also a kind of kinship, it was that of survival and of recognition. The importance of rishtey at the naka counters the idea of "primordial" caste or community relationships determining status and access to anything of value at the naka. Instead, the use of the concept of rishtey conveys the ways in which relationships at the naka were constantly being re/made by people who were related not by blood but by circumstance. Over time, it became clear that rishtey was enormously consequential for how work was pursued and paid at the naka, particularly in the absence of written contracts and official over-sight. The rishta that an individual worker could develop and maintain with those who meted out temporary contracts could be the difference between no work, some work, and regular jobs, as well as how workers were paid and what recourse they had if there was a dispute about pay-ment, the job, or any other matter associated with the job in question.

After I had crossed a certain threshold of familiarity at the naka, such that a subtle level of rishta existed between us, Shubha began to ask me, "Have you put my son's name in the cooperative's list for available workers? Have you told them yet? They think you're an important per-son, they'll listen to you." She again described how her husband had died when she was a young mother with four children, leaving her to ensure their survival on her own. "That's why I've ended up here, waiting for work. If I don't do this, I don't eat." I replied that, as far as I knew, there had been a local workers' cooperative, but it was now defunct. I prom-ised to check. (It was defunct.)

The importance of rishtey came up with Suma as well. She was one of the few women at the naka to have been born and raised in Mumbai.

Her family was from Dharavi, known at one time as the largest slum in Asia. Dharavi had been a flash point for communal tensions in Mumbai in the early 1990s, as the first area in the city to experience communal riots when the Babri mosque was demolished in the city of Ayodhya in 1992.[27] On one visit, we sat in silence for a while, watching people and traffic go by. It had been two days since Suma had been hired for a job. The job had turned out to be unloading a large dump truck full of broken rocks and cement. She described loading a steel pan from the truck, hoisting it onto her head and carrying it to a pile on the roadside, where she would dump it before going back to the truck again. In this manner, she unloaded half of the truck by herself in one day. She was paid 100 rupees, roughly equivalent to two U.S. dollars at the time.

"See," she said. "So much work, and only 100 rupees." According to her, domestic work was the best kind of employment. It was steady and did not require unloading or breaking rocks and cement. She once pointed to the apartment buildings at the edge of the hutments where she lived and said that women who live in the hillside slums often went there to look for domestic work. "There's always someone ready to do it. And if one person doesn't want to go, there's always someone else."

A standard minimum day wage rate had been provisionally "enforced" through an informal system of workers and contractors monitoring one another according to unofficial, citywide agreements about a standard minimum wage for a day's manual labor. To be sure, workers had a vested interest in keeping the highest standard minimum day wage rate in place. If the payment offered for any given job was below the accepted standard, workers expected each other to refuse the assignment or, at least, to haggle the rate up to the standard. However, the common industry standard was violated regularly and thus served as a source of tension between the various caste-based groups of people who used the naka, with different groups regularly accusing one another of undercutting the standard minimum wage. Ensuring a standard minimum wage became not only a matter of earning a fixed amount for temporary construction jobs but also a matter of honor and group affiliation.

The intersection of economic competition at the naka with notions of honor and gender was illustrated in an incident in which a Banjara woman virtually faced eviction from the naka. During "the season" for construction work in the city, this woman, who was a member of a community of seasonal migrants from Karnataka, said that the police had been called to remove her and other members of her community from the naka. The police were reportedly doing so at the behest of some of the Maharashtrian Nav Buddho women there, including Shubha. The woman who was subject to the attempted eviction recounted the incident:

> They [the Maharashtrian Nav Buddho women] called the police on us yesterday, who told us not to sit there anymore. The police, they were so white [*gora*], just like the Marathi people, so *gora*. The people I know there, the ones who just want to make trouble, they say that it's "their" naka, and they don't want anyone else to come and sit there. They say that the Banjara people shouldn't come and sit there, because we don't live here the whole year, and we should just go. They accuse us of just working for fifty rupees [per day]. Why would anyone just work for fifty rupees? We get work because we work harder than the Maharashtrian people. All they want to do is sit around and eat *paan* all day.

This woman's comments were in response to the repeated sentiments of the Nav Buddho community about seasonal migrants, who were usually from tribal Banjara and Lambadi communities and went back and forth between their villages and the city every few months. Their migrations to the villages were timed to occur after the monsoons, when workers would be needed to harvest sugar, tobacco, and other cash crops in rural areas throughout Maharashtra and northern Karnataka. Migrations to Mumbai were undertaken between harvest seasons in order to supplement the piece or day rate that workers could earn on the farms. Nonseasonal or permanent migrants, like the Maharashtrian Nav Buddho workers at the naka, regularly expressed anti-Lambadi or anti-Banjara sentiments in terms of other communities taking jobs that were rightfully theirs. Women of the Nav Buddho community complained that contractors hired women of the tribal communities "so very often" because "they go with contractors and do some bura kam. Then how are *we* expected to ever find work from here?" They argued that if women of one community traded sex from the naka, and were willing to work for half of the going day wage rate, other women soliciting work from the naka would be required to do the same in order to compete effectively for paid work.

The economics of the naka were fairly straightforward and provided a context for many of these intergroup antagonisms. Plentiful workers at the naka tipped the balance of power in favor of contractors, rendering the naka a buyers' market and reducing workers' leverage to negotiate the best rate for themselves. That tribal families often migrated together and brought their own food supply to Mumbai, gleaned from harvesting landowners' crops and bought by the meager day wages earned through farm labor, added insult to injury for Nav Buddho migrants, who resented seasonal migrants' access to cheaper staples in rural areas. Despite the differences of seasonal or permanent migratory status, however, all these people lived side by side in the hillside slums, with the same housing and financial needs. For everyone, having a rishta of some kind with a potential employer, or someone who could arrange employment, was often the most critical element of securing any kind of income.

Workers and advocates reported that a living wage for a family in a slum or temporary housing colony in the city was around 2,000 rupees per month. To earn this sum, which enabled just enough purchasing power for food, water, electricity, and basic household expenditures, the primary wage earner in a household would need to secure twenty working days in a month. However, most of the approximately fifty women who were heads of their own households and the subjects of formal interviews at the nakas consistently reported having only eight to ten days of paid construction work per month. Roughly half of the required monthly income required had to be raised through means other than day wage construction work.

The high competition for work mobilized the need for rishtey and *pehchaani* (recognition or acquaintance) to procure paid work from the naka. The ideas of rishtey and pehchaani were also interpellated as impropriety through overfamiliarity in verbal attacks deployed by the Nav Buddho community against Banjara women, whom they perceived as interlopers and economic competitors at the naka. This discourse functioned within a broader context of attempting to maintain access to a public space, where "public" was defined by sexual norms that included injunctions against women *visibly* selling or trading sex for work. This was considered morally suspect, at best, and was a matter of honor that, for women at the naka, was akin to monetary currency in that it was also earned and could be traded upon for socially legitimated work, including construction work. In light of these dynamics in garnering paid work from the naka, there is a relation between rishtey and capital that uniquely renders buyers and sellers of manual laborers' services within the same frame. This rishtey is not that of biological kin, nor of idealized dispassion between white-collar coworkers, but one produced and mediated through daily negotiations for survival.

Filling the Income Gap

The story of soliciting work from the naka is one of almost, but not quite, meeting one's economic needs. While the naka functions as a space with multiple meanings for migrated communities surviving in Mumbai, the primary purpose of the naka—offering a sustainable livelihood through day wage contract labor—is rarely, if ever, achieved by the majority of workers who use the space. Everyone who used the naka as a primary source of paid work found it necessary to supplement the income that jobs procured from the naka provided. This was particularly true for women, and it raised the question of how they met these livelihood gaps. One answer—episodic sex work and sex trade—offers a clear explanation for how the income gap left by construction work was filled. Nonetheless, it would be misleading to claim that this was the primary means by which the gap was addressed. Women engaged in a range of income-generating strategies, which included construction work, sex for work, and sex work, as well as engaging in small-scale business ventures and selling services other than construction labor by doing domestic work or piecework manufacturing.

Piecework was integrated into the daily lives of naka-based workers. Almost all of the homes in the hillside bastis also served as miniature manufacturing units. In extolling the virtues of Mumbai, Maya, another naka-based worker, had said, "You can do anything in Mumbai. There is so much work here! You can put designs on bangles, make earrings, make hairpins—there is so much work!"

People who lived in the hillside bastis of Sanjay Gandhi National Park participated in informal manufacturing largely by making cheap costume jewelry that would eventually be sold by individual vendors on local commuter trains and in street markets. Different homes participated in various kinds of commercial production. The home of Daya, another naka-based worker, doubled as a space for making earrings and *mangalsutras*, necklaces typically worn by Hindu women as a sign of marriage. The children there were regularly stringing together small black plastic beads and tin pendants plated with a thin layer of gold to make the style of mangalsutra that Suma proudly wore. She had been married for seven years, and the gold plating had worn off her pendant almost completely, revealing the tin underneath. All women at the naka, regardless of their religion, wore mangalsutras if they were married or partnered in any way.[28]

At Shubha's house, the storage space under the double bed in the front room was used to keep a hairpin-making machine. When they were not cooking or cleaning in the space, Shubha or Shubha's daughter-in-law made use of their time by sitting on the ground behind the machine with a pile of three-inch, narrow, black metal strips. The strip would be inserted into the machine, which had a pair of round pads attached to a series of gears and a lever. The lever, when pulled, would bend the metal strip around a small post, resulting in the strip being folded in half to form a hairpin with a clasp that would be decorated later. One kilogram of finished hairpins was worth two rupees. Shubha was seen as one of the more resourceful people at the naka when she also landed the job making sweets for Sankranti in early January.

All of this piecework supplemented the wage that Shubha earned from the naka, but only slightly. The main source of income remained the work solicited from the naka itself. Yet, with so much competition for work from the naka, the question remained as to how workers managed to distinguish themselves from one another in the eyes of contractors and other potential employers in order to compete effectively. A response to this question came from the larger naka in the city center, where a female contractor explained, "Without acquaintance, no one finds work." (*Pehchaani beena kam nahi milta hai.*) When I asked her if she ever had a problem with herself or her workers being paid on time, she replied, "Without trust, no one finds work." (*Vishwas been kam nahi milta hai.*) Both of these refrains took on a different shade of meaning in relation to the use of the term "bad work" (*bura kam*). During one interview, Giri was unequivocal about what she thought it took to secure paid work day after day from the naka, about the atmosphere of competition, and about why women continued to choose to go there to solicit contracts, despite the inherent uncertainties:

> Oh, the Banjara people, they work. They do double work. [*Double kam karte hai.*] They are of a different kind of work. [*Doosra kam ka hai.*] Some contractors who used to give work now don't. For four months, the Banjara people come; rain comes, and they go back to the village. They came and spoiled the naka. That's why Marathi women don't get work anymore. We used to get four or five days a week. A woman is ok if she has a man. If not, it's bad. The woman who laughs and plays, that's the woman who gets work. [*Hasnewallah, khelnewallah, voh aurat ko kam milta hai.*] That's the era [*zamana*] we're in. That's why Banjara people get work. Banjaras own land in the village, but just come here to make money. We're the ones who earn honor, they're

the ones who earn money. [*Izzat kamane walle hum hai, paise kamane walle voh hai.*]

Maintaining a standard minimum wage for work solicited from the naka was not only a matter of earning a certain fixed amount for temporary construction jobs but also a matter of honor and community affiliation, especially when tied to perceptions of women doing sex work or sex for work from the naka. Banjaras being targeted so clearly and directly in these discussions raised the question of how Banjara women would respond. When I attempted to make contact with Banjara workers, it became apparent that my familiarity with members of the Maharashtrian Nav Buddho community was perceived as an alliance. This precluded approaching a similar degree of familiarity with other communities at the naka, particularly one that had a competitive and even, at times, antagonistic relationship with Nav Buddho workers. However, some amount of contact was possible, and initiating contact with Banjara women at the naka led to a group interview of sorts, on a hillside near Jamrushi Nagar, with approximately thirty Banjara men, women, and children. Unlike their Nav Buddho counterparts, the Banjara settlement was much more temporary, resembling the campsite of a transient community more than the semipermanent shacks situated among well-worn paths in the more established sections of the settlements. During our interview, I attempted to delicately approach the charge that Banjara women were trading sex with contractors for work by asking about women's dealings with contractors, about how contractors treated the women who worked for them, about how challenging it was to find work. Much circuitous discussion was had in this vein. Eventually, in a moment of desperation, I asked if women they knew ever experienced anything "unusual" with contractors. After several more cycles of these kinds of questions, the woman who was acting as the spokesperson for the group replied impatiently, "Yes, yes, we know very well what you are asking and, no, we never ever do anything like that!" She said that there was no rain at all in Gulbarga (in northern Karnataka), and that her family had been going back and forth between Gulbarga and Mumbai for the past ten years. "When it rains, we get good work," she said. Then, clarifying her earlier comment about contractors, she added, "Some people are good, some are bad. We get work through having an acquaintance." (*Koi accha rehete hai, koi bura. Pehchaani se milta hai.*)

Secrets on the Street

The vagaries of soliciting paid work from the naka implicate both the space of the street and the notion of the open secret, a concept I discuss further in the book's conclusion. The street has entered the epistemological fray of anthropology relatively recently, as critical geography and new modes of ethnographic inquiry grapple with rapidly changing, deindustrializing, and expanding cities. The need for critical interest in the street was famously framed by Marshall Berman: "Unless we know how to recognize people, as they look and feel and experience the world, we'll never be able to help them recognize themselves or change the world. Reading *Capital* won't help us if we don't also know how to read the signs in the street."[29] I have taken up this methodological exhortation in the process of seeing "ethnographic knowledge as always already situated, and always a product of geographical change."[30] However, while I do not eschew Berman's interest in seeing the street as a site of resistance or revolution ("the shout in the street"), I have taken a slightly different tack here, in showing that the street is a unique site of multiply produced meanings, and that the spectrality of these meanings is sometimes the difference between surviving and failing to survive. The spectrality of sexual commerce at the naka may be thought of as an instantiation of the ways in which public space in Mumbai is contested, and produced through that contestation. As Gidwani and Chari write, "Henri Lefèbvre (1991 [1974]), whose insights, we have suggested, are at the heart of radical geography, saw the lived space of the street as potentially skewing the fit between dominant spatial practices and subaltern representations of space. The production of space under capitalism becomes one arena of contestation over the dialectics of capitalist development, in which ordinary people seek to remake place and spatial relations to some extent, but not under conditions of their choice."[31] If the differential uses of the naka signal the negotiations for survival that Mumbai's working poor negotiate, then the production of sexual commerce as the open secret of naka-based solicitation serves to facilitate the economic utility of the naka for workers. The silences surrounding sex work at the naka are necessarily rich, laden with innuendo, and coded for those who can hear.

SEX, WORK, AND SILENCE 111

Conclusion

> There is no binary division to be made between what one says and
> what one does not say; we must try to determine the different ways
> of not saying such things. . . . There is not one but many silences, and
> they are an integral part of the strategies that underlie and permeate
> discourses.
> —Michel Foucault, *History of Sexuality*, vol. 1, *An Introduction*

> "Closeted-ness" itself is a performance initiated as such by the speech
> act of a silence—not a particular silence, but a silence that accrues
> particularity by fits and starts, in relation to the discourse that sur-
> rounds and differentially constitutes it. The speech acts that coming
> out, in turn, can comprise are as strangely specific.
> —Eve Kosofsky Sedgwick, *Epistemology of the Closet*

I end this chapter by analogizing "the closet," not with the naka but with
the silences surrounding a certain practice at the naka. Eve Sedgwick's
invocation of this Foucaldian notion of silence serves to provide a rubric for complicating the relationship between speech and truth, while
it opens up a critical space to consider the multiplicities of silence and
what Sedgwick later references as "ignorances."[32] If silences are speech
acts, and nakas must be purposed for soliciting as broad an array of services as possible, then the silences surrounding the solicitation of sexual
services from the naka, the "back teeth," produce the naka multiply, under the sign of livelihood.

While this chapter serves to outline the connections between honor,
caste, and the stigmas of prostitution as they operate in the space of the
naka, the questions of unspeakability and of secrets remain. Although
the contours of selling or trading sexual services from the naka are outlined here, they are unspeakable in the spaces of the naka and the surrounding hillside communities. How, then, do we understand that a phenomenon is taking place while hidden in plain sight, rendered illegible by
direct speech, illegal by the state, and yet clearly signified and obliquely
named? One means of pursuing the discourse of sexual commerce in
the spaces of the naka is through an analysis of the silences surrounding
sex work and trade among naka-based workers. An analysis of sexual
commerce that centers silence troubles the idea that sexual commerce
consists of a series of objectively knowable truths that can be enumerated, cataloged, and ultimately acted upon in the same manner.

I have addressed the silences surrounding sex work at the naka by exploring the ways in which these silences are produced as an aspect of the discourse on sex commerce there. In examining the production of silence and sex work at the naka, I have also examined the social and caste-based hierarchies and norms of the naka as an urban, public space. In the following chapters, I compare this naka with other spaces in the city where sexual commerce is more openly discussed, where it is defined in a manner that is legible within the dominant, internationalized discourse of sexual commerce. An analysis of sexual commerce in these other spaces helps to elaborate the contours of silence surrounding sexual commerce at the naka, while raising doubts regarding conceptual distinctions that maintain the idea of sexual commerce as an exceptional case, belonging to a completely unique zone of existence unto itself, both economically and spatially. Taken together, the discourse of sexual commerce in all of these spaces suggests that sexual commerce exists on a continuum of income-generating options for low-income urban migrants and that, rather than delineating the parameters of "choice" and "force," these options are part of a broader set of negotiations that people living in poverty engage and manage in everyday life.

CHAPTER 3

SEX WORK AND THE STREET

This chapter further elaborates the range of services, and modes of remuneration and exchange, that occur under the auspices of sexual commerce, a concept that describes a continuum rather than a singular practice. The continuum of sexual commerce is part of a range of informal labor practices, where selling sexual services may be one of several income-generating strategies that people engage contemporaneously, or over a period of time. While some do rely on sexual commerce for the majority of their income, many use sex work more episodically, as a supplement to other income-generating strategies. This chapter considers the possibility that if sexual commerce is produced on a continuum, so too are the regulatory practices that are brought to bear upon the range of practices by which it is constituted.

The idea of a continuum of regulation for sexual commerce in everyday life countermands the idea that if sex work is somehow legally prohibited, then its criminalization is enforced in well-ordered and absolute terms. I follow this line of inquiry here by discussing the regulation of sex work on a busy city street near a hectic commuter railway station in another of Mumbai's northern suburbs. This discussion necessarily includes elaborating on the continuum of sexual commerce and the ways in which its illegality and social stigma are manifested through particular techniques and actors. In the case of soliciting clients for sexual commerce on this city street, actors who participated in regulating (i.e., controlling, inhibiting, stigmatizing, punishing) solicitation for clients included both local police and merchants whose shops lined the sides of the road. The harsh treatment meted out by police against street-based sex workers was the subject of numerous conversations among women who solicited on the street that forms the primary ethnographic frame for this chapter. Merchants whose shops opened onto the street provided a moralizing narrative for why the women who solicited there deserved this treatment. That there were two establishments in the same area where sexual commerce also took place—a brothel and a dance bar[1]—placed the regulation of street-based sexual commerce into sharp relief, and raised the question of what, exactly, was being regulated there. Noting contradictions in the ways that criminality functioned with respect to street-based sexual commerce in this space provides an opportunity to consider how prevailing theories of civil and political society may be further complicated through a critique that accounts for sexual commerce in the city. Such a critique would account for the ways in which official regulation of sexual commerce in public is uneven, patchy, and lacking coherence, dislodging the notion that law and practice amount to the same thing with respect to prostitution. I use the space of the street to stage this critique, extending the discussion that began in the introduction on the politics of public space in the city.

Migrants on the Street

The discourse of sex work on the street was a world apart from that of the *naka*. The street was located next to a major commuter railway station in Mumbai and was used as a "stroll" for sexual commerce by a roughly stable group of fifteen women, along with another twenty to thirty others who came and went more infrequently. According to women who solicited there, this street had been a place known for sexual commerce for several years. During the period that the ethnography describes, this area was a contested zone, with an active struggle being waged over the parameters of its proper commercial use and whether or not soliciting clients for sexual services could continue there. The moniker "street-based sex workers" was ascribed to these women by a local NGO that distributed condoms and did other HIV prevention outreach in the area, according to the outreach workers who introduced me to women there.² The regulation of the street by police, along with the NGO defining women as sex workers and women being seen to perform the attributes of solicitation, contributed to women being classified as a population of sex workers per se by everyone in the locality. This definitional parameter was something women themselves also used, facilitating their acknowledgment that their income-generating strategies included selling sexual services. Unlike the laborers' naka, where family members and long-term acquaintances would solicit paid work from the same space, women doing street-based sex work were geographically far from their homes and families. Women doing street-based sex work used this distance to mitigate against the stigma of prostitution, in many cases avoiding disclosing this aspect of their paid work to their families, including their children. Instead, they said that they were engaging in construction work or other nonstigmatized forms of generating income. Other women who traveled to laborers' nakas far from their homes to solicit clients for sexual services also made this claim to their families, that they were exclusively doing construction work to make a living. In the case of the city street that is of interest in this chapter, women were able to solicit there because they lived in different areas throughout the city. They came to this place to do sex work specifically because of the relative anonymity it afforded, especially in comparison to their areas of residence or areas where they did construction work among village-affiliated social networks. Like naka-based workers, these women also lived in close-knit communities of people who had migrated from rural areas and were now living in slums that were subject to demolition, and threats of demolition, by a combination of real estate developers and the municipality.

Doing sex work was a partially successful strategy for making ends meet, but, like construction work, it was not sustainable in and of itself. While this second research site was similar to the first in that both were used by migrated workers to solicit short-term contracts (primarily for sexual services, in this case), this street was used as a space where sexual commerce was more openly negotiated and acknowledged than it was at the naka. At the laborers' naka, the solicitation of clients for sexual services was invisible and disavowed, and the primary mode of solicitation for sexual services was via soliciting contractors for construction work, or by seeming to be doing so. In contrast, women used the street to directly solicit clients for sexual services, a practice they acknowledged more freely than did women at the naka. Women soliciting sex work from this street also reported earning money by doing agricultural labor in their villages, as well as other day wage work in the city, including construction work, which they solicited from laborers' nakas similar to the one discussed in chapters 1 and 2.

Women soliciting from the street and at the naka had several key similarities, including that they all officially belonged to Scheduled Castes (SCs) and Scheduled Tribes (STs), as well as belonging to the official grouping of Other Backward Castes (OBC). Although the street-based sex workers in this group were not from the same eastern Maharashtrian district as the naka-based workers, many of these women were also from rural SC and ST communities, living in economically depressed, underdeveloped, drought-prone districts in southern Maharashtra and northern Karnataka. Women doing street-based sex work at this site reported such factors as drought, lack of access to education for members of their caste, especially for women, and extremely low wages for landless agricultural workers as leading to their decision to migrate to Mumbai in search of work.

In their villages, these women had worked as landless agricultural laborers with their families, earning two to ten rupees per day, primarily serving as weeders and harvesters in areas where cotton and sugarcane were dominant cash crops. Almost all had come to Mumbai as young women and girls with their husbands, in search of more lucrative paid work in the city. Others came on their own, after being left behind in their villages by husbands who went to other towns and cities as seasonal migrants in search of work. These men had never returned, nor had they sent remittances back to their families left in the village. Their wives were subsequently heads of their own households, being either widows or "abandoned" by their husbands. Much like naka-based workers, they had found it impossible to support themselves and their children on the wages of a landless agricultural worker in the village. Lina, for example, spoke about her village in northern Karnataka, where she left her two children with her mother. She said that her husband had left her, and that "last I knew he was really sick. People were saying that he had AIDS, and may have died already. I don't know where he is now, but wherever he is, I hope he's happy and fulfilled [*sukhi*]."

Migration and Housing (Redux)

As at the construction workers' naka, women who solicited sex work from the street had done agricultural labor in their villages and often compared the village and the city in terms of varying day wage rates available in each place (ten rupees per day in the village compared with

fifty, a hundred, or more in Mumbai). The fact that the comparison between livelihoods available in the village and the city was clearly in favor
of the city corroborated the high levels of out-migration present in many
source villages, where every family had at least one working member
sending remittances home from wages that he or she earned in an urban
center. And yet, despite the possibility for earning more than ten times
the village day wage rate in the city, bringing the entire family to Mumbai was deemed unfeasible for many of the women who worked on the
street, because of the high cost of living and highly unstable housing in
the city. The most cost-effective strategy for survival, then, was for one
family member to earn city wages and to send cash remittances home
with trusted relatives or friends, or to take remittances back themselves
periodically.[3] The following exchange reflected a common theme in my
discussions with street-based sex workers on the relationship between
the village and the city.

Radhabai said she was off to her village.[4] When I asked whether she'd
be coming back, she waggled her hand in both directions and turned
down the corners of her mouth, indicating her ambiguity.

"We came here to fill our stomachs," she said, "and instead what do
we do here? Just walk up and down this street and eat slaps [*mar khatey
hai*]."

Shaini said that Radha hadn't had any work for two days, and that
her whole family was living back in the village. She said that Radha was
off to her village and may or may not come back. Almost everyone else
in this community of street-based sex workers was back in their villages
as well. I was told that this was "the time" for people to go back, for a
short while, at least. They would return soon, by and large, and later in
the year they would go back again to help with the harvest so that they
could increase the family's income for the season.

These kinds of exchanges illustrated several points about the cycle
of migration for the women working on this street. For example, rather
than describing a linear migration trajectory, in which workers leave
their villages once to settle permanently in the city, or describing a
trajectory of regular, "circular" seasonal migration like that of Banjara
tribal people working from the construction workers' naka, Shaini's and
Radha's movements between the village and the city were frequent and
somewhat less predictable. Their geographic oscillations were dependent on the agricultural seasons, as well as the amount of work available
in any given place. A glut of workers in the fields, or heavy police harass-

ment in the city, would prompt another round of migration, provided that it was financially feasible at the time. The harvest was a significant event for the income that it generated. Going back and forth was important for the opportunities it afforded for earning money, and for taking cash and gifts to family members. While none of these women lived and worked in Mumbai year-round, the city, and not the village, served as a base for these migrations.

When Radha was asked when, or even whether, she would be returning to the city, she was noncommittal, as were most of the women working from this stretch of pavement. The assertion that one could not know if one would return to the city reflects precarity in at least three registers—precarity in finding paid work; the precarity of one's own health and, therefore, the physical capacity to work; and the precarity created by the official management and control of urban public spaces, primarily via the police. Radha alluded to this last category of precarity when she said that they "only eat slaps" on the street. Other conversations referenced the instability of housing, like that of naka-based workers.

During another conversation I stood next to Uma as Shaini explained how they all come to this stretch of road in the late afternoon from their homes. In due course, she began reciting the localities throughout the city where each of them lived. Shaini pointed to the building across the street and said, "My house is nice, it's like that, it's a solid [pucca] room."

Uma said, "Shaini lives in a room in a set of solid-built dwellings [challi], I live in a hut [jopdi]. This is the way it is." When she referred to the hut [jopdi], I asked if one of the city's advocacy groups for slum dwellers works in her locality, as they do among people who live on the hillsides of Sanjay Gandhi National Park. She shrugged and said no, but "we do try and save our jopdis ourselves. They come to tear the jopdis down every so often. Mine is next to a market. But we put the children out in front when they come to break our houses because they wouldn't hurt kids." I imagined a confrontation between the bulldozers and the residents of the slum, with a large group of children constituting the first line of defense for the hutments. "The women cops are the worst," she continued. "They are the most dangerous, because they can actually touch the ladies, the male cops can't."

The housing instability described by Uma resonated with that of naka-based construction workers. The distinctions that women made between the different categories of housing—a challi versus a jopdi, a pucca room versus a temporary shelter—revealed a running catalog among women on the street of the hierarchies in economic standing that existed amongst them, measured in part through the type and level of stability of one's housing. Although pucca rooms (constructed of cement, concrete, or brick, literally meaning "solid rooms") were also subject to demolitions, it was more likely that a *kucha* (temporary or less solid) shelter would either be demolished or be swept away by the monsoon rains and poor drainage. The noncommittal approach to whether one would or would not return to the city following a visit to the village was informed by these differences and reflected the precarity that these women negotiated daily. While day wage construction workers also experienced and managed a significant degree of unpredictability in finding work, the seasonal nature of construction and agricultural work facilitated slightly more routinized patterns of movement between the village and the city. In addition, day wage construction workers almost always being surrounded by economically interdependent kin and village networks most of the time meant that there was a slightly greater degree of stability with respect to housing and supplying one's day-to-day needs, stability that came with less personal autonomy. As a result, it would not have been possible for women at the naka to solicit clients for sexual commerce in the manner of women who worked as street-based sex workers, without losing the community support upon which their survival often depended. At the naka, and on the street, this valence of community support was produced within the terms of *izzat* (honor).

Izzat

Radha did eventually return to Mumbai from her village in northern Karnataka, after the harvest season. Our conversation following her stay there addressed the question of izzat in the space of the street and prompted further queries regarding relationships between various modes of generating income.

Radha was older than most of the other women working from the street and had a perpetual white rash up and down her arms. When I asked her about it, she chuckled, as if going to the doctor was the last thing on her mind. I asked her about her time away and she explained that she had been in the village for the past month for the harvest. "How was it?" I asked.

She replied, "I was able to eat the bread of honor. It felt good." (*Izzat ki roti khaneki mili. Aachi lagi.*)

Another woman with a perpetual smile came up to us, also wanting to talk. She said she was from Nagpur and explained that she did both manual day wage labor (*begari kam*) and "this work" (street-based sex work), although there wasn't much work anywhere lately because things were "cold" (*thanda*) now. "And what do the people in the village know about what you are doing in Mumbai?" I asked.

She and Radha exchanged a smile. The woman from Nagpur replied, "They are told that we do construction work. They say 'she does day wage work in Mumbai' [*voh Mumbai mein begari kam karti hai*]."

Radha's use of the term *izzat* in the sense that she was able to eat food earned with her labor in the fields, and not by prostitution, was reminiscent of Shubha's comment at the construction workers' naka; in response to the question of women soliciting clients for sex from the naka, she had said, "Yes, you could sit inside your house with your izzat, but . . . ," then trailing off, refusing to discuss the matter further. Radha's comment was also consistent with the language used at the construction workers' naka and among the women doing street-based sex work, in which "bad work" (*bura kam*) and other such phrases ultimately connoting the loss of social capital were deployed to mean prostitution. Her friend's statement that people in the village understood that the remittances they received had been earned through doing construction work in Mumbai indicates the need to manage the stigma associated with prostitution. Radha's reference to "eating bread earned with honor" was significant not only for the conflation between honor and any commercial activity that does not involve sex but also for the manner in which sexual commerce and other income-generating strategies are evaluated against one another within the shared rubric of paid work. According to her formulation, these various modes of soliciting paid work were understood relationally; if she has earned the bread of honor by working in the fields during the harvest, she earned the "bread of dishonor" on the city street. For this reason, relatives in the village were told explicitly that these women did day wage work in the construction industry when they were working in Mumbai. Regardless of the livelihood strategy Radha employed, she made it clear that she had to earn in order to survive.

Negotiating Wages

The daily life of doing sex work from this street included constant negotiations for the space to solicit clients, primarily with the police. The limited access to this kind of space was exacerbated by the existence of two discrete brothels located close to the stroll used by street-based sex workers. Women primarily from Andhra Pradesh worked and lived in these brothels, located at the end of the street. Although women who did not live in the brothels could rent space to bring clients there for short periods of time, street-based sex workers reported availing themselves of this option much less than they had done before. As with the construction workers' naka, the strain between brothel- and street-based sex workers was produced by competition for an overlapping client base; this strain was sometimes manifested through clashes based on differences in caste and regional affiliations. Police harassment of street-based sex workers was both a product and a stimulus of these tensions. This matrix of pressures on women working from the street was a frequent subject of discussion among and with street-based sex workers.

As I approached a small cluster of women one afternoon, it was apparent that they were engaged in a heated conversation about someone who had taken one of the women's regular clients. One of them kept saying, "I never do this. I never make a fight over a customer." They were discussing a client who had been taken by a woman who also worked from the street, but who was part of another group of street-based sex workers, one that does not mingle with the women with whom I had been in contact.

"Who are they?" I asked Reyna, noticing a small number of women from the other group sitting on the steps in front of the tea shop.

"They?" she replied. "They're tribal. Look, they never wash or comb their hair, and they'll come here wearing the same sari every single day." I thought of Uma, who was of a Scheduled Caste, not tribe, whom I had seen wearing the same red and green sari with shining bits of zari (embroidery) work on it for the past several months. The other group of women saw this conversation, making no move to approach. They eventually rose and began walking the stroll, up and down the street.

The stakes involved in finding a minimum number of clients who would pay at least fifty rupees were made clearer as women described the wage structure for sex work in the area. On another occasion I saw that Sheila, a central figure among the women with whom I was in closest contact, was lying down on the raised platform in front of one of the closed shops along the street. "What's wrong?" I asked, as she heaved herself up slowly.

"I'm sick," she replied, nodding. Her hair was uncharacteristically unkempt, and she looked as though she were dragging herself just to sit up. "My health just isn't good."

Lina said that she was also doing poorly. When I asked her what was wrong, she hesitated and then said, "I got shivers in the night, and I couldn't sleep, and I had a bad fever." I thought of night sweats, and how she had said that her husband, she thought, had died of AIDS. Later, Sheila said that Lina had white discharge (*safed pani*), a common local term for yeast infections, and often the first opportunistic infections for women who have AIDS. They mentioned that one of the local NGOS had not come for some time to distribute condoms, and that the organization now sells the condoms through what sounded like a social marketing program, at one rupee per three condoms. The problem, in addition to the cost, they said, was that "the NGO gives the entire allotment to the brothel at the end of the road. The brothel sells the condoms for two rupees each to us. We can't afford to buy them even at one rupee for three."

I asked where the other women from their group were, and they pointed with their chins up the street in the direction of one of the brothels up the road. "Oh," I said, "how much do brothel keepers take?"

"Fifty."

"Fifty per hour?" I asked.

"Half hour," said one woman sitting next to Sheila. "Fifteen minutes," said another. "Ten minutes," said still another. "Sometimes not even ten minutes," came the last sardonic comment from Sheila, and I realized they were saying that the brothel takes fifty rupees of the amount paid to each woman *per customer*, no matter how long they used the space of the brothel. "Sometimes, not even ten minutes." Now there were smiles accompanying the statements on timings. Given that most of these non-brothel-based sex workers reported charging fifty rupees or less per customer, it was hard to imagine how one could afford the brothel fee as well.

The local politics of the brothels at the end of the street, and that of the dance bar in the middle of the block, were also part of the wage equation. The brothels, it seemed, did not serve as an option for street-based sex workers to find support, space, or shelter. They were, instead, a source of intense competition for street-based women working independently.

As I asked more about the brothels at the end of the road, Piru lowered her voice conspiratorially and said, "They take fifty rupees per customer at the brothel. When I first came here [four years ago] it was thirty. The brothel only lets us stay on the road until seven in the evening, when it's getting dark."

"They only *let* you stay until seven? How can that be? They can tell you how long you can stay out here?" I asked.

"They give the police bribes [*hafta*] on one side, so that they get us off the street by evening. That way there's less competition for their own women. . . . Women on the street are bad for the brothels' women," she said bitterly.

"So," I asked, "the police get hafta from the brothel on the one hand, and then they chase you off the street, and," I speculated, "they get hafta from the dance bar girls, too?"

"Yes."

Given that using space in one of the brothels was not an option for the women working from this street, other spaces were sought, including lodges and guesthouses, for which the client would pay, or private homes. Some women explained that the lodging house on the street, next to the movie theater, used to be a discreet and affordable place for taking clients, until this option was also foreclosed. Piru said, "Once there was a fight there, and so we can't take clients there anymore." After that, Piru had had to set geographic limits for her clients, such that she would never agree to go beyond a certain suburb with any of them. "Sometimes I take someone else with me, so she can wait outside the door, just in case." This informal system of women protecting one another was also in effect while they waited for clients on the street. This was exemplified by an interaction on the street that was reminiscent of the day I was told to leave the naka after a certain hour, lest I be mistaken for someone soliciting.

The interaction occurred on a day that I had unusually not seen Sheila but learned from Reyna that she lived with Sheila and Sheila's three children. Reyna explained that Sheila is known as Varsha by her biological family. Reyna's time that day was split between talking with me and avoiding the extremely inebriated man who was begging her, or any one of them, to leave with him. He was stumbling and falling over, while repeating that he wanted to take one of them somewhere else. I touched Reyna's left forearm, the inside part, where she had a new tattoo. The raised green letters spelled "Sheila" in Devanagari script. She spoke about Sheila with deep warmth and regard, describing all the ways that Sheila encouraged her to stop chewing tobacco and to stop her other "bad habits." That the name Reyna had had tattooed was the name Sheila used with her friends and clients from the street, and not the one she had been given at birth, seemed significant, indicating a kind of memorialization of Sheila among this particular group of people at a time when she was very ill.

Night was falling, and we were all clustering around an electrical transformer next to a street barber who kept shooing us away. The inebriated man who had been hovering around Reyna earlier found us and insisted on buying tea for everyone. The women humored him, while Reyna stood behind a large electrical transformer with a big wad of tobacco in her cheek, trying to avoid him completely. He stumbled off, only to return with a confused boy from the tea stall carrying a full pot of tea and five empty glasses. Despite our protests, the tea was poured, and we accepted grudgingly. A half-full glass materialized in my hand, and I drank it fast; the women started urging me to leave with repeated assertions of "Madam, it's getting late . . ."

"These women are all my sisters!" the man slurred, as if in response to these exhortations. Turning to me, he said, "Maybe you want to come and see my house?" Before I could answer, the women took the glass from my hand and propelled me toward the train station, urging me to leave as quickly as possible.

Assessing Income-Generating Strategies: *Majburi* and *Mehnat*

Sex work from this street was a component of layered negotiations for economic survival among women who solicited there. These negotiations often took the form of assessing extant options and attempting to create options where none had existed before. Taken together, these assessments and evaluations constituted a local discourse of work that integrated prostitution.

Shaini explained that she "got into this line" through Radha, who is her aunt by marriage. "I didn't have work, and still I had to feed both of my children," she said. When I asked what, if anything, she would rather be doing for work instead, she replied, "All we have is *majburi*[5] [compulsion, constraint, helplessness, obligation] and we say 'fifty rupees,' and maybe they'll wear a condom, maybe they won't." She chuckled ruefully. I noticed that she chose to use the word *majburi* and not *jabardasti* [force].

We had been standing midway down the block, and I wanted to continue our conversation somewhere slightly more private. I suggested a cup of tea from one of the local stalls. We walked over and ordered a "one by two," a common local term for asking a tea seller to split a single serving of tea into two even portions. When Shaini offered to pay, I insisted that she put her money away by saying, "When I suggest tea, it means I'm buying, OK [*theek hai*]?"

She smiled and replied, "You people, you don't have any tension. You do a job [*naukri*], you make 5,000 rupees a month, you have no worries. For us, it is just majburi."

Over tea, Shaini spoke about her two children—her daughter, who is married, and her young son, still in school. Both are living in the village.

After her husband left the family, she decided to come to Mumbai for work. She lived in another suburb with a man to whom she refers as her husband as well. Her husband here in Mumbai has a construction job. I thought of her earlier comments about majburi and asked, "All of you here usually say, 'If we don't get work on the construction naka, then we come here for this work.' Why is that? Do you like that better than this?"

"Yes," she said, as though it were obvious. "That's hard physical labor [mehenat]." She raised her arms at right angles on either side of her body, doing the motion that women did as they lifted vessels of wet cement and rocks onto their heads at construction sites. "This? What's this? Sometimes you get a good man, sometimes a bad man, sometimes there's no work here at all, sometimes they refuse to wear condoms . . ."

Shaini's assessment of hard manual labor, such as that done by women on construction sites, being more desirable than doing street-based sex work might seem to conform to an argument against prostitution. However, Shaini's reflection revealed a complex process of negotiation in engaging different kinds of solicitation. While her expressed preference was for doing construction work rather than paid sex, the way in which this preference was articulated resisted compliance with normative injunctions against prostitution. Shaini located the greatest hazard of prostitution in clients who refuse to wear condoms, and the greatest problem in the lack of stable income, thus making mehenat better than paid sex, which, she implied, is something other than hard labor. At no point did Shaini say that she was subject to force (jabardasti) in pursuing day wage labor and prostitution. The difference between force and compulsion in this context was paramount, marking the difference between individuals exercising force (jabardasti) and structural factors forming constraints (majburi) that elicit a compulsion or need, in this case, toward certain livelihood options.[6] Shaini's assessment of mehenat as being "better" than sex work was ultimately evaluated through a different set of parameters than those used in discourses that deem prostitution inherently violent and exploitive, or as constituting a loss of dignity and worth for female sex workers and, by extension, for women "in general." Because Shaini located the problem with sex work in "bad clients," we may surmise that "good clients" (i.e., those who wear condoms, appear regularly, and pay fifty rupees or more) would make sex work comparable to or even more desirable than construction work.

In their discussions of construction work and sex work, the women doing street-based sex work were clear that these two types of solicitation were not mutually exclusive. Everyone had done both construction work and sex work during their working lives, along with many other income-generating activities, and were familiar with a range of episodic labor. Rather than being distinct earning strategies, these various modes of solicitation were concomitant for this group of women. These modes of solicitation enabled and constituted one another as commercial activities, their viability assessed at any given point in time with respect to the amount and type of work available, to the wage offered, and to the time it would take to complete. In a later interview, Radhabai was explicit about the relationship between construction and sex work: "All of them all have impure/sinful thoughts in their guts. [*Sub pet mein haram sochte hai.*] All of them. Me, I came to Mumbai ten, twelve years ago. From Akola. I came with my husband and two sons. I still have to marry one son off. I did manual labor when I arrived. Sometimes we still go to the naka to look for work."

"Does sex work [*dhandha*] happen from the naka too?" I asked.

"Yes, yes. No one gives work for nothing. He [the contractor] will say, 'Will you listen to me?' ['*Meri baat soonegi?*'] 'Yes.' ['*Hahn.*'] 'Then let's go.' Then they'll give you tea." She paused to laugh, saying, "We'd lay on the work from the front, and they'd 'lay it on' from the rear." (*Hum age se lagate the, aur voh peeche se lagate the.*)

She went into a long description about household expenses, how much for rice, how much for wheat, oil, kerosene. "Then? With all those expenses, how are we supposed to survive?"

"So, do you make more money working in begari kam, or in this work?" I asked.

"No, it's not like that. It's like, for that work, there will be ten women sitting there, and they only need one, so they'll say, 'You, will you listen to me? Then come on.' It happens all the time. Like for me, I had to take a loan to pay 30,000 rupees for my son's house, a house like that," she said, pointing to a shack behind us.

"How much do they take back when you repay the loan?"

"Oh ho! How much? Listen, if you don't pay it back within seven months, they take another 30,000! Otherwise, its 10 rupees for every 100 you borrowed." (In other words, 3,000 rupees to repay against a 30,000 rupee loan, due within seven months, averaging 4,714 rupees per month).

The comparisons and relationships between various modes of work were based on a cost-benefit analysis that included time, money, how much income can be reliably earned in a given enterprise, and the conditions under which that earning takes place. To this end, it was helpful to have a sense of how much income construction workers and sex workers reported making. Although mapping the income from construction work was fairly straightforward, with income levels being corroborated and fairly consistent among naka-based workers, achieving a similar level of corroboration and accounting with this group of street-based sex workers was much more difficult. While street-based sex workers seemed to agree that one benefit of doing day wage construction work was the potential for earning a monthly income of 1,200 to 2,000 rupees, there was little agreement about how much a woman could earn doing street-based sex work. Earnings reported by women doing sex work ranged widely, the differences being tenfold, at least. These inconsistencies can be attributed to a number of factors, including women's own earning capacity changing significantly from month to month or, for some, not having an accurate record of their own earnings. Inconsistencies in reporting earnings or the frequency of securing work also indicated a strategy women used for managing their relationships with NGO workers and researchers seeking to systematically document this kind of information.

Sulochana said that she entered "the line" two years ago, when she stopped working at a hospital. She had been an outreach worker there, working with people with drug addictions. Although she found the work rewarding, she said she left that job because "they only paid something like 2,000 rupees per month, and that's not nearly enough to make ends meet."

"How much do you get here?" I asked.

"Sometimes 9,000, sometimes 10,000."

"Really?" I asked, surprised at how high the figure was. Most of the social workers I knew were making 2,000 to 5,000 rupees per month, 6,000 if they were lawyers. I explained that my research was also being done at a construction workers' naka and described how people there described their monthly incomes, mentioning that one of their chronic complaints was that they never get work.

Sulochana replied, "People will always say that, but it's not right. They will say they get one day of work when they actually get three. It's like that."

"Why do they do that?" I asked.

"Who knows? I never do that. When these people [from local NGOs] come and ask how many [clients] we've had that day, I say. If I've had two, I say two. If I've had none, I say none. I figure, it's better to tell them the truth, in case you ever really need their help."

During the time I spent with women on this street, it became evident that "needing their help" could refer to any number of situations on this street that women needed to manage. Many of these situations were brought about by local merchants and police. Police were often aided by the merchants, as complaints from shopkeepers about sex workers pulling down the neighborhood's status, and therefore its commercial viability, enhanced the police's ability to carry out sweeps and to use violence or the threat of violence more freely as they made arrests, which resulted in each woman paying a fine of 1,200 rupees per arrest.

Police

All of the women, including Uma, Radha, and Shaini, told vivid stories about being chased off of the street by the police. Uma related one incident about a police officer from the local station who had been transferred to this area some three months earlier. His harassment of street-based sex workers at his previous posting was apparently legendary. "Once he chased us down the road with his scooter, nearly ran me over. Another time, we ran so hard, I thought that old woman with us was going to die for sure. She was breathing so hard." Uma went on to describe a woman whom the officer had beaten with his night stick (*lathi*) so badly that she could not walk for several days. "Someone should ask him, what wrong have we done?" she said. "We're doing it for the stomach." (*Usko puchhna chahiye, humne kya galti kiya hai? Pet ki liye karte hai.*)[7] When I asked the chief inspector at the local police station about the chasing and beatings, he replied, "Who can tell who is a good woman and who is a bad one? This is a family area. There's a movie theater on that street that families like to come to. We have to keep the street safe for them."

These women were ostensibly deemed by the police to be a collective threat to respectable, middle-class families for whom the area had to be kept "safe" (i.e., free of sex workers), while they were also reportedly taking bribes to protect the client base of the brothels and the dance bar. Whereas the laborers' naka was deemed a respectable public space from which only licit and legal commerce took place, the presence of street-based sex workers on this block signified moral and even commercial degeneracy that the police were justified in using force to control. Over time, Sulochana's, Shaini's, and even Radha's comments demonstrated that doing street-based sex work was not only a stopgap economic measure to supplement income or a necessity for securing legitimated day wage labor. It was also a commercial activity in which women could earn potentially better wages for the amount of time they worked, with potentially better working conditions. However, their stories also made it clear that while doing sex work could afford a higher monthly income, it exacted a price in the form of heightened police harassment.

Thinking the Police

While contemporary debates on sexual commerce have addressed a broad range of issues, including the formulation of an appropriate social response to the exchange of sexual services and money, such debates have primarily focused on the juridical regulation of this exchange. More often than not, their specific focus has been on individual laws, or on policies that provide a template for laws, that criminalize, decriminalize, or legalize prostitution. In recent years, these three juridical poles have been narrowed to two, as scholars and activists principally debate the merits of legalization versus criminalization. If attention has been paid in these debates to the social meanings of sexual commerce, these have been mobilized in the ultimate service of arguing for or against a certain juridical outcome.

Given the need for a legal framework for sexual commerce that accounts for sex work as a livelihood strategy, and the potential crisis that sex workers face as laws and policies seeking to abolish sexual commerce gain traction, the urgency of engaging with the question of the law with respect to prostitution is convincing. Like the LGBTQ rights movement in India, which has found it necessary to focus vast organizational resources on reforming the antisodomy law (Section 377 of the Indian Penal Code) such that it may no longer be used to harass and intimidate nonheterosexual and gender-nonconforming people,[8] any group of people whose existence is criminalized must necessarily focus on decriminalizing that existence in order to achieve any other social or political gains. At the same time, there is an argument to be made against utilizing an exclusively legal focus in thinking through the vagaries of sexual commerce (and the politics of sexual orientation and gender identity, for that matter) because this potentially overlooks wide swaths of the everyday lives of people who inhabit stigmatized social categories and economic spaces.[9] Here, I aim to describe the spaces of dissonance and congruity between juridical discourses on prostitution in India and its governance in everyday life by discussing the ways in which sex work is policed in Mumbai, and how this policing informs the production of sexual commerce in the city. This analysis avoids eliding the practices of local police and the aims and intents of the law by maintaining a clear distinction between speaking about the ways in which the law provides parameters and deputes authority for policing the street, and the practices that take place under the auspices of law enforcement. In this analysis, the police are an instantiation of the state on the street, constituted between official regulatory regimes, the political economy and social norms of the Mumbai police, the daily life of the city street, and all that lies in and among these touchstones for the practice of policing in the city.

In seeking to understand how policing helps to produce sexual commerce in myriad ways, it bears recalling that police draw their legitimacy and authority not only from the legal sanction of their office, but also from their particular association with the law as a normative social code. The ostensible purpose of the police is to enforce the moral code contained therein. The production of the police as arbiters of moral codes pertaining to sexuality in public becomes apparent in the existence and practices of police vice squads in the West, for example. It also becomes apparent in the ways in which police have historically worked on parallel but not coterminous tracks alongside other arms of the state—e.g., border control—in the service of working toward a shared utopic vision of national security.[10] In this case, that vision increasingly entails rendering prostitution invisible, through the rhetoric of its elimination.

The instantiation of a common rubric of security has been of interest for scholars of urbanization and Mumbai, primarily within the context of critiquing communalism following the Bombay riots in late 1992 and early 1993. This literature offers a perspective on the Mumbai police that pertains to a critique of the governance of sexual commerce there. Thomas Blom Hansen's *Wages of Violence: Naming and Identity in Postcolonial Bombay* discusses the composition of Bombay's police force with respect to the politics of caste and religion in the city, and to the ways in which the police are a site of articulating and enforcing difference in these registers. Sujata Patel and Jim Masselos's *Bombay and Mumbai: The City in Transition* and Patel and Alice Thorner's earlier collection *Bombay: Metaphor for Modern India* also center questions of religion, caste, and ethnicity in thinking through the modes of governance that shaped the phenomenological terrains of Mumbai at the turn of the twenty-first century.[11]

The groundwork for these critiques of the police in Mumbai near the end of the twentieth century is to be found in earlier historical work. In his piece on the police in late nineteenth-century Madras, David Arnold provides an overview of the history of the police in India during the colonial period that offers an important genealogical thread for contemporary policing practices.[12] Arnold traces the history of the police in India through the mutual imbrications of British imperialism and industrialization. Police in England had served as a means to monitor and control a new urban workforce, one that was forming in the wake of industrialization, whose presence constituted the growth of the first industrialized cities in Europe. The suppression of class warfare was explicit in the police's mandate, being instituted to "curb urban crime and discourage working-class political activity."[13] The military was deemed inappropriate for this task because "the English bourgeoisie had a long-standing objection to using soldiers in internal disturbances."[14] The new London Metropolitan Police, founded in 1829, was modeled after the Royal Irish Constabulary, which "was intended to crush agrarian unrest and sporadic terrorism directed against British rule [in Ireland]. . . . In India, the Irish police model was first introduced in Sind in 1843 and, in modified form, it was applied elsewhere in British India in the following twenty years."[15]

Arnold argues that local police in India took on a greater role when troops were in short supply during postwar economies in the early twentieth century.[16] The origins of the police in the United Kingdom, and their direct linkage with maintaining class hierarchies and imperial interests provide a genealogical link between the historical purpose of the police there—to maintain the interests of the colonial state by protecting its military and economic interests—and the ways in which police forces were institutionalized in South Asia. The importance of this genealogy was not lost on the arbiters of Indian independence in the 1930s. However, proposals to significantly reform the institution were met with resistance, as described by Arnold:

> Attempts to change the character of the force would jeopardize the efficiency and internal cohesion of the force as the British had created it: the Congress could not afford to juggle with the organization of the force as long as it served the ministry faithfully. This it did, partly because the Congress ministers as much as the senior police officers were coming to regard Communism as the major threat to both British and Congress interests in India. Indeed, it could be said that the Congress ministry of 1937–39 demonstrated that the loyalty of the police was no longer solely to the British Raj. It was fundamentally a loyalty to the propertied classes, to the interests of the industrialists and landlords in particular, and for this reason the resignation of the Congress in 1939, the party's return to office in 1946, and the transfer

of sovereignty in 1947 did not produce any sharp break in the character and functions of the Madras police.[17]

This purpose of the police, to protect the interests of the propertied classes, was accomplished in British India primarily through devising systems of racialized spatial containment, whose legacies are reflected, for example, in the demarcation of cities on religious and class lines, as well as the continued maintenance of distinct zones where sex work should not, and should, be practiced.[18] This system of demarcating sanctioned and prohibited areas for sex work operates through a matrix of localized relations of power, including ideas about soliciting clients in public, which cannot be neatly explained as the direct enforcement of the letter of the law on the street. The differential regulation of the brothels and the dance bar in the case at hand, due, at least in part, to the bribes police allegedly accepted in exchange for protecting the client base of these spaces, demonstrated this and was confirmed in the explanation given by a member of the local police for the beatings inflicted by one of their cadre upon street-based sex workers: "Who can tell who is a good woman and who is a bad one? This is a family area." The statement does not evoke the law at all; rather, it speaks to the habitability of the street for families, defined in opposition to women who are doing sex work, all of whom are classified in the statement as "bad" women. The statement corroborates the idea of extant criminal classes, defined, in this case, through inhabiting the category of "street-based sex worker," while also clarifying this police officer's vision of the purpose of his organization as necessarily exceeding the bounds of law enforcement.[19]

The criminality that sex workers inhabit by virtue of their sex workerness has been a trope of sexual commerce since the start of the nineteenth century, when all exchanges of sexual services and money were beginning to be consolidated under the sign of prostitution. The criminality of sex work today, including that of visible, (re)cognizable sex work in Mumbai, is part of a long historical process that reflects the ways in which the question of sexual commerce has been highly contested discursive ground. The ways in which abolitionist and nonabolitionist perspectives have vied for space within this discourse are evident in internationalized debates on whether most sex workers are, or have been, victims of trafficking. Abolitionists have called for the removal of sex workers from the spaces where they live and/or work under the sign of "rescue." Rescue in this context entails extrajudicial removal and detention in remand homes, often through raids conducted by a combination of police and antitrafficking NGOs. For the purposes of our discussion on the practices of policing on this city street, it is important to note that the new internationalized ideal of rescue is being deployed within a geopolitical context in which increased police, security, and militarization are offered up as solutions to any number of social phenomena, including poverty, migration, prostitution, and intersections thereof. An uncritical emphasis on police as a means of intervening in the lives of sex workers has thus become a shared characteristic of both governmental and nongovernmental antitrafficking discourses. At the same time, abolitionist as well as anti-abolitionist advocates have reported that police accept bribes and "pimp" girls for the purposes of prostitution. This calls the reliance on police and criminalization as a major tactic of abolitionist responses to sexual commerce into question, while also providing an abolitionist rationale for the necessity of NGO involvement in antitrafficking interventions, including brothel raids.[20]

The question of the police in relation to sexual commerce is complex, to be sure. A critique of the police cannot be overlooked in a critique of sexual commerce, nor can the institution of the police be simply conflated with a unitary notion of the state. Of all the issues of police themselves and the practice of policing sexual commerce that could be subject to debate, the vexing aspect of police demanding and accepting bribes from sex workers, brothel owners, and other middlemen has been emphasized and, indeed, takes center stage in discussions that aim to complicate what the police mean to regulating sexual commerce. There are two problems with this emphasis. First, the emphasis on bribes in critiques of the police has generally produced bad or corrupt policing as exceptional, thereby maintaining the idea that there is a basic status quo of consistency in juridical systems. This analysis runs counter to the idea that policing is idiosyncratic, and that an experience of the law as consistent, predictable, and functional is contingent upon social and economic status, citizenship, and subjective legibility within the law. The second problem is in reference to the idea of what a bribe, roughly translated in Hindi as the word *hafta*, is. While there is broad agreement that bribes are an aspect of policing prostitution in Indian cities, there is vast disagreement on what a hafta means in this context. Do haftas in and of themselves indicate an incompetent police force that works for the highest bidder? Or that there is no rule of law or juridical oversight in a place like Mumbai, save that which is paid for on the open market? I suggest that it means neither of these, that instead the hafta indicates that the rule of law is contingent, specific, and compartmentalized, that it serves not only those who bribe but also those who embody hegemonic ideals of sexual normativity, civil society, and, in this case, "*the* public" on this particular street, where the public were families and local merchants. It also means that the police are embedded within an economic and social web, one in which haftas are considered, by some, to be a natural perk of a job that does not pay a middle-class salary, and in which the police understand where the letter of the law must be enforced (in public) and, perhaps more pertinently, for whom it must be enforced.

Merchants and Hegemonies of the Local

After a week in Delhi, I went back to the community of women soliciting from the street and saw Uma on the road first. As I walked toward her, I saw that she was sitting on her own. While I was still some distance away, a man in a dhoti and Nehru cap walked up to her, leaned forward, and raised his eyebrows. I heard her say "fifty" softly. He turned and walked away. I approached and sat next to her as he was leaving. She looked at me and said, smiling, "You can't even get fifty these days."

We held hands while we sat there chatting. During our conversation, three children walked by, going from the juice stall to the fruit vendors along the roadside begging for coins. When I asked Uma where the other women were, she replied that they were sitting farther down the street. She was sitting on her own because, as she explained, "Nothing comes of us all sitting together in one place like that."

Uma's phrasing indicated that, in fact, for women doing street-based sex work, sitting together in a cluster, as women and men did at the naka, would do much more than "come to nothing." It would lead to a police raid of the area, in which women would be arrested en masse, ostensibly for violating the antisolicitation clause of the ITPA, though it was understood that being visible as street-based sex workers would, at worst, lead to arrest or, at the very least, to harassment. Women arrested for soliciting clients for sex were required to pay a 1,200-rupee fine before they were let go, causing a huge financial loss, in terms of both the fee and the time lost that could have been spent earning, or attempting to earn, for the day. To avoid these risks, the women strolled up and down the street, both to attract the attention of clients and to blend into the flow of pedestrian traffic, especially in the late afternoon and evening.

In another conversation, Sulochana, who also solicited from this street, had emphasized her good relationships with her relatives. I chose not to ask whether or not they know she sells sexual services. She had stayed close to me that day, choosing to sit with me and talk rather than walk up and down the road. "I don't usually sit like this," she said, "but I decided to sit today because of you." As we sat chatting about her work, her family, and the street, she asked, "How does it feel, you sitting here with us like this? Don't you feel strange, the way everyone stares?" Being stared at had become, by then, a regular feature of my daily life in the city. Experiencing Mumbai as a female-bodied gender-nonconforming person, and often traveling alone, within a culture of public sociality in which directly looking at another person was much less taboo than it was in New York City, I had become accustomed to regular and fairly constant staring almost everywhere in Mumbai. Reflecting on the potential convergences between being the object of staring as a gender-nonconforming person and as someone who might be read as having a relationship to sex work, I said only, "No, I don't feel strange."

The stares of passersby and merchants alike, the ever-present threat of police harassment and arrest, and the possibility that clients would not patronize a sex worker who could so clearly be identified as such were all constitutive of sex work on the street. Local merchants were especially critical of this use of what they deemed to be public space and often called the police when street-based sex workers became too conspicuous, either by lingering in front of their shops for too long or by gathering in numbers greater than three or four. Merchants described themselves, and were understood by local police, as members of a respectable middle-class citizenry who were waging a struggle to eliminate street-based sex work from the neighborhood. Ethnographically, they served as observers who held collective memory about the changes over time in their locality, and in the city as a whole. As such, merchants were integral to the production of local discourses and knowledge about the practice of sexual commerce. The merchants there consisted of the tea stall owners, fruit and juice vendors, and shop owners and workers. Shop owners claimed the most economic power, social credibility, and physical space, with their stores selling household necessities, nonperishable food, and services that included repairing commonly used electronics. Although the local dance bar was also a part of the space of the street, it remained somehow discreet, its only conspicuous aspects being the men who walked in and out of the front door, and the imposing security guard who kept watch outside. The movie theater across the road from the dance bar provided a commercial anchor for the block; with its mainstay of the latest Bollywood releases and its accessibility via the local train station, it was a draw for people from many surrounding areas.[21]

The tensions between merchants and street-based sex workers were illustrated, and explained, on one occasion when I went to sit by the older juice vendor who observed the block's activity from his trolley, which was usually parked near the theater. I had become acquainted with him when, after seeing me regularly for a month or so, he had decided to call me over to ask why I repeatedly came to this street to talk with "these bad women." Since that first meeting, when I had tried to explain the nature of the research I was conducting, stopping by to have a chat and a *nimbu pani* (a perfect mixture of just-squeezed lime juice, water, sugar, and chaat masala that he tossed into a rinsed glass) became part of my routine upon arrival there.

As I went there more often, the juice vendor, who sat in a row of juice and fruit stalls by the side of the road, would announce my arrival to his colleagues, saying, "Yeah, it's her." (*Hahn, voi hai.*) While I was sitting near his stall one day, he went into a diatribe against the local police for not doing more to prevent the area from being "run down" by these women. "The cops aren't doing anything to control them. And these women aren't even top of the line. The top of the line girls are in the dance bars; he [the police] gets hafta from them anyway."

I asked why he thought these women did this kind of work, and about their refrain that if construction work is not forthcoming, they come here "for the stomach."

"That's an excuse," he replied, "that they do this if they don't get the other work. No one could do this unless they liked sex [*sex pasand hai*]." He said this with visible disgust and then launched into his own history of migration from Benares to Mumbai in search of work. "Look, me, I worked on a government employment scheme in a factory making auto parts near Pawai [a suburb of Mumbai], but I went back to my village for a year in '72 and lost that job. I did lots of other stuff in between, and now I'm running this juice stall, because what else am I going to do? See, now, these women, they say it's for the stomach, but they could do anything else. Instead, they're spoiling the good name of this street. [*Yeh rasta ka nam badnam karte hai.*]"

Like the police, who were concerned about families visiting the movie theater not feeling comfortable coming into the area, the juice vendor reflected the sentiments of many of the merchants on the street. For merchants on the block, the visibility of street-based sex workers constituted as egregious a transgression as exchanging sexual services for payment. Men walking by who were familiar with the area reflected these sentiments as well, often shouting at street-based sex workers, "You people have ruined this street. Get away from here!"

In the course of chatting with the women one afternoon, before clients were around, several asked if I go to the movies, if I wanted to go to the theater on this block, perhaps? The latest Bollywood blockbuster, *Talaash*, meaning "search" or "quest," was playing. I looked up at the marquee and replied, "It's *Talaash*," as if this answered their question.

One of the women laughed, "Yes! It's a *talaash*, and sometimes you find them, and sometimes you don't, and sometimes they hit you, and if they don't hit you, then sometimes they don't come around, either." (*Talaash hai, aur kabhi milta hai, aur kabhi nahi . . . aur kabhi admi bhi mar dalta hai, aur agar nahi dalta hai, toh atey bhi nahi.*) She said this all in a singsong way, flipping her palm toward the sky and the ground with each lilting phrase. Then she asked seriously, "That's a good film, have you seen it?" She pointed up at the movie poster. It was a gigantic image of Akshay Kumar swinging Kareena Kapur on his hip and firing a gun, her midriff covered by his bulging forearm. "They are brother and sister in it," she said. (They are not.)

Sheila arrived then and greeted me warmly. They all asked again where I stayed in the city. It seemed to be one way of making conversation. "Mahim," I said.

"You come by train?" asked Sheila, looking concerned. "Remember, you should always have a ticket. Otherwise they'll give you a fine."

"I have a monthly pass," I replied. This exchange prompted Uma to recall how many times she'd been caught on the local trains without a ticket.

"At first I used to cry," she said, laughing at her younger self, "but then I got smarter because I knew they'd just pull me off the train and shout at me. Now when I get caught I say, 'No, I don't have a ticket. What can I do? I don't have a ticket.' They threaten to put you in the lockup, say they'll give you a fine, but we don't have any money, so how will they give us a fine?"

The metaphor of a talaash could also have been extrapolated to the women themselves, who were targeted as criminals by almost everyone on the street, except potential clients. The basis on which this talaash was taking place was unclear at first, given that the raids on the street conducted by the local police seemed to be prompted by little more than the women's visibility increasing somehow when, for example, they congregated on the street, and by a generalized yet unmarked set of parameters by which it was understood that they were soliciting clients for sex. The codes for illegal and illicit solicitation were made plain by one of the proprietors of the local provision and grocery shop, set into a prominent storefront on the road. It was run by a diminutive set of men behind the counter and a plump, healthy-looking woman in a bright yellow nylon sari. I had seen them all asking Sheila about me, and had seen them carry on their conversation as Sheila pointed at me, looking like she was explaining something. I had walked over when I thought it appropriate to intervene in the conversation. One of the men immediately brought a chair for me to sit in next to the woman in the yellow sari. "Please, sit," they insisted. The woman was speaking in Gujarati with most of the people who came up to the shop, except Sheila, with whom she spoke in Marathi. The man who ran the shop was Gujarati as well, along with almost everyone who came to buy their provisions there. While I was sitting there, and the woman in the yellow sari was still talking to Sheila, a police officer in full uniform came by. The woman pointed at him and said to Sheila, laughing, "Look, there's your father-in-law!" (*Dekh, tera sasra agaya hai!*) Sheila pursed her lips and drifted away up the road, while I remained seated in front of the shop.

The woman in the sari and I chatted for some time about where I was from and the research I was doing. Then she asked me in a hushed, almost conspiratorial tone, "So, what do you ask them?"

I launched into my standard description: "I ask them what their situation is, what they feel they need, what they think about different kinds of work, things like that." I felt myself being vague in my effort to be concise and elaborated further. When I mentioned women in the construction industry possibly doing sex work as well, she nodded as if this were common knowledge, and said that there had been a lot of complaints from the people who live on this street about women standing here waiting for customers.

"So, have they been here doing this for very long?" I asked.

"No, just three or four years."

"So," I asked, "how do people here know what they are doing? I mean, if all they do is stand on the road."

"Oh, people know," she said with confidence. "When the police come, they run. When they are on the street, they don't really go anywhere. And there are always a lot of men following them around. You can just tell. That's why I told you to come and sit over here with me. Within two minutes, you'd have had a swarm of men after you, too, if you had just stood there by yourself."

After some time, I excused myself and returned to the women. "What was she asking you?" asked Sheila.

"This and that," I said, "what am I doing here, what am I asking all of you, stuff like that, and I thought, if I talk politely with her, then maybe she will bother you all less, right?"

"That's right," she said, without conviction. "That's right."

Near the end of the day, as I was leaving one of the local tea shops with another woman who worked from the street, I saw Lina and noticed her tattoos. I said hello and, pointing to the image on her arm, tried to show her my own. I began rolling up my sleeve when she stopped me.

"No," she said, "don't do that. Why would I want to see? This [the tattoo] is all you take with you when you die anyway. When you die, all they will ask is 'was she good, or was she bad?'" Putting her fingers together in a pinching motion, she said, "For this much they are ready to call you bad, but how much you have to do to be called good, isn't it?" (*Itna mei bura bolne ka tayar hai, leykin aacha bolne ke liya kitna karna padta hai, nahin?*)

The Civil, the Political, and the Politics of the Governed

My ethnographic discussions in this chapter on a group of female sex workers who use the spaces of a city street to solicit clients for sexual services has dealt primarily with the ways in which local police and merchants together regulated these women's access to the street for the purpose of solicitation. At the same time, I have discussed the ways in which the law enforcement in this area was uneven, idiosyncratic, and even irrational, especially as two establishments in the area where sex work took place were allowed to function with relative sanction. The ways in which sex work was policed and regulated unevenly on this street draws a critique of the state, particularly with respect to the ways in which regulatory actors, in this case merchants and police, worked to differentially regulate some sex work, but not all. This critique begins by asking, what does thinking about sex work do to help us (re)think the state? Staging this question requires reconsidering the question of the relationship between and constitution of civil and political society in India.

The larger questions of civil and political society in India are being articulated in relation to the putative distinction that these terms represent, through the metaphor of separate spaces, in which each discrete but related sphere is said to operate in the unifying equation of governance. Aditya Nigam frames these questions in a review of Partha Chatterjee's discussion of the problematics of political society in *The Politics of the Governed*:

> The first set of issues revolve around what [Partha] Chatterjee concedes are "analytical refinements obtained through productive engagement with actual empirical situations on the ground." Among these are Nivedita Menon's proposal that civil and political society are better seen as two distinct modes of engagement with politics, rather than as domains that can be neatly separated and that of Stuart Corbridge and others, which sees these as "interlocking political practices." Clearly, these proposals arise from the difficulty of thinking of the civil and the political in terms of the spatial metaphor inherited from western political theory, which does not seem to work beyond a point.[22]

I suggest that the problem of the uneven regulation of sexual commerce on this street may offer some measure of the "analytical refinements obtained through productive engagement with actual empirical situations on the ground," not only with respect to the problem of seeing the civil and political as distinct domains but also of contributing to critiques of how these conceptual domains are constituted. Framed in terms of the subject of this chapter, the questions that inhere in these problematics center on how local police and merchants (political and civil society, respectively, in the Gramscian sense) intersect in regulating street-based solicitation on this city street, where such solicitation was actually marked in relation to two other sites of sex work there, the beer bar and the brothels. How may we use a critique that accounts for sexual commerce on the street to analyze the ways in which police and local merchants together produce street-based sex workers as a population that requires an exceptional degree of police regulation? Was sex work per se being policed on this street, or, perhaps instead, did the combined actions of local nonstate actors and the police result in protecting the client bases of both the beer bar and the brothels while erasing sexual commerce from public view? These become questions of political theory when police and merchants are provisionally understood to function and to be produced within the respective milieus of political and civil society.

Fundamental to feminist and postcolonial critiques of state formation and governance have been the idea that states are uneven in myriad ways, that there is no one "state," that states are not octopi, with a central brain and many limbs that do its bidding in every geographic and conceptual corner of the nation. One of the ways this has been shown is through the often great distance between the letter of the law and the practice of its exercise. In the languages of juridicism and democratic governance, that distance is the distance manifested in differential access to the rights of citizenship. Some are more completely apprehended and recognized as citizens than others, the state is working for some and not for others, but not in predictable ways. For example, on the street I have discussed here, the state as it is represented by and deputes authority to local police is working for local merchants, who do not directly pay the police for their services, but it is also working, in a sense, for the brothels and the dance bar, who both probably do pay, in the form of haftas. That ostensibly respectable citizenry do not pay haftas and are served in some sense by the police seems to be corroborated by the police themselves in this context. Consider the statement of the police officer earlier in the chapter, about the street needing to be protected for families. His rationale for beating sex workers invoked not the law but, rather, a hegemonic sense of morality regarding the police's right to exercise coercive force to suppress visible street-based solicitation. The differential and somewhat irregular nature of regulation on the street suggests that police, local merchants, and sex workers all inhabit multiple zones of morality/immorality, legality/illegality, and regulation. A consideration of this multiplicity, especially in the context of the regulation of sex work in public through the regulation of solicitation, allows us to further Partha Chatterjee's challenge to "dirty one's hands in the complicated business of the politics of governmentality."[23]

The work of the Subaltern Studies Group renders the people on this street who were selling sexual services legible, in a sense, with respect to theories of governance, because they conform to the classical definition of the subaltern subject, the numerous and necessary critiques of that term notwithstanding. The women who were selling sexual services on this street were all from communities of landless agricultural workers who were SC or ST in official enumerations. In *The Politics of the Governed*, Chatterjee builds a theory of political society around the subaltern in the city, the rural peasant now become the urban slum dweller. Of his definition of political society in this argument, Chatterjee writes:

> Some of you may recall a framework used in the early phase of the Subaltern Studies project in which we talked about a split in the domain of politics between an organized elite domain and an unorganized subaltern domain. . . . To say that there was a split in the domain of politics was to reject the notion, common to both liberal

and Marxist historiographies, that the peasantry lived in some "prepolitical" stage of collective action. It was to say that peasants in their collective actions were also being political, except that they were political in a way different from that of the elite. Since those early experiences of the imbrication of elite and subaltern politics in the context of the anticolonial movements, the democratic process in India has come a long way in bringing under its influence the lives of the subaltern classes. It is to understand these relatively recent forms of the entanglement of elite and subaltern politics that I am proposing the notion of a *political society*.[24]

Soon after this reminder of the foundational intervention of the Subaltern Studies Group, Chatterjee alludes to the possibility of spectral apprehensions of the figures that inhabit his version of "political society" in commenting on Gramsci's originary definition of this concept: "My intention was to point out the possibilities that exist in that normatively nebulous zone that I have called political society. When I use that term, I am always reminded that in the *Prison Notebooks*, Antonio Gramsci begins by equating political society with the state, but soon slides into a whole range of social and cultural interventions that must take place well beyond the domain of the state."[25] Chatterjee's understanding of "political society" is illustrated through a number of case studies, prominently featuring slums along railway lines that are similar to the slums I have described throughout the book, places that, in my discussion in this chapter, served as housing for the women who worked as streetbased sex workers. Chatterjee uses this understanding of political society in his discussion of the ways in which the "entanglements of elite and subaltern politics" are manifested via producing the urban poor as various kinds of populations that must be managed through modern means, ostensibly with the purpose of literally pulling them into modernity. Chatterjee's argument on the relationship between citizens and populations is instructive in this regard:

> Unlike the concept of citizen, which carries the ethical connotation of participation in the sovereignty of the state, the concept of population makes available to government functionaries a set of rationally manipulable instruments for reaching large sections of the inhabitants of a country as the targets of their "policies" . . . . Indeed, as Michel Foucault has pointed out, a major characteristic of the contemporary regime of power is a certain "governmentalization of the state." This regime secures legitimacy not by the participation of citi-

zens in matters of state but by claiming to provide for the well-being of the population.[26]

Produced simultaneously as populations to protect and to protect *against*, sex workers are also simultaneously apprehended within the auspices of contemporary governmentality as "slum dwellers" or "encroachers," "people with HIV risk," "poor laborers in middle-class areas of the city," and "rural migrants in the city." In other words, women who do sex work may embody a divergently mapped set of populations to be regulated and are, within the contexts I have described and analyzed thus far, regulated as criminals. To be sure, all of these subjective categories are accorded via the technologies and tactics of enumeration, tactics that are set to intensify under the push to bring a biometric identification system into being in India.[27] Chatterjee's history includes "the enumeration of population groups as the objects of policy relating to land settlement, revenue, recruitment to the army, crime prevention, public health, management of famines and droughts, regulation of religious places, public morality, education."[28] While public morality does not mean the same thing as prostitution, it evokes the histories and practices of regulation, enumeration, and eventual attempts to erase the solicitation of sexual commerce from public urban spaces. It is striking to consider this history of enumeration in relation to the history of producing and regulating prostitution in India, where regulating sexual commerce was constitutive of the early rhetoric of regulating Indian polities and populations, providing a host of theoretical frames both for the early colonial state and for the contemporary regulation (and production) of populations and cities.

Criminality

Chatterjee acknowledges in his critique that in "the field of popular democratic practice, crime and violence are not fixed black-and-white legal categories; they could be open to a great deal of political negotiation," while also saying that he does not discuss what he calls the "darker side of political society."[29] His example of slum dwellers who break the law in the service of securing urban land for shelter and facilities like electricity and water, but who are otherwise engaged in legal and licit income-generating practices, actually runs the risk of producing a hard boundary between the criminal and the noncriminal or, at least, between criminals and those who engage in legitimated illegal activity necessary to securing shelter. He describes the actual populations that form the bases for his critiques and definitions of political society as follows: "They may live in illegal squatter settlements, make illegal use of water or electricity, travel without tickets in public transport. In dealing with them, the authorities cannot treat them on the same footing as other civic associations following more legitimate social pursuits."[30] If this runs the risk of reinstantiating the boundaries between the licit and illicit, and the legal and illegal, Chatterjee's argument also provides a way to critique this reinstantiation as well. This nod toward the somewhat fuzzy line between what is legal and what is not helps stage the question of how a consideration of sex work would further complicate the nebulous zone of criminality and, in the process, the notion of political society. How does the daily existence of people who live in the settlements he mentions, and also regularly solicit clients for sexual commerce, modify or more enhance our understanding of the vagaries of what "political society" aims to describe? By accounting for sexual commerce in particular, and sexuality in general, in a critique of governance, we may also extrapolate how the performance of morality, produced in no small part by eschewing sexual commerce, at least overtly, is a compulsory and minimal cost of accessing any services at all for the members of "political society." The exception to this imperative to essentially trade an acknowledged or overt acceptance of sexual commerce as an aspect of daily life for access to the rights of citizenship in some shape or form would be found in the political society that is constituted by sex workers in red-light areas, which constitute a unique and instructive case in urban planning and regulation in India. In the context of both naka- and street-based sex workers, it is crucial to remember that everyone is particularly aware of the necessity to perform normative morality, while living in an economic context in which sexual commerce is an available economic lifeline, a fallback for many, and a central mechanism of survival for others. Effectively eliding a critique of sexuality in this milieu precludes the possibility of recognizing the ways in which honor and respectability for women, for example, must be continuously managed, negotiated, and performed. We are left with the vague sense that each urban subject is somewhat like the next, save for being marked by poverty; that they are all heterosexual, gender conforming, monogamous, and normatively moral, even if they are not apprehended as full citizens.

In his analysis of the genealogy of the concept of civil society, Sunil Khilnani discusses Hegelian ideas of social recognition, and the challenges of building a cohesive civil society in the face of fracture and fragmentation and, in the Indian context, the lack of a shared conceptual frame of the right and proper workings of civil society.[31] However, Khilnani notes, "the point is not that such a common frame of reference never existed; it is, rather, that rival conceptions have entered into a lethal confrontation."[32] The phrase "lethal confrontation" presumably references communal violence, which has been a dominant theme in the scholarly discussion on civil and political society in South Asian studies.[33] I suggest that this idea of a lack of a shared frame of reference, of rival conceptions of civil society, and governance, may be a way to think about the lack of a shared frame of reference for how sex work should be apprehended—as a criminal activity that is detrimental, geographically locatable, and geographically actionable, or as something else entirely?

We know that abolitionist perspectives on sexual commerce render sex workers as victims within theories of the civil and the political look. In this light, they are simply excluded, from citizenship, services, recognition, and apprehension. But what happens if people who sell sexual services are considered to be agents who occupy multiple subjective zones of, for example, slum dweller, construction worker, and sex worker? How may we think about the civil and the political, or governance itself, when we think about all the moving parts as they are moving? Do women have an imperative to be moral non–sex workers in order to be apprehended within a theory of governance as something other than abjected and marginal? These theories would seem to currently say that women are out of the bounds of governance if they sell sex. However, if people are understood to occupy multiple locations at the same time, then parameters of the civil and political must shift in order to account for a measure of this spectrality.

Conclusion

Ultimately, how does the existence of sex worker politics and subjects impact a conceptual universe that is constructed through theories of the civil and the political? What do the coexistence and imbrications of all of these phenomena call into question or complicate? I have attempted to show that, at the very least, the complex existence of sex workers within the urban milieus I have discussed thus far calls into question the idea that subjective social categories (like "sex worker") are stable and clearly apprehendable in every context they inhabit. I have also attempted to show that the underground of the civil and political in Indian cities must include a critical consideration of sex worker subjectivities, and that the differential production of sex worker subjects casts doubt on the idea that there is a stable boundary between the legal/legitimate and criminal/

amoral that serves as a kind of universal referent. In the following chapter, I continue to probe the paradigm of political society through a focus on the spaces of Mumbai's main red-light area, Kamathipura. This focus assesses the ways in which an idealized notion of prostitution in the city is constituted in its most formal and iconic sense, and how this impacts less visible and more episodic engagements with sex work and sex trade at the nakas and on the street.

CHAPTER 4

RED-LIGHT DISTRICTS, RESCUE,
AND REAL ESTATE

This chapter is drawn from a decade-long ethnographic engagement with two of Mumbai's main red-light districts, Kamathipura and, to a lesser degree, Falkland Road. Over the course of India's postindependence history, both came to represent prostitution in Bombay/Mumbai and, in some sense, prostitution in India as a whole. By the 1980s, to evoke Kamathipura or Falkland Road was one way to evoke an image of sexual commerce in India writ large, especially through the dissemination of images of the infamous "cages" of Falkland Road. That these images also included cropped photos of women sitting behind the ground-floor entry grates of the houses that lined the lanes of the area was rarely discussed. The various contractual arrangements and the range of autonomy and servitude in which women were working (from independent sex work to severe forms of debt bondage) were also largely excluded from representations of sex work in these districts.

Red-light districts are at the heart of policy discourses on prostitution, to be sure, but perhaps more fundamentally, they are at the heart of the imaginary of prostitution. In India, this imaginary has been especially indebted to discourses on prostitution in Mumbai, produced within numerous milieus, including public health campaigns, Hindi films, newspaper reportage, gossip and rumors that circulate throughout the city, and, since the early 1980s, scholarly research and documentary films and photography. When I began this project in 2002, daily life in the brothels of Kamathipura and Falkland Road was largely as it had been for decades, with the addition of a stepped-up schedule of regular visits from peer educators and public health outreach workers. Both places were still the centers of sexual commerce in the "island city" of South Mumbai, their lanes lined by women soliciting clients in the early evening, additionally populated by shopkeepers and outreach workers during the day. Clients who purchased sexual services still represented the broad range of men who worked in the city; many would visit a brothel after the working day, before boarding a commuter train to go back to their homes in the suburbs.

By 2012, these areas were markedly changed, with only a fraction of brothels still in operation, the lanes filled not with women soliciting clients but with migrant men who worked in the small-scale industrial units that had replaced many of the brothels. I was told that the profile of clients had been changing over the course of the preceding four years; whereas clients had previously worked in a broad range of jobs, earning a commensurately broad range of wages, clients in the red-light districts now were primarily migrant laborers, whose earnings were relatively meager. The less clients earned, the less brothels could charge, which ultimately meant a more meager income for sex workers as well. Some of these changes were attributable to sex workers being officially and unofficially evicted from the brothels, which were also their homes, through the increasing occurrence of brothel raids. In addition, redevelopment plans had been circulated in the area since 2009 by a prominent Mumbai real estate developer; the plans envisioned a district of lucrative high-rise residential buildings and shopping malls, in place of prostitution. This chapter traces Kamathipura's transition from a place that had an active sex trade and, perhaps, an equally active network of organizations seeking to intervene in that trade, to a place that is, by many accounts, in the last stages of a transition from being a red-light district to becoming an upper-middle-class residential and shopping area.

We may derive competing sets of meanings from diminishing brothel-based commerce in South Mumbai, depending on which theoretical framework we employ. One set of meanings may be derived from abolitionist understandings of prostitution, in which prostitution is understood to be a form of violence, and is therefore understood to be a form of trafficking per se. From this perspective, brothel closures equal less violence against women. However, if prostitution and violence are conceptually disaggregated, that is, if violence is understood to be a contingency that sex workers navigate in the course of earning a living, then brothels are places where people live and work, and potentially become places where people selling sexual services organize collectively for various purposes, including the elimination of violence from clients, brothel owners, middlemen, and police.[1] In this latter formulation, the eradication of brothels poses a threat to public health promotion efforts, at the very least, while also decreasing access to the limited services that are currently available in red-light districts for sex workers and their children, via the various (abolitionist and nonabolitionist) organizations working in these areas. In analyzing brothel-based sexual commerce and the possibility of its erasure in South Mumbai in this chapter, I build on the book's central premise: that sexual commerce must be understood in relation to migration, housing, and daily negotiations for survival. I argue that emptying brothels must also be understood within the context of the politics of urban land use in contemporary India. The closures of the brothels are part of a larger urban land grab occurring throughout India, which is perhaps constituted most apparently by slum demolitions and the displacement of people living there.[2]

In 2005, I wrote of exceptionalized brothel-based prostitution in Mumbai by critiquing the production of the spectacle of Kamathipura. I argued that the spectacle of brothel-based sex work in general had produced prostitution, and red-light districts in Mumbai, as exceptional, while cohering the rest of the city through its categorization as the opposite of a red-light area, as a set of spaces where prostitution ostensibly did not take place.[3] The spectacle of Kamathipura has been produced through an extremely complex, layered set of visual, juridical, and biomedical discourses that have developed over a long period. These discourses have been produced in part through the network of organizations that have operated in the spaces of Kamathipura and Falkland Road, a network that includes HIV-related surveillance and prevention programs being conducted by the municipality and NGOs working in the area. In addition to providing health education and some health services, some of these initiatives also quietly monitored new entrants into the sex trade in these areas, and particularly aimed to prevent the entry of minor girls. Over time, the existence of explicitly abolitionist NGOs has increased in the area, with the goal of eliminating prostitution altogether. As we will see, some of these programs were effective in curbing the incidence of STDs, including HIV infections, as well as curbing the presence of minors doing sex work. At the same time, some of these programs have also facilitated the heightened occurrence of brothel raids, conducted in conjunction with local police.

Drawn from these observations, the argument in this chapter is built around two distinct lines of inquiry. The first line of inquiry focuses on how to situate brothel-based sex work within the conceptual spaces of migration and economic informality. On the one hand, my ethnography of Kamathipura and Falkland Road from 2002 to 2003 showed that while prostitution is discursively produced as sociologically, medically, and geographically exceptional, this idea is undermined by accounting for the considerations of everyday life in these districts, and by the livelihood and migration histories of the women who live and do sex work in the brothels located there. While each person had a unique narrative, these narratives were linked through similar histories of poverty and rural landlessness, as well as similar economic responsibilities of providing for families in their villages. That numerous women with whom I spoke, and whose stories I relate here, had solicited manual labor jobs from nakas and clients from the street before arriving in the red-light district offers a conceptual space to think of brothel-based sex workers as migrants working in the informal economy, negotiating differential levels of economic precarity, violence, and the possibility of violence.

The second line of inquiry focuses on the decline of brothel-based sex work in South Mumbai. While women working in the red-light districts do so in a diversity of contractual and daily circumstances, the idea that brothels are places of unilateral violence and abuse has contributed to producing the necessity to eradicate brothels as common sense. The common sense of eradication has developed alongside economic changes in the city that have enabled profits from real estate development on an unprecedented scale. While a narrative that relates the decline of brothels to the efficacy of abolitionism is certainly available, I argue that the decline of brothel-based sexual commerce in one of Mumbai's potentially most lucrative real estate markets is the result of a complex convergence of interests between real estate developers, politicians, local police, the municipality, and abolitionist NGOs.

A Brief History of Kamathipura

Although it is well known in histories of Bombay/Mumbai, it bears repeating that Kamathipura is named for the Kamathis, a community of migrant laborers from what is now Andhra Pradesh who began settling in Bombay in the late eighteenth century.[4] The Kamathis settled in an area of the city bounded by Falkland and Bellasis Roads, near what later became areas where colonial administration took place, and where colonial residences and the military cantonment were located. The Kamathis came to Bombay in search of paid work, finding it in the city's first large-scale infrastructural development project, the immense land reclamation scheme, which began in the eighteenth century and ended in the nineteenth, to unite the archipelago of seven major islands into the continuous landmass that would constitute modern Bombay/Mumbai.[5] Some sixty years after the arrival of the Kamathis, when the American Civil War halted cotton exports from the United States, a broad range of migrant and local workers, including descendants of the Kamathi migrants, were absorbed into the city's then-nascent textile industry, when Indian textiles became a vital component of the global cotton trade.[6] By the end of the nineteenth century, Bombay's textile mills had expanded beyond its southernmost hub and into the growing suburbs, and Kamathipura became designated as a red-light area in the city center frequented by both non-European men and by British soldiers.

There are many local narratives regarding how Kamathipura became a red-light district. On one visit to Kamathipura's Fourteenth Lane with a mobile health clinic serving sex workers in the area, a physician providing medical services there commented, "Don't you know about the history of this place? It all started because of the British. They wanted this as a place where their soldiers could come and visit prostitutes. It's been here for more than a hundred years." The idea that the area began its life as a red-light district as a response to the desires of "foreign" men is embedded within local origin stories of Kamathipura. The idea resonates with the British government's documented concerns about its soldiers having familial relationships with "native" women and encouragement of soldiers to become clients of sex workers instead, shown in work on the Cantonment Acts and the Contagious Diseases Acts.[7] This move toward institutionalizing prostitution through official colonial military policy had a number of consequences, including that of heightening official concerns about maintaining racial "purity." Historian Philippa Levine has shown that these concerns were contemporaneous with the era's disciplinary and discursive entrenchment of allopathic medicine, public health, and humanitarian social work. One nexus of these discourses, she writes, was embodied by the figure of the degraded sex worker:

> The prostitute fulfilled a role as the most degraded of women, a polluted and despised wretch removed from decency but nonetheless

providing a "necessary" outlet. As masculine and feminine roles became more sharply defined in the nineteenth century and as fears of VD grew, the prostitute as a social problem acquired greater urgency. Weighted down with a confused medico-moral baggage tied to long-standing conceptions about gender, class, and race, prostitution symbolized difference. As such, it could also serve to yoke "lesser" populations to ideas of sexual disorder, offering a veritable commentary on the savagery and barbarism of colonized peoples.[8]

That prostitution would be produced as naturalized and endemic to colonized people is particularly astonishing given the long historical route by which sexual commerce in India was reduced to a singular, geographically sequestered activity during the rise of the British Raj, as elaborated in the introduction. The idea that "the prostitute" was the most degraded of women was constitutive of the continuing consolidation of the category of prostitute in the late nineteenth and early twentieth centuries.

The narrative of the degraded "native" sex worker and the exploitive British soldier rely on the idea of racially homogenous clients and sex workers. However, in her historical account of prostitution in Bombay, Ashwini Tambe shows that the red-light districts there are better described as having been an agglomeration of people from vastly different places, rather than as places where everyone selling sexual services was a South Asian woman, and everyone buying was European:

> A racially stratified sexual order thus emerged with the state's formal approval [of prostitution]. The most explicit expression of official tolerance for European brothels is found in the writings of Stephen Edwardes, who was the police commissioner of Bombay from 1909 to 1917. Edwardes declared that without European prostitutes, British men would increasingly "resort to" Indian women, a possibility that "could not be regarded with impunity by those responsible for the general welfare of India" (Edwardes 1924/1983, 81). As he explained, "the growth of European populations, and the government's disapproval of liaisons with Indian women made authorities accept European brothels as a necessary evil. No direct steps were taken to curb it" (Edwardes 1923, 85).[9]

There is a great deal more to say about the history of the area, especially at the point of its potential demise as a red-light district. In light of these few facts, the theme of migration to this part of Bombay/Mumbai is pronounced. In a sense, it is a place that was founded by migrant workers, and it continues to be a space for migrants who, like their predecessors, were also landless in their villages and came to the city in search of a sustainable livelihood. However, the story of migration in these areas has been increasingly subsumed under a narrative of harm. I argue that while nothing about the rise of this narrative was inevitable, its power has been bolstered by the iconicity of prostitution in India, and by the spectacle that this iconicity has contributed to producing.

Spectacular Kamathipura

Located a short distance from the Mumbai Central commuter railway station, Kamathipura's role as the penultimate, iconic Indian red-light district has been unrivaled. This iconicity is defined in relation to the idea of prostitution as an inherently heterosexual phenomenon, with the embedded assumption of female sellers of sexual services and male buyers of those services. The nearly ubiquitous tropes of fallen, dishonored, and disreputable female sexuality that animate legal discourses on prostitution demonstrate the ways in which conceiving sellers of sexual services *as women* is required to maintain the current discursive matrix of prostitution, which also turns on the notion that women who sell sexual services have never engaged in any other livelihood strategy.

Kamathipura has been produced as an iconic red-light district in this historical moment through its circulation in print media and television, public health programs and, since the mid-1990s in particular, through its circulation in abolitionist antitrafficking discourses. At the same time, stories about the district continually circulate throughout the city, forming a cascading, generalized awareness about the existence of Kamathipura and the business conducted there. This awareness is informed by histories of the area that blur into myths, memories, and reports of real episodes of violence and brutality, all of which are interpolated within fantastical narratives of coercion and desire. These stories, circulated through local networks of gossip and rumor, produced in schoolyards, between neighbors, and in street corner conversations, have resulted in a relational understanding of red-light districts vis-à-vis the rest of the city, an understanding in which prostitution occurs primarily in Kamathipura and Falkland Road because it does not, ostensibly, occur elsewhere in Mumbai.

In an article on Kamathipura, I argued that the district has been at the center of the spectacle of prostitution in India, a spectacle that produces the rest of the city as being a space where prostitution does not occur, in relation to Kamathipura, which is overdetermined as a site of sexual commerce in the process. I emphasized the ways in which Kamathipura is spectacularized through numerous discursive routes, including public health discourses focused on HIV prevention, media coverage of the area, a steady stream of volunteers from different local agencies and universities, as well as a flow of students and researchers from the West whose numbers swell the lanes of the main red-light districts during summer and winter intersessions: "A key element of the definition of a 'spectacle' in this sense is that, rather than being mobilized to action or concern, the audience—in this case, 'the public'—participates in acts of shared voyeurism. . . . using the notion of spectacle as that which 'maintains the status quo,' it is plausible to think of these representations as sets of practices which reiterate and maintain norms vis-à-vis gender and sexuality. In other words, whereas 'the public' is not a euphemism for 'the bourgeoisie,' the 'public' does become a way of naming non-sex workers."[10]

In a more recent critique extending this notion of spectacle as it may be attached to the ways in which Kamathipura is conceived in discourses of prostitution in India, I explored the role of documentary films that circulate outside of India in producing this spectacularized image, including the widely screened *Born into Brothels*. I argued that this documentary and others like it constitute a subgenre of contemporary documentary filmmaking on India, and that this subgenre has played a major role in shaping the perception of sex work in India. At the same time, I offered this caveat:

> To be clear, this is not an exercise in positing ethnographic truths against filmic ones. Rather, if the ethnographic body of work shows anything, it is that sex work in India cannot be reduced to the set of unitary and fixed ideas of prostitution-as-violence. If anti-prostitution films are able to traffic in these kinds of reductive truths, it is because these truths serve a narrative function, because they tell a story that may be apprehended in the same manner, time and again, by a vast audience. The storyline that animates these documentary films is, in turn, permeating filmmaking that is self-consciously fictional, finding sound footing in umpteen television serials and feature-length films that have an anti-trafficking/anti-prostitution theme.[11]

This is especially pertinent to understanding Kamathipura which, unlike red-light districts in other Indian cities, has the unique distinction of being the subject of numerous visual representations of prostitution in India. Kamathipura enjoys a unique, if caricatured, filmic legibility, particularly in Hindi films, perhaps due to it sharing the city with Bollywood.

The Hindi film industry has had a long-standing interest in Mumbai's red-light districts. In addition to the courtesan and the prostitute serving as archetypes in Hindi films, red-light districts were spaces from which to recruit female actors during the early years of Hindi filmmaking, in the first few decades of the twentieth century.[12] Then, as now, red-light districts were also spaces to set stories, backdrops for dramatic narratives of rescue and redemption. The contemporary Hindi film industry regularly refers to Kamathipura by name in numerous films, or alludes to sex work and the district in dialogues that euphemistically conflate women and girls waiting or standing on a road with the idea of inherent urban danger. In a passing reference in the film *Saathiya* (2002), a male character's father express his disapproval of his son's marital choice by remarking that his son must have found his fiancé "standing by the roadside." Kamathipura has merited more direct appraisals in less mainstream Hindi films, such as Shyam Benegal's *Mandi* (1983), Mira Nair's *Salaam Bombay* (1988), and, later, in Madhur Bhandarkar's *Chandni Bar* (2001). If *Saathiya* is indicative of a foregone conclusion that Kamathipura is a place of danger, these other films, as well as *Chameli* (2004), indicate something else, that working in a red-light district is complex, that there are attendant harms and dangers, and that people negotiate these dangers while earning a livelihood.

One of the most recent mainstream Bollywood films to include a reference to Kamathipura is *Talaash: The Answer Lies Within* (2012). The film is loosely described as a sequel to *Talaash: The Hunt Begins* (2003), the film that was briefly discussed in chapter 3, and includes several characters who are referred to as "sex workers in Kamathipura."[13] The actress Kareena Kapoor, who also acted in the first *Talaash*, plays a character known alternately as Rosie and Simran. It is eventually revealed that Simran is a ghost who has been leading the protagonist toward the resolution of the film's key mystery. In my conversation about the film with women engaged in street-based sex work, one of my interlocutors used the metaphor of "the hunt," derived from the film's title, in describing the lives of women who solicited from the street. Sex workers "hunted" clients, and police "hunted" sex workers. Nearly a decade after the original film had been released, the sequel provided another metaphor for sexual commerce in the city. Now, the sex worker was a ghost, and Kamathipura was potentially subject to physical erasure.

The discursive elisions between Kamathipura, danger, and prostitution, evident in a number of films made in and about India that far exceeds the very short list I provide here, were also evident in conversations I had throughout fieldwork. These usually began with the journey to Kamathipura itself. When I hired a taxi and gave Kamathipura as my destination, the driver's reply would often be a worried or confused, "Madam, why do *you* want to go *there*?" The injunctions against visiting the district included the belief that the area as a whole was immoral and dangerous, and that any woman's respectability was suspect by virtue of entering the lanes, day or night. Women who served as outreach workers for one of several local HIV prevention projects working in the area negotiated this by walking through the lanes in teams, wearing bright yellow or white vests emblazoned with the logo of their respective organizations over their saris.

Sex Research Tourism

Programs for HIV prevention in red-light districts like Kamathipura have their institutional roots in the early 1990s. This historical moment also coincides with the time when economic policies designed to "liberalize" India's economy, such as reducing tariffs on foreign imports, were beginning to be adopted in India. The early 1990s were also the time when India was shaken by the destruction of the Babri Masjid (Mosque) in 1992 in the northern city of Ayodhya, which presaged communal riots in Bombay, as it was then called, and the rise of Hindu nationalism within Indian electoral politics. During this period, funds for HIV/AIDS prevention and surveillance efforts in India began to flow from abroad, initially from sources that included the Norwegian, Dutch, and Canadian governments. The story of foreign funding for then newly founded HIV/AIDS organizations is a complex one; activist collectives working in feminist movements at the time were seriously debating the implications of accepting foreign funding before choosing, or not choosing, to work as externally funded entities, a discussion that permeated organizing efforts on sexuality- and gender-related issues. In feminist movements, the decision whether or not to set up funded organizations had direct bearing on the ways in which these movements were institutionalized. Similarly, money for HIV/AIDS work shaped the ways in which LGBTQ and sex workers' organizations began building their institutional infrastructure. Some of the groups that were the first to be funded for this work are still in existence; most organizations' work exceeded the narrow mandate of HIV prevention to include advocacy and social programs as well. By 2003, entities within the Indian government, including the National AIDS Control Organization (NACO), as well as nongovernmental organizations were attracting much larger sums from a range of governments, foundations, and individual donors. These included UNAIDS, the Joint United Nation's Programme on HIV/AIDS; the U.S. government's *President's Emergency Plan for AIDS Relief* (PEPFAR); the Global Fund to Fight AIDS, Tuberculosis and Malaria; and the Bill and Melinda Gates Foundation, which, in 2003, committed US$67.5 million for HIV prevention efforts in India for the following five years; by 2009, the Foundation's total commitment to funding HIV/AIDS prevention efforts in India had increased to US$338 million.[14] This funding trend changed drastically in 2011. Arguing that the job of reducing HIV infection rates had been accomplished, and that India should deal with the epidemic on its own, the Gates Foundation ended its funding abruptly in that year. Funding for HIV from a number of other significant donors also ended or was reduced in 2011. This occurred alongside much more stringent governmental restrictions on how NGOs received funding from abroad.[15]

The funding that came to India for HIV-related work from the early 1990s onward was accompanied by a discourse on sexual commerce that was being shaped by the long-standing notion that sexual commerce constituted exceptionally high HIV risk. The added financial support for transmission prevention programs and the growing interest in sexual commerce from funders, academics, and activists (also due to the rise in the influence of antitrafficking frameworks for understanding prostitution) had a number of consequences. These included an uptick in the number of researchers from abroad visiting red-light areas in India as part of research programs and projects that aimed to investigate HIV/AIDS prevention efforts. While people in Kamathipura were not strangers to people coming to the area as clients, missionaries, or social workers, the phenomenon of a higher volume of researchers coming for short-term, informational visits was relatively new.

To be sure, my own continued presence in Kamathipura in 2002 and 2003 was a part of this landscape. Each time I went to the area I was legible as a researcher, albeit one with a slightly unusual status. Unlike many of the researchers I encountered, who usually came once, asked a fairly standard set of questions, and left, I was a more regular presence, particularly at that time. This difference did result in some advantages, including the ability to observe the same dynamic between sex workers and numerous groups of researchers in the same settings. These observations made apparent the generalized research fatigue of many of the residents of Kamathipura. This was particularly true of peer educators in the area, who were usually older women who had been sex workers in their youth and now worked for local HIV prevention programs. Their employment in these programs seemed to be a kind of retirement strategy, mitigating the inability to secure clients for sexual services. The peer educators for the government-run HIV/AIDS outreach program in the area were often the first people introduced to foreign researchers aiming to meet sex workers in Mumbai. Having been asked similar sets of questions repeatedly by people doing research in the area, these women had a set list of answers, which emphasized the ideas that Kamathipura was easily apprehendable, and that it was something other than a place of exceptional harm. Observing these interactions over time, it eventually became clear that the women's answers formed a narrative in the most fundamental sense, replete with tropes, formal conventions, and a clear message. I was able to document a version of this narrative during a visit by a group of three American university students to Kamathipura, some six months before the end of my longest stay in Mumbai. The students were in the city for a week and were visiting NGOs working on HIV/AIDS. By the time they arrived, the informal network of HIV-related projects in Mumbai had shared information about this group, such that their itinerary was common knowledge. This particular visit entailed meeting with the peer educators. Some of these peer educators had been facilitating health-related service provision and outreach in Kamathipura since the early 1980s.

On the day the students had scheduled their research visit, I spent my afternoon in Kamathipura with some of these peer educators. On this occasion, like many others, I had joined the women for lunch. We finished eating, when three white Americans, two women and one man, were shown into the room. They were invited to sit in chairs that were quickly unstacked from the edge of the room and placed facing the group of women who continued to sit on the floor. At first, I continued sitting with them on the floor as well but, sensing the urgent stares of the staff in my direction, I moved to a chair. The women usually returned from doing outreach at around three in the afternoon and spread a rug on the floor to sit and have their midday meal together. I had observed that, generally, the staff members, who were middle class, college educated, and non–English speaking, sat in chairs while they were in the office, while the peer educators did not. This observation required me to make a choice, which I made based on the possibility of chatting informally with the women before they left for the day, sometimes while sharing food. A member of staff had noticed this choice and insisted that I have a chair. We eventually struck an unspoken compromise over the course of my visits, such that I had to move to a chair only if visitors came by.

The three Americans, I later learned, were students from an American Ivy League university. For this visit, the staff had organized a performance of the HIV awareness skit that the outreach workers perform at cinema halls in the area. The peer educators performed the skit in the office as the students watched earnestly, even though it was performed in Hindi and without translation. After the skit ended, I was asked to translate an informal interview between the two female students and the peer educators. The staff member who facilitated the interview encouraged the students with vigor, saying in English, "You can ask them anything! Go ahead!"

All three students cringed slightly and looked at one another. One of the women looked at me and said, hesitantly, "Can you ask them . . . how they started doing this? I mean, if it's OK. We don't want to make anyone uncomfortable."

"Yeah," the other woman echoed, "we don't want to make anyone uncomfortable."

They repeated this sentiment several times throughout the interaction, even as they gained momentum and began asking questions more easily.

"Did they know they would be doing this when they came to Mumbai?"

"Did they come on their own, or were they forced?"

"How did they know what they would be doing here?"

"Did they know there was such a terrible disease as AIDS before they came?"

"Do their families know what they are doing?"

"Are they married?"

One woman from among the peer educators sat near the front of the group on the rug and answered all of these questions as the sex workers' representative. She spoke as a practiced interview subject, one who had heard these queries many times before.

"Yes, I knew this is what I was coming for."

"People were always coming and going between the village and Mumbai, and they had money and jewelry when they came back to the village."

"No, we didn't know about AIDS before we came here."

"Yes, our families know."

"Yes, I am married."

The students took copious notes from the interview. Near the end of their visit, I realized that they had not said what the interview would be used for. When I asked, they said simply, "It's for a report."

"Will it be published?"

"It might be," one replied.

Thanking everyone, they left.

This kind of interaction was fairly emblematic of research interviews that were conducted throughout the area, though this does not describe all research interactions, to be sure. The interaction was emblematic in several registers: the brevity of the encounter between the students and the women; the line of questioning that the students [ultimately] pursued, which drew a clear discursive boundary around the questions of force and choice that were at the center of their inquiry; the idea, possibly conveyed by the staff, that all of the women there were current sex workers; and the apparent lack of disclosure to the people being interviewed about how these interviews would be used. This interaction was also marked by my own discomfort in being potentially associated with these American students, an association that was liminal in such moments, as I was marked as both Indian and American, the former by virtue of my skin color, mode of dress, and language skills, the latter largely by virtue of my gender nonconformity, the questions I asked, and my mode of speech. Although I attempted to augment any non-foreignness through strategies like insisting on sitting on the floor with the peer educators, chatting, and having lunch, these had limited effect.

This interaction exemplified several problematics that are produced through research conducted in Indian red-light areas. The first of these is the tensions between insiders and outsiders that are uniquely emphasized in these spaces, as evinced in my discomfort at being associated with the students who were, in that moment, über-outsiders. While all ethnographic research plays on this tension and indeed uses an outsider positionality to draw out themes and questions that otherwise remain embedded within the vagaries of daily life, this tension is much more pronounced in a context in which the question at hand concerns a semi-legal, illegal, or illicit activity that is highly stigmatized. In this context, occupying an unreconstructed outsider-ness means that people being interviewed may deliver a standardized narrative, as in this case, or it may mean that no interactions or observations are at all possible, or something in between. This is not to support the abolitionist claim that if sex workers do not reveal accounts of trafficking or physical violence, then they are dissembling, or deluded, or simply lying. It is to account for the structure of power in which these research interactions take place, and to ask, what kind of conversation is possible between researchers and people selling sexual services in illicit and illegal zones, where researchers are necessarily produced as middle class and non-stigmatized? What kinds of conversations do these differences elicit, particularly when it seems that a version of the same questions is being asked repeatedly? In chapter 3 I showed that, after some time, I was invited into a position of more liminal outsider-ness, in which individuals began to quietly reveal where and how sex work took place at the naka. While there is a body of work on red-light districts that has produced information that goes far beyond the delivery of standard narratives, I suggest that the issue of research fatigue is particularly pronounced in these areas. This means that the elision or erasure of the physical presence of researchers and NGO workers from scholarship on red-light areas ignores a critical parameter for analyzing the qualitative and quantitative data that these interactions produce. Locating researchers in the spaces of the red-light district would mean accounting for the limits of speech in conducting this kind of research, which includes accounting for research fatigue among brothel-based sex workers, in particular. To be sure, this fatigue is the result of years of people coming and going from these spaces and asking repetitive questions, but the fatigue is also caused by the steady decline in working and living conditions that has intensified, despite the research and interventions that have been conducted here.

Sex Work in Kamathipura: Migration, Livelihoods, and Remittances

Unpacking the gaze on Kamathipura is key to unraveling the persistence of two pervading assumptions in most health- and livelihood-related interventions targeting sex workers. These assumptions are, first, that women who do sex work do no other income-generating activities at the same time and, second, that women who primarily do sex work to earn money have always done so, and have rarely, if ever, engaged in any other income-generating activity. The question of origins for doing sex work ("How did you start doing this?") is ubiquitous in research and journalistic representations of sexual commerce. Whether or not the question is deployed as a means of reinscribing a moral injunction against selling sexual services, this line of questioning succeeds in maintaining a categorical boundary between having sold sexual services and not having done so, a line that crosses from purity to pollution at the moment of initiation into sexual commerce as a seller (but, notably, not as a buyer).

The interviews and interactions I discuss in this section are drawn from research I conducted over the eighteen-month period of fieldwork that spanned 2002 and 2003. Since that time, Kamathipura has undergone dramatic changes. As of 2012 there were many fewer brothels operating than ever before, and people were being encouraged to leave, through both brothel raids and lease buyouts. The version of Kamathipura I present here no longer exists, although other, much less visible forms of brothel-based sexual commerce are emerging in Mumbai. These newer forms of sexual commerce are all traceable through Kamathipura because some of the same people are involved, and because the slow erasure of Kamathipura has prompted their inception. The narratives that I present here are thus rendered as foundational artifacts of the new ways in which brothel-based sexual commerce takes place in the city. In a sense, these narratives capture a moment of transition, when the effects of rendering Kamathipura a spectacle and a target of intervention were becoming dramatically manifested.

These narratives show that sex work in Kamathipura may be productively understood in relation to the phenomenon of migration, and that many people who sold sexual services there had worked as naka-based day wage laborers at some point in their working lives. They also show that people in Kamathipura, like those at the naka and on the street, were enmeshed in a matrix of earning livelihoods, keeping secrets, and sending remittances to friends and family living in rural areas. This matrix did not preclude the experience of violence; rather, women managed and sometimes endured violence in the course of navigating their survival. In addition to the matrix that describes daily life in Kamathipura, these interactions and interviews also problematize the production of knowledge on prostitution. Sex workers in Kamathipura have been targeted with public health and social work programming for years, as well as being the subjects of media and scholarly interest, which has contributed to the volume of people passing in and out of the area. Many of these programs and projects have reified the moment at which women began selling sexual services, regardless of how long ago that may have been. Taken together, all these interventions and research interactions have resulted in sex workers in Kamathipura constituting an extremely experienced group of research subjects, as well as their being expert consumers of social work and "social improvement" programs. This provided an important context for my conducting interviews, which were aimed at discerning livelihood and migration histories, as well as the daily life of the area with respect to accessing housing and water. By emphasizing questions about housing, migration, and livelihood, I aimed to avoid centering the question of origins, as has often been the case in interactions between researchers and brothel-based sex workers, by way of avoiding reifying the moment of entry. Not only has research on sexual commerce been saturated with this question, but the reductive analytics that the question produces (either reinscribing a narrative of powerlessness or laying claim to an unfettered free choice) led away from questions of migration, livelihood, and housing. These questions may include discussions of when and how someone began doing sex work but, rather than framing the moment of beginning sex work as causal, foregrounding these kinds of questions means understanding this moment with respect to the structuring contexts in which it takes place. However, despite my best efforts, almost all of the women I interviewed eventually said they had not been forced to do this work, often emphatically, seeming to be alarmed that the interview was about to end without the question having been raised. This answer was delivered with a twist when I visited Kamathipura after the end of my primary research period in Mumbai.

After the end of my main period of fieldwork, in early 2004, I attended the World Social Forum (WSF), which was held in a large open area near the edge of the city. Because of the vast distance between this venue and South Mumbai, I was able to return to Kamathipura only briefly from the WSF. Najma, whom I had interviewed months earlier, took my hand upon seeing me again and led me to the group of women she was hanging out with that day. They were sitting next to a man with a huge metal container of *idlis* (a soft rice cake) and another huge container of *sambhar* (a lentil and vegetable stew). He was selling servings of three idlis with sambhar and fresh chutney wrapped in newspaper for two rupees. Najma bought a newspaper-wrapped packet and put an idli into my mouth, not waiting for me to say whether or not I was hungry. With my mouth full, Najma's friends began asking me what I was doing there. I finished chewing and replied that I was doing research on what women in Kamathipura did for money before they came here, and whether there were women in the city who were doing construction work or some other kind of work and this *dhandha* at the same time. A woman in the group who had initially mistaken me for a man shook her head and said, "Madam, your question is very difficult." (*Madam, aap ka sawal bahut mushkil hai.*) Two younger women, one wearing a sheer black sari, approached arm in arm and also asked what I was doing there. When Najma explained, one of the younger women smirked and, joining her hands theatrically, began shouting, "That bad pimp [*dalal*], he brought me here! And sold me into dhandha![16] *Ai hai!!*" She and her friend doubled over in peals of laughter.[17]

Women who did sex work in Kamathipura were in constant dialogue with narratives of trafficking and violence, a dialogue that was especially present in dealings with outsiders who asked questions about the lives of women selling sexual services there. These exchanges demonstrated the ways in which research in Kamathipura was nothing new for the people who were its subjects, and perhaps even verged on being over-determined. In order to discern issues of livelihood and housing more clearly, while aiming to avoid prepackaged answers to questions that had clearly been asked numerous times before (e.g., "Are you here by your own choice?"), I conducted formal interviews with a core group of ten women, whom I contacted through an NGO that conducts a free mobile clinic for women living and working in red-light areas throughout the city. Over six months of meeting women through this organization, the number of formal interviews grew to twenty-five. Initial formal interviews with groups of women, a year's participant observation with peer educators in the government HIV/AIDS unit, and subsequent formal interviews with individual women constituted the basis of my research in the area. My written notes from Kamathipura documented informal interviews with more than fifty people, including shopkeepers, NGO workers, brothel owners, and sex workers, as well as many, many interactions with people in the lanes and on the street in front of brothels, such as the exchange during my visit in 2004. Most of the formal interviews were conducted in the brothels where women lived and worked. Najma was one of the first women I had met, and she became a more familiar contact over the course of this research. Here I offer a description of our first meeting, more than a year before the WSF.

Accompanying the mobile medical clinic, I went to the Fourteenth Lane in Kamathipura. In local circuits of gossip, the Fourteenth Lane was one of the best-known and "infamous" places in the area. On any given evening, it was jammed with women standing outside of the door-ways of the buildings along each side, waiting for customers. There was a school at the end of the lane, near a larger building, nearly twenty stories high, which served as a landmark for the boundaries of the district. The larger building was white and green, with dome-shaped arches along each side on the top floor and smaller arches framing the windows on every floor. Based on its architectural aesthetic, I had initially wondered if it was a very tall mosque (it was also a school). I later learned that it marks one of the invisible boundaries of the city; Kamathipura and Falkland Road, I was told, inhabit the nexus between Hindu and Muslim areas of South Mumbai. I learned that these red-light districts also inhabit the nexus between the rich and poor areas of South Mumbai, as Kamathipura and Falkland Road border some of the wealthiest neighborhoods in the city.

Accompanying the doctor who worked with the mobile clinic and one of his assistants, I approached the relatively nondescript entrance of a building at the other end of the Fourteenth Lane, walking past the *paan wallah* sitting just outside. Next to the *paan* stall was a row of young women sitting and standing on the pavement. They let the doctor and his assistant pass without notice but gave me that hard stare reserved for strangers, social workers, and nonclients in the red-light area. The entrance to the building was sandwiched between a mechanic's stall on one side and a restaurant serving nonvegetarian food on the other. Women were scattered up and down the street. It was around two in the afternoon.

The base of the staircase just inside the entrance was illuminated by light from the doorway, but because the stairs were perpendicular to the entrance, we were plunged into nearly total darkness as we began to climb. Without any lighting in the stairwell, and with the especially bright sun outside, my eyes adjusted to the darkness slowly, as I followed behind my companions, who trotted upstairs easily. Feeling my way through the semigrayness, I noticed that the wooden banister had ornate carvings and a smoothness that must have come from daily use over many years. The smells of uncollected rubbish and neglected street maintenance that had accrued outside faded as we climbed. The whole building had a very old feel, and the doctor said that it was from the "original" days of Kamathipura. "This building has always been a brothel," he explained. He dated Kamathipura's existence as a red-light area from 1872.

Unlike the residences and shops along the Fourteenth Lane itself, which consisted of *chawls* (a type of building) with rooms partitioned into tiny, sometimes bed-sized living quarters, this building had a wide staircase that led up to an equally wide landing on each floor.[18] There was a shared toilet at the end of each offshoot of hallway, along with a small window that let in the glow of daylight. Outside of the rooms, which were also partitioned to house any number of beds, was a long wooden bench where up to three people could sit comfortably. I was reminded of the waiting area in a dentist's or doctor's office.

Najma was a peer educator for the NGO for which the doctor also worked. That day's entire outreach team came and sat on the bench outside her room, which today would be used for the mobile clinic. Shirin, a neighbor, started pounding up and down the hallways telling people the doctor had come, while Iccha sat with the gray briefcase open on her lap, dispensing pills into little white envelopes. The doctor, Dr. Raj, sat with a notebook in his lap, writing each woman's name, her ailment, and what he was prescribing. I sat on the bench opposite Najma's room, taking it all in, asking a few questions here and there of the people who had gathered for treatment, and then joined Dr. Raj and Shirin, who were teasing Najma about her cooking. She had set up a portable kerosene stove in front of the doorway to her room to prepare her midday meal. Half of the stove served as container and funnel for the fuel, the other half consisting of a ring for the cooking vessel and a circular burner underneath. I had seen many people who worked at the naka struggle with older versions of stoves like this one. Shubha often sat in front of hers wielding fine metal instruments and pliers, trying to equalize the flow of fuel and air to the burner to achieve that fast, hot, blue flame that makes a loud rushing noise under the pot. The pot on Najma's stove was full of green chilies, some pieces of cut vegetable, and water. "What are you making, green chilies *sabzi* [a vegetable dish]?" asked Dr. Raj. Najma laughed and, mildly defending herself, said, "No, no, there's vegetable in there, too."

Najma

Unlike many of the women in the area, it was possible to interview Najma at some length and in private. The location of her room, at the end of a long corridor, plus her slightly older age meant that she was able to access a greater level of autonomy than younger women in the area. Najma said she was from a small village in West Bengal and identified herself as Muslim. At this point in time, it was known that women from Bangladesh were working in Kamathipura, most likely having crossed the border by bus into West Bengal. To avoid trouble from local authorities, all claimed to be from the Indian side of the border.

"The village," she said, "feels very different. There, people have honor [*izzat*]." When I asked about her childhood, she said, "It was very hard. I didn't have a mother, I had a stepmother." She described the ways in which her stepmother treated her badly, such that Najma took care of herself from a very young age. When I asked at what age she had started earning, she replied, "Four." In the village, she earned doing domestic work; both in the village and in the cities, where she lived later on, she did building construction work. Of doing construction work, she said:

People would see me working like a man, and point to me, and talk about me, and make fun of me. So I thought, "What's the point of trying to work like this and protect my honor, when no one thinks I have honor anyway?" Eventually I had to decide between honor and filling my stomach. So I decided to go to and stand in the *bazaar* in Calcutta. After all, I was responsible for myself, for the soap I used, for the oil to put on my body and in my hair. In Calcutta, I begged, I washed dishes. I also did day wage labor [*begari kam*]. I could get *vada pav*[19] from the naka. Like everyone else, I also did *dhanda* [sex work] with the contractor.

Najma explained that she used to have sex with contractors not for money, but for more building work. If she would have sex with them, she would get work "for the *whole* month. . . . Lots of people got work this way, it was common. I got lots of offers like this. In Calcutta, I was also working with my friend washing dishes in a restaurant. The brother-in-law of my friend said, 'Why are you working so hard? Your hands will go bad from all this dishwashing. You could have good clothes and good food!' So he sent both of us to do dhandha in Delhi."

Najma eventually left Delhi, saying that there was too much drug use in the red-light district there. "It didn't suit me," she said, deciding to come to Mumbai instead. She said that her family back in the village believes she is doing construction work. She currently earned 100 rupees per day (3,500 rupees per month) and listed her expenses: food, clothes, her son's school fees, 200 rupees to the woman who comes to sweep and mop her room each morning, as well as "bribes [*hafta*] to the police, and raids cost money, too." I asked what happens when the police raid the brothel.

"My son protects me," she said. Najma's son was around ten or eleven years old, a shy boy who had his arms around his mother's waist whenever I saw him. "He hates going to school," she said. "He just wants money and to wander around on the streets all day." When the police come, she explained, her son, who goes to a Marathi medium school and speaks fluent Marathi, says to them, "She's not Bengali, she's Marathi," so they don't arrest her. She explained further: "The police are in each building, every day. They wait where people will run [to hide], ask for a photograph, ration card, take everyone away at least once a month. There's no law saying they should *hit* people, but they do it all the time."

A Note on Privacy and Interviews

Unlike this interview, in which I was able to speak with Najma alone, most of my interviews and all of my conversations with women in the area were conducted with greater or lesser numbers of onlookers nearby. In the interview with Meena, five other people were present. The lack of privacy constituted a significant aspect of interviews conducted throughout this project and is especially important to critique in relation to interviews that took place in these brothels. From an abolitionist perspective, the lack of privacy afforded women while they were being interviewed would indicate the oppression they suffered, perhaps at the hands of people who profited from their doing dhandha. This may have been the case, especially in the interview with Meena that follows. However, even in this interview, for which Meena had been awoken, and during which she seemed uneasy, fear and oppression do not tell the whole story of the encounter. While we spoke, people watched me write in my notebook, nodded or shook their heads during various points in the conversation, and distracted Meena's child, a rambunctious toddler, during our conversation.

The suspicion with which privacy was treated in these kinds of interviews may also be read as suspicion on behalf of people whose existence is legally liminal because they are engaging in criminalized activity. Although I was eventually able to conduct interviews in Kamathipura with a greater degree of privacy, the overall lack of space (as demonstrated in living conditions in the brothels) and time (as women were usually working, sleeping after working, or doing household chores) also created challenges for achieving a space that could facilitate longer conversations and address more nuanced questions. Beyond interview settings, privacy generally was eschewed in this place where so much space, information, food, and clothing were shared.

Meena

I arrived at the building and plunged into the pitch darkness of the stairwell again, my eyes adjusting only when I emerged onto the slightly brighter first landing. I couldn't remember which floor I needed to reach, and having gone alone this time, I had to ask a couple of people for directions. It felt different to be coming here on my own, although the people who worked for the mobile medical clinic had introduced me here the day before. It was early afternoon, and I thought there would be more people around who would be willing to speak with me. When I eventually made it to Najma's, she began loudly explaining that she had told some other girls that I'd be coming today, but that they never turned up.

As I spoke with her, two men approached, collecting money from everyone on the floor. Najma started scolding them and complaining to the one collecting money about their tardiness. "You said you'd be here at one, and here it is so late!" She kept complaining, gathering momentum, until she shouted, "I'll give you such curses [*gallis*], you never heard such curses in all your life, I swear!" The man turned to look at me with a tired, bemused expression on his face. This was clearly routine. She gave him 100 rupees, an amount which he wrote down in a little notebook, before moving on to the next doorway. I noticed from the hallway that inside Najma's tiny room there were many partitions, including one that seemed to divide the room into portions from top to bottom. To reach the top half, one would have had to climb up a ladder inside Najma's enclosed bed space and crawl up into the space above, which had a little open window looking out into the hall where I sat.

Najma explained that the men were collecting their monthly dues. It was unclear if this meant rent, or a portion of the income from herself or someone else selling sexual services. She referred to both of the men as "the boss" (*sheth*). After the sheth had left, Najma put a padlock on the compartment containing her bed and led me down a flight of stairs, now lit by broad daylight, to the floor below. I was instructed to sit in the outer room of one of the "apartments" that led off of the main hall. The inner chamber of this apartment held a bunch of beds crammed in together, and a little storage space above for bags and clothes. The outer room had pictures of Hindu gods, Bollywood film posters, and posters of snowcapped mountains and blue rivers. All of them looked to be cut out from magazines and calendars. I waited there with an older woman who exuded an air of power, by virtue of her age and her arms-akimbo posture. Her physical gender ambiguity (it was unclear to me, at first, if I was talking with a *hijra* person or an old woman with whiskers) also lent her an air of authority. We chatted a bit while I waited for whomever Najma was bringing to speak with me. In response to my asking her where she was from, the old woman said she was from a little village in Northern Karnataka and that, no matter what, she preferred Mumbai, and not only Mumbai, but Kamathipura, above all other places.

"Why?" I asked.

"Because," she said, "in the village, if you ask someone for a kilo of millet [*jawar*] or some other ration, they'll just say that they don't have it. In Mumbai, you ask for something, and someone is always willing to help you. Especially in Kamathipura."

Najma eventually came back with a young woman she introduced as Meena. Meena came in with her toddler son, a big, healthy boy with a shaved head and several big black dots of kohl on his face to keep away the evil eye. Meena was around twenty years old and stunningly beautiful. Her hair was piled up on her head in a bun, and she was wearing a loose *salwar khameez* that looked like her nightgown. Her eyes looked weary, and I apologized for having awoken her. Our interview was short but began to reveal a personal history that most women who were interviewed seemed to share.

When asked about her family, Meena said that her parents had been day wage laborers who had gone each day to a naka to look for work. Her parents had taken her along as a child, as she did not attend school. She measured the time when her parents worked this way according to the wage they received. "It must have been ten years ago," she recalled, "because the rates [for day wage laborers] were eighty rupees [per day] for men, and fifty rupees for women." Women would be hired for cleaning bricks, while the men were hired for breaking rocks. "We would get a full month's work then, not like now," she emphasized. When asked if she had ever done any other work than sex work, she replied by saying that she had been married. When her husband left her, she thought about doing construction work. Instead, her friend introduced her to "this line."

The old woman with the air of authority had stayed to listen to us talk; two men also entered the room and sat down. Another younger woman stood behind me and looked over my shoulder as I wrote. I realized later that she might have done so simply to watch someone writing in fluent English, a skill that relatively few people around her possessed. All in all, there were around six people in the tiny room, including Meena. Meena seemed stressed at various points during the interview and was clearly exhausted. At times the room was silent, except for the sounds of everyone's breathing and my notebook shifting as I wrote. Meena's son played around us, picking up things like plastic garbage buckets, which everyone, especially the women, kept shouting at him to put down. If Meena had not told me he was her son, I would not have known because everyone seemed to be sharing the responsibility of disciplining and amusing him.

Especially significant in this experience of interviewing Meena was the old woman telling me the merits of Kamathipura, emphasizing the material generosity that she said was lacking in her village. Although this was never a question asked of her, I understood her desire to volunteer this information to an outsider asking questions, who was writing it all down in a notebook, within the context of widely disseminated perceptions of the district as a place of organized crime, danger, greed, and immorality. In relation to these perceptions, recorded interviews became a method of self-representation, a venue for telling an alternative narrative, at times a reactionary one, at least in parts. People's willingness to participate in any interview process mobilized the dominant discourse of sexual commerce in Kamathipura, a discourse in which agreeing to an interview was an attempt to intervene in that discourse. While these interventions may be seen as a way to preserve and protect an illegal and exploitative business, the older woman's choice to speak of people's generosity with food did not directly address the issue of prostitution itself. Rather, in saying that people in Kamathipura share rations, while others do not, her comment addressed the question of sociality, of character traits, including kindness and generosity, that are excluded from public representations of "fallen women" living and working in the red-light area. At the same time, the presence of people who were older and seemingly more powerful than Meena did not contribute to an open or relaxed interview, although the interview itself was significant for its resonances with women soliciting construction work at the naka. Like women soliciting clients for sexual services from the street, people living and working in Kamathipura had also attempted to earn money primarily through day wage labor, but had found such labor to be insufficiently available. All engaged with sexual commerce in some way, as migrants to the city.

The supervision we experienced in this particular interview gave rise to a number of methodological questions. For example, what kind of research is possible in such a highly overdetermined space, one whose name had become coterminous with trafficking and violence? The hegemonic narrative of a place like Kamathipura being only and always a place of unimaginable horror permeated each conversation between sex workers and non–sex workers. The narrative entered each conversation, such that it was difficult to speak outside of its bounds. That everyone insisted on saying that they had come to Kamathipura out of choice, that it was a place of generosity and care, evinced a powerful hegemonic lens that I, as a middle-class English-speaking researcher, embodied for the sex workers, brothel owners, pimps, and clients with whom I interacted. My verbal self-presentation as someone who did not necessarily subscribe to the hegemonic view of prostitution may have contributed to mitigating the dominant narrative I was seen to embody, although I eventually realized that it was folly to imagine I could ever shed it completely.

Hina

Hina also worked as a peer educator for the NGO running the mobile clinic. She lived in the Fourteenth Lane, on the second floor of a chawl. I went to meet her in the early afternoon as well, having learned not to go earlier. People would have been working until four in the morning and would not have awoken until noon; after six in the evening, "people are filling their stomachs." As I reached the building, Hina waved at me from her window, which looked out onto the lane. I went up to her "room," which was a tiny six-by-three-foot enclosure, one of three or four in a partitioned room on the second floor of an extremely weathered but solid building. There was no running water or indoor lavatory, and I could see several kerosene stoves scattered in front of the enclosures. Hina's space was big enough for a single mattress, with a shelf tacked up on the wall for a glass and a couple of vessels, a hook on the low ceiling above for hanging clothes, and pictures cut out from magazines and newspapers on the walls, including several images of Hindu gods that were reminiscent of naka workers' homes.

When we sat down on the mattress in her enclosure to speak, she called to a young boy in the hallway and reached into her sari blouse to give him some money for a cold drink for me, despite my refusals. "Pepsi? You'll have Pepsi? You have to have *something*," she said.

"Then I'll have water," I replied.

The boy came back with a plastic bag filled halfway with soda, tied closed with string, and inflated like a balloon from the carbonation. It had been dispensed from a two-liter bottle at one of the stalls in the lane.

"What is this?" she asked, annoyed. "I told you to get a bottle!"

He mumbled something about the stall not having bottles, and then about her not having given him enough money for one. I insisted that it was all right, that I would drink this soda, and it would be fine. The boy lingered for the duration of our interview, just out of sight outside the door that led into her windowed enclosure. As I was leaving, I noticed that an older woman had also been sitting nearby.

"No, madam," Hina said. "I'm not giving you something to drink from a plastic bag." (*Nahi, madam, mei aap ko plastic bag se nahi pilati hoon.*) We compromised by agreeing on a metal cup for the soda, which she filled by biting a corner of the bag carefully, and squirting the contents into the vessel.

Hina began by explaining that she was from Bijapur district, in Karnataka, the state that shared Maharashtra's southern border. Her mother and father both did agricultural and other day wage labor, until her father died of a heart attack when she was a child, causing great constraint (*majburi*) in the household.[20] Afterward, one sister had done agricultural labor (*matthi ka kam*), while the other did day wage labor (*begari kam*) to help the family survive. Hina also solicited work from the naka in her village, until she married.

Hina had come to Mumbai with her spousal family to find work fifteen years prior to this interview. Her husband had been violent and left the family, including his own parents, herself, and their four children after divorcing her ("giving *talaaq*"). When the family had first arrived in Mumbai, they lived in a slum close to a naka, where she began doing day wage labor. The whole family worked from the naka, where they solicited paid work from private contractors, and also did day wage labor for the municipality.[21] The day wage rate from the naka for women at the time was twenty-five rupees. When asked about working conditions for the women who were soliciting work from the naka, Hina said, "Some men are good, if the girls were to stay innocent [*aam*], then the men would, too. If the girls don't, then the men don't either. The contractors don't do any wrong work [*galat kam*; prostitution] with the girls."

Hina's father-in-law died shortly after they arrived in Mumbai. When the municipality demolished all the temporary housing (*jopdis*) in their locality seven years earlier, her mother-in-law returned to the village. Hina and her friend (*saheli*), whom she met at the naka, toured Mumbai; they visited Haji Ali and saw the city. Hina said her saheli had explained that "this and that happen here," an oblique reference to sex work, and had finally asked her, "What *else* are you going to do? There is majburi."

Hina's children were sent to live in the village and attend school there, to be looked after by her mother-in-law. Hina's mother-in-law visits twice a year and takes money to support the family. In the village, Hina said that they believe she is doing begari kam. When asked whether she prefers the village to the city, Hina said she prefers the village, "the family life, the feeling of seeing familiar people [*mil jhul*]." Throughout the interview, and especially near the end, Hina punctuated her story with the statement, "I came here of my own choice." (*Mein marzi se ai idder.*)

Hina's story was that of a migrant laborer in the city sending regular remittances to her family living in the village, like most, if not all, migrated workers in Mumbai. Many families had sent children to their villages to be raised by other relatives, citing factors like the high cost of living in the city, as well as the perception of greater safety and virtue in rural areas. Hina's family believing, or saying they believed, that she was earning money through day wage labor in Mumbai was a common refrain among women working throughout the red-light area. At the same time, "working in Mumbai" was a common euphemism for "doing sex work" in villages throughout Maharashtra and Karnataka, particularly if the worker was a woman.

A recurring theme in Hina's story was the difference in living conditions between the village and the city, and the problem of housing in Mumbai. After her family came to Mumbai, they settled in a slum, like thousands of other poor migrants in the city. Having settled in an affordable area, the family found that housing became unsustainable when the municipality demolished the homes there. When the family decided to go back to their village, Hina reported difficulty in finding an affordable place to stay for herself alone. For poor women living away from their immediate families, living in a brothel was one of few viable housing options. To be sure, many nuclear and extended families lived in Kamathipura as well, although the proportion of female-headed households and single women was higher there than in other parts of the city. At the time of this interview, Kamathipura still offered relatively secure housing, especially compared with the slums in Sanjay Gandhi National Park and others throughout the city that had been targeted for demolition.

Shirin

Shirin also lived in the Fourteenth Lane in Kamathipura, across from Hina's chawl. She lived on the other side of the lane, where the only structure was a concrete wall lined with jopdis—which were, in this case, temporary shacks made of wooden frames, with corrugated metal walls and net cots secured diagonally across the structure with brown twine. A year ago, Shirin said, the jopdis on that side of the lane had been torn down by the municipality. Some of the displaced tenants had been given rooms in a suburb of Mumbai, in housing that had been built as part of a resettlement scheme for people whose jopdi had been demolished. I asked if she would go there, wondering if she would mind being shifted so far from the place she knew. "Why not?" she replied. "If they're giving nice rooms in a good area?" Despite the resettlement scheme, Shirin was living in a rebuilt jopdi, on the same spot as before.

Shirin was born in Andhra Pradesh, in a village that was a twenty-four-hour journey by train from Mumbai. Her family had been extremely poor, and she had never gone to school. She was the youngest of three girls and one boy. Her family had never had their own land and survived by doing agricultural labor and herding goats in the village. In the fields, workers would be given lunch, and two rupees per day for harvesting or weeding, or three rupees per day for well digging. Although only the men did building construction work there, both men and women worked in the fields.

When Shirin was thirteen or fourteen years old, fifteen days before her wedding, she left her village to search for her brother, who had gone missing. She became lost on this journey and was befriended by an older woman. The woman introduced her to a man who eventually brought her to Mumbai. She did not know why she was being taken there. The man left her in a house, which she later learned was in the Falkland Road area. From inside a room in the house, she could hear this man making a deal for her, speaking in Hindi with the brothel owner. As a Telugu speaker, she could understand little of the conversation. The brothel owner eventually spoke to Shirin in Telugu, saying, "If you work, you will get 3,000 rupees per month." Two months later, the man who had brought Shirin to Falkland Road brought another girl. Shirin heard him say in Telugu, "What happened to that girl I brought?" referring to Shirin. This, Shirin said, was the moment at which she understood that what had happened to her was part of the man's business of bringing girls from Andhra Pradesh to this place.

At first, Shirin said she wouldn't go near any men, and would hit them if they tried to come close to her. Eventually, she said, she did sex work, and continued for four years, paying off the amount that had been paid for her by the brothel owner, with interest. By the time she paid off the debt, she had a daughter. She said it was "the same year that Indira Gandhi was killed" (1984). When the baby was six months old, Shirin had a fight with the brothel owner, "on the day of Ganesh Chaturthi," and left the brothel.[22] She boarded a train to go back to her village in Andhra Pradesh with the baby, but only went as far as Pune, a four-hour drive southeast of Mumbai. She said, "I thought, I have a baby, what will the people say?" She boarded another train for Mumbai and returned to Kamathipura.

As Shirin was roaming the area looking for a room for herself and her baby, a woman asked her in Telugu, "Do you want to do dhandha?" (*Dhandha karna hai?*)

Shirin replied, "Yes, I have a child." (*Hahn, bachcha hai.*) She worked in the woman's brothel, splitting her earnings equally between herself and the brothel owner. She saved money over the course of a year and returned to the village, having decided to tell her kinfolk there that she was married, so they would accept her and her child. She now went back and forth regularly.

Shirin said that she eventually stopped doing dhandha when she started working as a peer educator for the NGO. Shirin had worked for at least three organizations active in the area, serving as an outreach worker and peer educator. Through this work, she acquired a number of skills, including running a crèche and boarding facility and doing HIV education. She remarked that there were "at least ten different organizations" working in the area. Comparing her village as it was in her youth and as it was when we spoke, she said, "Ten or twelve years ago, most girls came to Mumbai not knowing what they were coming for, like me. Now, the girls in the village see that the girls who come back from the city have nice clothes, and they think, 'We'll also go!' They leave their families and husbands to go. A girl might bring her saheli, one girl brings two, it's like that."

In the course of her work with the NGO, Shirin had done outreach at one of the largest railway stations in the city. She discussed meeting women there who came from their homes to do sex work during the day, who were known as "flying sex workers" in the jargon of sex work–related organizations. These women took customers to local guesthouses and charged around thirty rupees for one hour. They would accept condoms from Shirin. "Sometimes, police used to come [for condoms] too," she said. Like the circuits of knowledge about Mumbai in the village, the police had also changed since she first arrived in the city. "The newer cops hit the girls, but the older ones say that the girls should do dhandha on their [the police's] terms. If the government wanted, they could stop this, but they don't want to. The police help this business, they get money from the brothel owners for the girls there." She compared the interests of the police in the area to the competing agendas at play among the local NGOs. Referring to an abolitionist NGO working in Kamathipura, she said, "What does that organization want? They want a court case. What do the cops want? They want money."

Shirin's story was a chronicle of twenty years of living and working in Kamathipura. Like most narratives of arriving and working as a sex worker in the district, her story was complex and not easily reducible to a singular paradigm. When Shirin described her departure from the village as a girl of thirteen to look for her brother, she said, "My brother disappeared, and I thought he might have been arrested by the police for selling country liquor." Her story does not imply that she was kidnapped exactly, although it contains elements that could be slotted into a narrative and legal definition of trafficking. While she was clearly held in debt bondage by the first brothel owner, she reported having freedom of movement in the area and having the resources to eventually pay off the debt.

Shirin's history of her working life, from field laborer to sex worker to outreach worker in Kamathipura, reflects some of the economic and political changes in the district over the previous two decades. Whereas twenty years prior, one or two NGOs had worked in the area, by the time we spoke, there were, as Shirin said, more than ten. This meant that working for an NGO as a peer educator or outreach worker itself became a viable livelihood option, a competitive job that came with a regular monthly salary, won on the basis of qualification, experience, or a degree of familiarity with people in the area. While NGO work created a new, albeit small, niche for sex workers to work as full- or part-time peer educators, Shirin's narrative also pointed to NGOs as significant players in the politics of the district. With so many different NGOs working in the area, these variously resourced organizations functioned as new power centers, each with their own agendas, in addition to the brothel owners, middlemen, sex workers, and police, who also had stakes in how the area operated.

In Shirin's village, the police were part of the local system that controlled illicit commerce in goods, to the point where she feared that her brother had been arrested and she set out in search of him. Over the years, Shirin experienced the police as people who supported the sex trade in Kamathipura by profiting from it. Seema, an older woman who had also come to Kamathipura as a girl from Andhra Pradesh, listed the regular payments made to the police along with other monthly bills: "electricity [batti], food [khana], water [pani], payments to the police [hafta], rent for my room [kamra ka kharach] . . ." This long-standing relationship changed as the police became, according to Shirin, "more violent."

Slum dwellers across Mumbai experienced the violence of the police and the municipality, the demolition of their homes by bulldozers often being preceded by the looting of their jopdis or vandalism of their possessions. In recent years, the demolitions had become more brutal, with people being given little or no intimation, and not being allowed to reclaim anything that was inside the jopdi even after the demolition.[23] Although rehousing schemes have been in place for displaced slum dwellers who qualify for resettlement, the shortage of these new flats, along with irregularities in their allotment, meant that, like Shirin, the majority of people who lived in areas targeted for demolition simply returned to the space they originally inhabited and rebuilt, if they could. Nearly ten years after this conversation with Shirin, the issues of housing and land use had become even more paramount for understanding the vast changes in Kamathipura and in red-light districts elsewhere.

The Ghost of Kamathipura

By 2012, the face of Mumbai was changing, perhaps more rapidly and visibly than ever before in the city's long history. High-rise apartment and office buildings seemed to be cropping up everywhere, their skeletons shrouded in burlap and blue tarps, rising tens of stories into the sky. Along Belassis Road, the main road leading from Mumbai Central past Kamathipura, the school that was my landmark—the tall green and white building with the arches—was now obscured by an even taller building in front of it. Roadwork clogged major traffic arteries in key areas of the city. Large-scale construction, several orders of magnitude greater than any project for which the naka workers I discuss in chapters 1 and 2 would be employed, seemed to abound.

While some would argue that all this construction signals rapid and universally beneficial economic growth, others point to these changes as signs of the consolidation of wealth, which does not necessarily lead to real economic growth, as evidenced by the miles of empty office blocks that began to populate major cities the world over in the late 1990s.[24] One real effect of the construction boom in Mumbai was the displacement of people in slums and low-income housing all over the city.[25] Resettlement packages were being offered to some of those who lost their homes, although qualifying for resettlement schemes was not always straightforward and usually benefited only a fraction of those displaced. This scenario was in keeping with similar demolitions, displacement, and construction in New Delhi, Ahmedabad, Pune, and Bangalore.[26]

The Kamathipura of 2012 was greatly changed from that of 2002; by some estimates, the population of brothel-based sex workers in the area had dwindled from 30,000 (or 15,000, or 50,000, depending on the source) to roughly 2,000. Small-scale industrial units had replaced many of the residences that used to line the lanes of the area, some of which had been brothels in the past. Redevelopment schemes for the area had been circulating since 2007, though landlords acknowledged that it would be difficult to shut down the brothels and displace people living there. These schemes had now gained traction, as the South Mumbai red-light districts in general had been dwindling, and redevelopment of the area seemed to have become a foregone conclusion, mainly because of the money that could finally be made from building in these areas. Journalist Neeta Kolhatkar offered this account of changing perspectives on real estate development in this part of the city: "In an earlier time, builders had stayed away from this part of central Mumbai. Ownership and tenancies were notoriously difficult to establish and in any case nobody wanted to shift out. But changing trends have made the area a veritable gold mine for its location. No one will confirm this, but the word is that the current quoted rate on the periphery of Foras Road [also a red-light area] is already between Rs 10,000–12,000 per sq ft and this could go up when the buildings come up."[27]

These "changing trends" included rapidly changing rules regarding how much square footage individual companies are allowed to build, as well as changes to zoning rules. Overall, there was a trend toward relaxing previous restrictions on the size of new construction, such as how many floors a building can have, and where it may be located. The result was new possibilities for profiting from real estate in prime areas of the city.

The media discourse of the attrition of sex work in the South Mumbai red-light districts largely exploited the explanatory power of the AIDS epidemic, with numerous journalists suggesting that areas like Kamathipura began to decline in 2005, due to AIDS having claimed so many lives by that time. While the impact of HIV/AIDS on sex workers is not disputed, HIV/AIDS is one component of a complex set of events and actors that, together, have resulted in Kamathipura, and areas like it, rapidly disappearing. These events and actors include stepped-up brothel raids, more violence from the police, the continued presence of HIV/AIDS and ways in which it was managed in Mumbai's red-light districts, and, of course, changing governmental policies regarding building construction limits, the manufactured availability of prime land, and the new price of real estate.

Raids

Builders and the municipal government had sought to redevelop the areas that have housed the South Mumbai red-light districts for some time. However, long-standing restrictions on new construction, put into place during the days of Nehruvian socialism, plus the disreputability of these areas for middle-class people, had resulted in the assessment that, despite their prime location, redevelopment would not be profitable. In the late 1990s, this assessment began to change as the AIDS epidemic gathered momentum in Mumbai's red-light districts and building restrictions eased as part of a broader program of economic liberalization. The municipality's response to the AIDS epidemic, which included a clear agenda of reducing the size of Kamathipura, is a key component of what happened in South Mumbai real estate after the late 1990s. Journalist Clara Lewis reported that the municipality (the BMC) considered this agenda to have been dealt with by 2010: "Dr Jairaj Thanekar, Chief Executive Health Officer, BMC, who worked in Kamathipura for 15 years to implement the AIDS intervention programme, says the corporation played a key role in reducing the number of prostitutes. 'From organising raids on the Yellappa markets down south—the main source of girls for Kamathipura—to raiding the brothels, we made it difficult for prostitution to function,' he says. 'From 1999 onwards, the number of sex workers started dwindling.'"[28]

If slum demolitions were a route to displacing slum dwellers and acquiring the land that once housed them, brothel raids had a cognate effect in red-light areas. By 2002, brothel raids in Kamathipura had become more frequent, although they were still a relatively new phenomenon in the South Mumbai red-light districts. Raids were conducted there from the mid-1990s onward in earnest, with the rationale that they would be the only way to both remove underage girls from the brothels and stop HIV transmission there. This was a radically different approach than that taken in Calcutta and in Sangli, Maharashtra, for example, where prevention and education efforts, including condom distribution and condom use policies, were enforced by sex workers in whole areas.

By 2002, brothel raids had become an increasingly common aspect of life in Kamathipura, as had added police surveillance.[29] From an emic perspective, police raids were a disruption of everyday life; they often targeted the daughters and other young female relatives of adult female sex workers who worked in the district, along with teenagers who were working voluntarily and had extremely circumscribed options for surviving and supporting their families. Residents of Kamathipura spoke of brothel raids as forced evictions that led to extrajudicial detention. In recent years, local organizations reported that police raids had included a demand from people being raided for their "official" papers, such as leases and rent receipts. Several residents experienced police confiscating documents that could have been used to prove their residency in the area, and that therefore could have been used to access resettlement programs, should the area be fully redeveloped.

Because of the highly polarized nature of the discourse on prostitution, it is difficult to evaluate the efficacy of raids in preventing or intervening in cases of kidnapping or coercion in red-light districts, although the efforts of local organizations did, as a brothel owner I will call Daya said, have the effect of reducing underage prostitution in the area. Raids are part of an abolitionist discourse of "rescue and rehabilitation," and women and girls who are rescued in a raid are taken to "remand homes" in Mumbai. Remand homes are operated both by the municipality and by NGOs. Some rumors about remand homes extend to accusations that they are poorly run and maintained, and that girls are held there in a state of indefinite detention while they are "rehabilitated" from doing sex work. The language of rehabilitation that inheres in discussions of raids and rescue moves understandings of sex work far afield from questions of livelihood, and into the discursive realm of individualized criminality, the possibility of "recidivism," and the psychological effects of selling sex. Among sex workers living and working in Kamathipura in 2003, the frequency of the raids was perceived to have increased over the previous few years. A brothel keeper in the Fourteenth Lane, who was known as Didi (older sister) and oversaw much of the business conducted there, had spoken of the raids in no uncertain terms.

In 2002, I spoke with Didi, whom I usually found cooking on her kerosene stove outside of her solidly constructed room, where she lived with her husband and young son. When I asked about what they did for work when she was in her village, she said, "You could make twenty-five to thirty rupees there, harvesting or watering in the fields. They would give fifty rupees a day for begari kam." As Didi spoke, she saw John Webster, a Norwegian filmmaker known at the time by many of the women in the area. His film *Rooms of Shadow and Light* (2001), which represented life in one of the nearby brothels in spare detail, was seen as a balanced presentation of daily life in Kamathipura. Seeing him, Didi said, "Look! One white man gives life, and another ruins it!" (*Dekho, ek gora jeevan dete hai, dusra gora barbat karte hai!*)

"What does that mean?" I asked.

She replied, "White people [*gorey lok*][30] take girls if they seem young, take them and put them in Chembur."

"What's Chembur?" I asked.

"If they put you in Chembur, you'll never come out again." (*Chembur mei dalenge, to kabhi nahi niklenga.*)

Seema, another Didi, was standing nearby and listening to the conversation. On hearing this, she added, "The police picked up two girls recently. If they see us on the road, it's 1,200 rupees. Where will we get that kind of money?"

Chembur, a suburb of Mumbai, was the location of one of the city's remand homes for sex workers.[31] For Didi, Chembur was simply a jail without reprieve, a place where girls were taken, never to return.

Daya

In the summer of 2012 I returned to Kamathipura, aiming to understand how the area had changed since I first began speaking to people there, and, specifically, why Kamathipura's obituary was already being written.[32] Walking around the Thirteenth and Fourteenth Lanes one afternoon, I saw one or two women I recognized, as well as a few of the brothels I remembered from previous visits. These brothels, also home to sex workers' families, still had charpoys (rope cots with wooden frames) in front of the doorways, the doors open, with people chatting or women brushing their hair while standing outside, watching people go by. In the Fourteenth Lane, the chawl still faced the brick wall at one end of the lane, along which jopdis (temporary shelters, in this case) had once again sprung up. Walking farther down, there were observable changes as well. Next to a brothel on the ground floor, opposite the jopdis, there was now an industrial unit of some kind, with men loading and unloading building materials from it, similar to the storefront industrial unit next to the naka. It had been a brothel and home when I was there last, in 2007, like the one that still remained next door. I was told later by the organization that had run the mobile clinic that industrial units were useful for redevelopment purposes because they were much more easily displaced than a brothel, and still generated income for landlords until new construction could commence. Numerous brothels had been replaced by these kinds of units all over Kamathipura. Unlike the industrial units, which were essentially temporary commercial spaces, people who lived in brothels could prove tenancy, and had a measure of protection from tenant's rights laws.

On this trip, the organization introduced me to a brothel owner I am calling Daya, who was one of the group's peer educators. The organization now also rented Daya's former home, an apartment in the Thirteenth Lane, to use as a permanent clinic. Daya explained that she discounted the clinic's rent for the space because it was providing a needed service to people in the area. The days of the mobile clinic in the van and treatments in the hallway seemed to be over.

Daya and I sat on a charpoy at the end of the Thirteenth Lane. I explained that I was interested in knowing what was happening in the area, and that I had been there years before, doing research for this book. She regarded me with skepticism until I mentioned my association with sex workers' rights organizations in other parts of India, and particularly the sex workers' organization in Calcutta. She seemed satisfied then, placing me, as I had placed myself, within a certain discursive context with respect to the politics of prostitution in India. "You'll have a cold drink?" she asked, by way of agreeing to speak with me further, and ordered a Mangola (a mango soda) from a man standing nearby, whom I had not noticed earlier. He appeared seconds later with a cold bottle and a straw.

"What do you expect to do for the women now? It's all over!" Daya said, gesturing up the lane in the day's fading light. "There are no women! Look at this lane—there are only men, living seventeen to a room!"

I looked up the lane and had the sensation of my eyes adjusting as I tried to see what Daya was showing me. The change that I had perceived but had been unable to articulate suddenly became clear. It was early evening, the time when these wide alleyways should have been lined with brightly dressed women waiting for customers. Instead, it was filled with young men, playing music from computers and MP3 players, chatting in front of the open doorways, and walking briskly from shop fronts to the main road. There were no women in sight. I asked how this had happened, wondering if builders were trying to evict people in order to profit from the redevelopment of the area.

"It's the landlords that give the most problems, not the builders," she said. "The landlords probably talk to the police and tell them where there's a new girl, and then the police raid that place. The landlords have made the rates [for sex work] fall in the area with all these raids."

"Do any of the local organizations help?" I asked.

"They raid *any* place, whether people are there by force or by choice. Look, before, the organizations [*sansthas*] would tell us that it wasn't good to have underage girls, and we don't keep underage girls anymore. That was good. But all the sansthas are the same—they say they want to help, but they keep kicking you from behind. Now they will look and say 'There's a new girl!' and then make a raid!" She named two such organizations, neither of which I had heard of.

"Two girls who came to my brothel, they got picked up in raids," she continued, "and they were taken from sanstha to sanstha to sanstha. They were eventually dropped in the jungle somewhere! Their parents had come with ration cards and all their documents and everything, and still didn't get to take them back. The sanstha didn't send them back to [their home in] Assam or anything."

I asked whether the raids alone could explain the transformation of the area.

"No, see, the landlord comes to people and says, 'Here, we're getting twenty lakhs [$45,000] from the builder, we'll keep ten and give you ten to leave,' and so people leave. They go back to their village, to Bhiwandi [on the outskirts of Mumbai], to wherever. The raids caused a lot of stress for women in the area. Two young women I knew of died from heart attacks, worrying about the raids. They dropped dead, right there on the street."

She said that in this lane, there used to be 150 houses, using the word *ghar* (house/home) for brothel. Now there were 5. Daya said that today, most dhandha happens in private apartments, in five-star hotels, and in bars, not in red-light districts. Looking up, I saw the high-rise building that now shadowed the Thirteenth Lane. I learned later that it had been built with an excess of the allowable Floor Space Index, with a number of illegally built "extra" floors. A court case against the builder was pending, leaving the building empty as the case dragged on.

Conclusion: India's Red-Light Districts in Decline

Sexual commerce in Mumbai has been conducted in many different kinds of venues, and with varying degrees of visibility. The most visible spaces of sex trade in the city—the red-light areas in South Mumbai—created numerous zones of vulnerability for sex workers while also offering stability with respect to housing and basic amenities, such as access to water, that migrants in other areas of the city found sorely lacking. The decision for women to sell sexual services, and to live in a red-light district, was contingent on these factors and was folded into a complex set of evaluations that may or may not have been undertaken by themselves, by their families, or as a joint decision involving several people. Women's decision-making power in this process ranged from full autonomy to no power at all, and included all points in between. The structuring frame for this evaluation was long-term sustainability for themselves and for the networks of people who relied on them for material survival. With this stability under attack through raids and slum demolitions, and with the conditions of rural poverty and urban migration intensifying, conditions now exist for less visible forms of sexual commerce to expand in the city, including those I discuss in the preceding chapters. While these forms of soliciting clients for sexual services are more episodic and, in some senses, expose sex workers to even greater vulnerability (e.g., as street-based sex workers), these forms also offer the advantage of being less visible to public scrutiny and regulation. From the perspective of doing work on HIV/AIDS, this development will make prevention and intervention efforts more difficult. From the perspective of advocates, the disappearance of red-light districts also renders collective mobilizations among sex workers more difficult as well. These mobilizations have been on a smaller scale in Kamathipura than those in other cities but have included sex workers availing themselves of newer initiatives in the area, such as an NGO-run cooperative bank and health services offered by at least two NGOs and one government-run clinic.

In a 2012 article in the daily newspaper *Live Mint*, journalist Gayatri Jayaraman reported on new forms of underground sexual commerce in the city arising in the wake of Kamathipura's demise:

> "The arranger" meets you at the McDonald's opposite Chhatrapati Shivaji Terminus station. She produces an album; two girls to a page. You only have to pay her Rs.100 each way for the commute. The girl will contact you. The rate is Rs. 1,500 onwards for a session. She cannot be arrested, she says, because she has only asked you to reimburse her travel. There has been no money transaction through her. If a man and woman choose to sleep together and he happens to give her money, who is she, or the law, to interfere in a personal transaction that she knows nothing about? This is the nature of the new Mumbai sex trade.[33]

The redevelopment of the red-light districts in South Mumbai has echoes in other Western cities and states in India. In 2004, the red-light area in Baina, a beachfront area in the coastal Goan city of Vasco da Gama, was bulldozed, dispersing sex workers who had lived and worked there. The area had been an unofficially regulated red-light area for some forty years. A journal article published by the Royal Dutch Geographical Society explained the motivation for the demolitions: "Baina's location on the shore was a logical choice for some exclusive seaside hotels and resorts. Sanjay Banerjee . . . reported in a *Times of India* article that the then Chief Minister Parriakar wanted to develop a highway and use the beach to promote tourism. In the course of the demolition, migrant neighbourhoods behind the red light area were demolished and migrant families evicted."[34]

Residents of one of the only red-light areas in the state of Gujarat, Chakla Bazaar, in the city of Surat, were subject to evictions in 2003. Despite protests from sex workers who had been evicted, as well as their having documented proof of residency, they were unable to reclaim their homes.[35] Local AIDS activists claimed that Chakla Bazaar has been a red-light area for four hundred years. The *Times of India* speculated on the reason for the evictions: "'We do not rule out that some people from the builder lobby may be behind the episode,' says councillor Padmaben M. Kantwala. However, an even bigger concern of NGOs active in AIDS control programmes is that once sex-workers are scattered, controlling the disease will be difficult. Now most of these 600 displaced women and nearly 70 children are staying on the streets."[36]

An ongoing struggle over the existence of the red-light district has also been taking place in Pune's Budhwar Pet, in the city center. A legal advocate who had attempted to intervene said that the brothels are disappearing there, replaced by storefronts and, for the moment, industrial units. Over the course of the past decade, Pune's transformation as a city, like Bangalore's, has been dramatic, with shopping malls and new residential buildings multiplying rapidly.

It is more than a little ironic that the form of the urban red-light district was initially conceived as a solution for the vagaries of urbanization in the late nineteenth century because it was imagined that a place *for* prostitution would mitigate the even greater imagined horrors of interracial marriages and repressed male sex drives. Over the course of the twentieth century, red-light areas became spaces where sex work, and sex workers, could be surveilled, regulated, and, in significant instances, provided with needed services. In a few instances, red-light districts also became spaces that fostered the collectivized mobilization of sex workers.

By the late twentieth century, the red-light district, at least in India, had become a proxy for prostitution itself; its eradication became the eradication of sexual commerce writ large. If red-light districts in Mumbai are now seen as sites of exceptional harm that should be eradicated for the greater good, this is the culmination of a process that began more than a century ago. In Mumbai, this eradication is being accomplished through a convergence of interests rather than through the machinations of a single rhetorical strategy or set of actors. Raids, conducted by a combine of police and abolitionist organizations, have worked in tandem with the interests of local government and private entities in erasing the red-light area. What could not be accomplished through wholesale displacement is commencing through attrition, as well as a generalized agreement that the erasure of red-light districts would, on the whole, be worthwhile. This hegemonic view has been produced in no small part through the spectacularization of places like Kamathipura, a process that has defined red-light districts in Mumbai as exceptional spaces of prostitution and harm, while concomitantly defining the rest of the city as normatively respectable.

The eulogy of Kamathipura, perhaps to be written in coming years, may no doubt tend toward romanticism. For example, in an "obituary" of Kamathipura in *Open Magazine*, the author relates a telling conversation with a *hijra* brothel owner:

> "They have quoted Rs. 40 lakh. I know the property is worth much more. They want a clean place so they want us out. All redevelopment plans are a farce," she says. "Many have left. It is just a matter of time before everyone else goes. Sex will sell on the streets, in parks and under bridges. I give Kamathipura two more years. But the claim that organised sex trade and exploitation will be wiped out is a myth. We all know that." . . . I buy them bangles, and they buy me mehendi cones. They offer me tea, and they want me to remember Kamathipura for its gracious eunuchs and its tales of love and loss. When the towers come up, remember us, she says.[37]

Kamathipura has always been a complex space, one that could never be reduced to simple tropes of harm or pleasure. The sweep of my argument here, drawn from ethnographic encounters and discourse analysis that spans a decade, shows the ways in which Kamathipura has constituted a space for survival in the informal sector, especially for women who migrated to the city from rural areas. This chapter also demonstrates the ways in which red-light districts comprise a commercial sector that generates remittances for people living in those rural areas. The power of the spectacle has marginalized analytic connections between brothel-based prostitution and informal economies, in favor of rendering brothels as exceptional sites of harm, and rendering their eradication as commonsense policy. If prostitution is properly understood as one of several livelihood options that poor rural migrants deploy in the city, then the spaces for prostitution will now disperse, rather than disappear, while the land that housed red-light districts is rebranded and resold for far greater profits than it ever generated before.

AGENCY, LIVELIHOODS, AND SPACES

The aim of this book has been to mobilize an analysis of sex work through a Marxian frame that accounts for sexual commerce in terms of livelihood, a category that emerged from conversations with people who sell sexual services and from observations of spaces that serve as sites of solicitation for women seeking male clients of those services. The frame of livelihood accounts for questions of violence and survival that structure sex work while it remains both criminalized and highly stigmatized. At the same time, the book contributes toward making analytic space for questions that presently run the risk of evaporating completely from scholarly and juridical discourses of sexual commerce, questions that concern pleasure, art, sociality, and the complex local discourses of sex acts and their meanings for sex workers and their clients, and the problem of identifying selling sexual services almost exclusively with cisgender women.

In choosing to avoid a didactic rejoinder to the abolitionist framework, I have endeavored to offer an alternative to the authoritative conflation of prostitution and violence by drawing on categories of analysis that emerged from my conversations and interactions with women selling sexual services in three distinct contexts in the city. This entailed centering questions of livelihood, migration, space, housing, and water in understanding how sex work operates in Mumbai, and why the different spaces in which it operates matter. Historiographically, sex work in India has been produced as occurring in or through *kothas*,[1] temples, and brothels—in *spaces*, but not in *sectors*, where sex work may instead be understood as existing along a continuum of livelihood strategies. While Marxian theories of space have been crucial in elaborating the mutually constitutive politics and political economies of space and class, the relationship between space and sex work has remained undertheorized. The marginalization of a critique of space and political economy in relation to sexual commerce in India has given rise to a regime of brothel raids and "rescue" as preferred methods of dealing with prostitution, a regime that is leading to the erasure of brothel-based prostitution in Mumbai and elsewhere. Whereas the relationalities between space and class remain undertheorized in scholarship on sexual commerce, the idea of space has been powerful in organizing historical and contemporary understandings of prostitution in India, in that prostitution in India has been thought to mainly occur in spaces that are exclusively purposed for sexual commerce, where everyone selling sex is (1) a woman or girl and (2) identifiable as a full-time sex worker. These ideas have worked to reify the iconicity of the brothel, and of female sex workers within it.

At its inception, I designed the research project from which this book is drawn as a means of critically engaging with what I perceived to be antiprostitution advocates' disavowal of sex workers' agency by critiquing the production of the figure of the iconic, brothel-based Indian sex worker. I reasoned that the increasing emphasis on female sex workers as victims of human trafficking, rather than as economic migrants, served to construct female sex workers as the ultimate embodiment of powerlessness and a lack of agency. In formulating an argument against this position, I attempted to construct a project that would recover the agency of Indian sex workers by framing them as both subjects and migrants, rather than as trafficked victims.[2] This initial attempt at reworking the question of powerlessness in debates on prostitution was soon transformed by the complexities of the ethnographic field and, initially, by learning how the field was constituted in the course of gaining entry into networks of migrant sex workers via local organizations and institutions. Because sex work is criminalized and highly stigmatized, local organizations offered one of the few routes to making initial contacts with networks of sex workers in different spaces. My first productive obstacle in this regard was that there were no local institutions of any kind that framed sex workers in terms of migrancy. Had my goal been a project on sex work and HIV, or on sex workers as victims of trafficking, the institutional support and direction would have been unambiguous. In the end (or in the beginning, as it were), my research on sex work and migration was facilitated by a migrant workers' organization whose outreach workers introduced me to people who solicit contracts for day wage construction work. Organizations working with street- and brothel-based sex workers facilitated contacts in those areas.

This book, the result of that project, has examined livelihood strategies that include sex work for three groups of women who had migrated to the city from rural areas throughout the country. These women were located in different areas of the city and engaged with sexual commerce variously. All were living in poverty and classified as belonging to a Scheduled Caste (SC) or a Scheduled Tribe (ST). At the construction workers' *naka*, women primarily earned their living as construction workers from the day wage labor market and supplemented both their income and their employability from the space by selling or trading sexual services episodically. On the street where women solicited clients for sex, some women also sold their labor at construction workers' nakas and returned to their villages seasonally, when extra work was available there. In the brothels of Mumbai's main red-light areas, women's entire income came from selling sexual services. At some point in their working lives, women in all three sites, including the red-light area, had solicited paid manual labor from one of the city's numerous day wage labor markets. Almost all those who sold sexual services were migrants in Mumbai and were originally from families living in rural areas, where they did not own or control any land, and where they themselves and everyone they knew worked as agricultural laborers.

Arguing that sexual commerce is part of a matrix of negotiating survival, I have shown that people who do sex work in Mumbai currently have also engaged in myriad other income-generating strategies. Some of the people with whom I spoke, whose primary livelihood strategy is now sex work, had started working at the age of four or five in roadside restaurants, washing dishes or serving tea. Almost all who grew up with their own parents began accompanying them to construction sites at a very young age, playing with other children among heaps of building materials while their mothers and fathers carried gravel, sand, and bricks around the skeletons of new buildings. Many had stood on a naka at some point during their working lives soliciting short-term contracts for manual labor. Describing and analyzing the relationships between sexual commerce and other, legal, less stigmatized, and often less financially sustaining strategies for earning a living has constituted a major thread of my discussions throughout the book, a thread that shows that stigma is part of the matrix of considerations that poor migrants to the city must navigate as they engage multiple livelihood strategies.

The book's focus on women was part of an attempt to engage something of the abolitionist framework's reduction of sexual commerce to the female body, and was analytically retained because women soliciting male clients for sexual services were part of daily life in each of the three research sites. That all of these women were landless SC and ST agricultural workers from rural, drought-prone areas to the south and east of the city was also crucial for understanding people in all three sites as sharing strikingly similar social milieus, livelihood histories, and economic responsibilities, both inside and outside the city. In Mumbai, they did piecework, worked as day wage laborers on small-scale construction and building repair projects, as street-based sex workers, and as brothel-based sex workers in South Mumbai's red-light areas. While the book shows the ways in which day wage labor and sexual commerce are linked, the book's focus and rhetorical strategies could be taken to suggest that sexual commerce is at the end of a linear trajectory of livelihood strategies for workers. In fact, people in all three sites moved in and out of different forms of generating income for as long as they were able to work. A serious consideration of these spaces and contexts, as part of the shared setting in which poor migrants must negotiate survival, has demanded thinking of sex work as something other than a discrete or autonomous space, while it also demands thinking of negotiating livelihood as something other than linear or static.

The project eventually became a way to draw political, economic, and conceptual connections between these three groups of workers, along the axes of livelihood, housing, migration, caste, and class, while repositioning, rather than eschewing, a discussion of violence. Violence serves as a primary interpretive lens for understanding the exchange of sex acts and money per se within an increasingly hegemonic discourse on prostitution in which prostitution is conflated with human trafficking. Rather than responding to this position by arguing that sex workers somehow do not experience violence or harm, I have aimed to analytically reposition violence, such that it serves as a lens for understanding the harms that arise not only from abusive clients, pimps, or brothel owners but also from the effects of criminalizing and stigmatizing sex work and migrancy. These effects include police harassment, social stigma, housing insecurity, and exclusion from key municipal services, such as schools, potable water, and access to opening bank accounts.

Sex, Work, and Silence

Nakas, public day wage labor markets that form throughout Mumbai for four to five hours each morning, have been central to my argument throughout the book. Nakas are unique as spaces, where people looking for work may gather in large numbers in the public urban spaces of street corners and railway stations without attracting unwanted attention from police and middle-class passersby who also inhabit these spaces. Women who waited for work at the naka were primarily perceived as using the spaces of the naka to solicit contracts for construction work. It was also common knowledge among naka workers and contractors that some women used the relative safety and legitimacy of their being coded as naka workers to solicit clients for sexual services, and that some women were thought to be doing both kinds of solicitation at the same time, regardless of whether or not this was the case. Reading the latter perception as a disciplinary narrative shows that women were seen to be fundamentally transgressing norms of propriety by openly seeking manual labor from a public place in the city. Inhabiting public space and using that space to solicit work from anyone who may visit the naka was seen as an indicator of abject poverty and transgressive of the relative seclusion of home. However, rather than suggesting that women were simply objects of this reading, the book shows the ways in which women at the naka both deployed and were subject to these perceptions. These deployments showed that women at the naka were necessarily in dialogue with a set of discursive practices that interpellate economic abjection, "untouchability," and gender in the perceptual category of "prostitute."

In 2005, I was introduced to a woman at one of the larger nakas in Mumbai. She explained that she was a single mother in her fifties, and that she came here to do sex work because she needed to earn money for her children's dowries.

"I make 300, 200, 250 rupees when I come here," she told me. "At first I came for *begari kam* [manual labor], but no one would hire me. And then I saw all these women just standing here, so one day, I asked them what they were doing, and they told me, and they said you can just sit here, and no one will bother you. There are lodges all around here where people go. Everyone knows about it."

When I asked why she didn't go to live and work in the red-light area, she replied, "Those women, they don't live with their families. If you live with your family, you can't go there. My family doesn't know I do this. I come on the train to this place, it's far from where they live. They think I do construction work." At one point in our conversation, she remarked with a smile, "See, these men, they still want an old woman like me."

My argument that there are multiple uses, attributes, and discourses surrounding the naka, the street, and the brothel is drawn from an ethnography that included as much speaking as it did silence, as much deflection as it did articulation of the kind evinced in this conversation. The parameters around which information was withheld or freely given varied with respect to each location, although information on negotiations for pay, condom use, and numbers of clients in any given day was never easily available, regardless of the location or type of space. This was especially true at the naka, where even the idea that sex work took place there was excluded from public discourse about the space. When naka workers eventually began discussing sex work more openly, they did so in lowered voices, away from the main spaces where naka-based workers gathered. Because brothels were ostensibly defined as spaces where sex work took place, it seemed more likely that one would obtain specific information about sex work there, that rapport would equal information freely given. I learned quickly that this was not to be, as women spoke extensively about their villages and their work histories, elements of their lives they had rarely been asked about, but were much more reticent about their incomes and issues such as condom use, which have been at the center of research agendas on prostitution.

I noticed that other researchers seemed to have a similar experience in attempting to speak with people in red-light districts. At brothels in particular, researchers regularly encountered roadblocks when pressing for details that may have veered into the areas of income levels and the ways in which specific sex acts take place. These observations and my own experience of conducting research in these areas countermanded the idea that researchers can establish individual, unmediated contact with brothel-based sex workers and gain clear information in a short time. Indeed, research on sex work in the main red-light areas of cities like Mumbai or Calcutta is not possible without the assistance of local organizations that have maintained regular contact with sex workers over a period of several years, at least. Even with this kind of assistance, it remains difficult to obtain numerical data on the working lives of individual sex workers. At a public event, one researcher explained that

FIG. CONC.1. Press conference at the National Sex Workers Conference, Thiruvananthapuram, Kerala, 2002

no contact could be made with sex workers in a particular red-light district without the presence of the researcher's chaperones, who were peer educators of a local HIV/AIDS organization, and that even then, only specific, approved questions could be asked. While these kinds of issues pertain to the problems of middle-class non–sex workers conducting research with people who work in sexual commerce who are stigmatized and criminalized, as well as the problems of needing to rely solely on local organizations for help in conducting interviews, they also pertain to research fatigue in red-light districts, of which I give an account in chapter 4. This is not to say that research with people living in red-light districts is not possible: an important body of work has been produced that relies on quantitative and qualitative data garnered from sex workers living and working in these districts. It is to say that the existence of a field of scholarship that addresses sexual commerce in India, and the ways in which this scholarship has been used to craft policy and interventions that target sex workers, potentially belies the ways in which gathering information on sex work, particularly when it is brothel based, is often a highly mediated event. The idea that clear information on the inner workings of sexual commerce is readily available produces sexual commerce as an essentially knowable practice that is clearly demarcated. From this perspective, stigma and criminality are no bar against knowing, and seeing, the truth of sex work.

One of my aims in the book has been to disrupt this idea of knowability in relation to sexual commerce, which also necessarily disrupts the idea that there are clean definitional lines around the exchange of sexual services and money. Knowability became a problematic within *Street Corner Secrets* as it emerged through the subterfuge and silences that formed a significant aspect of my daily life as an ethnographer in these spaces. Despite or, perhaps, because of these silences, I emerged from the spaces of the naka, for example, "knowing" without a doubt that sex work took place there. This knowing is partially accounted for by the circuits of gossip, rumor, and open secrets that constituted important elements of local discourses on sexual commerce. Secrets, and "open secrets" in particular, facilitate the partial knowledges required for multiply coding a space as being simultaneously normative and transgressive. The open secret produces the silences that, as Eve Sedgwick argued, are rendered as speech acts: "The fact that silence is rendered as pointed and performative as speech, in relations around the closet, depends on and highlights more broadly the fact that ignorance is as potent and as multiple a thing there as is knowledge."[3] The problems of associating "the closet" with the spaces for sexual commerce notwithstanding (the brothel is not a closet, nor is the naka, nor the street), I am interested in the mutuality of silence and speech in Sedgwick's critique. If "ignorance" can be directed toward an ostensibly generalized ignorance of where, and by whom, sexual services are solicited in Mumbai, then we may understand the silences and denials regarding this solicitation as constitutive of the continuing economic viability of sex work. Even in the red-light area, sex work is an open secret, one that those who engage in sexual commerce as buyers and sellers share to a much greater degree than do non–sex workers who engage in these spaces, including NGO workers and researchers. In contemporary Mumbai, sex work is produced through the rubric of the open secret, one that aims to protect the sellers of sexual services from the harms associated with criminalization and stigma, while producing a public in which knowledge about where and when sex work is solicited is shared. In the end, I knew that which I was never verbally told, in many instances, because of my own slow and, ultimately, partial absorption within a particular knowing public. This is a public that shares in the open secrets of sexual commerce in Mumbai, a public that is neither buyer nor seller, yet one that sees the contours of solicitation for sexual services in the city.

Majburi, Marzi, and Agency

In the summer of 2007, I was in Kamathipura talking with a woman who was from either Calcutta, in India, or Dhaka, in Bangladesh. She would not reveal her nationality for fear of being marked as an illegal cross-border migrant. Had local authorities been able to prove this, the law would have allowed her two choices—to be identified as an illegal migrant worker, or to be identified as a victim of trafficking, both of which may have resulted in her deportation and "repatriation," and would definitely have resulted in her arrest or detention. I began asking about her livelihood history, what she had done to support herself when she was younger, and what she did now. She said that, having worked for a number of years in the red-light area as a sex worker, she was now a madam; she was roughly in her early thirties. During the course of our conversation, which was conducted in Mumbai's unique version of Hindi, she, like Shaini, whom I discussed in chapter 3, used the terms *marzi* (choice) and *majburi* (a compulsion or set of constraints) in what I initially took to be an interchangeable manner. I noticed that she never used the word for force, *jabardasti*, as she related her livelihood history. I eventually interrupted her to ask, "When you talk about how you have earned, you say marzi *and* majburi. Why do you use both of these terms?" She had been reflecting on the deeply circumscribed lack of options for survival in her home village, and all of the strategies that she had used in her lifetime to earn a living, including construction work and sex work. She paused and then replied, "Over there [in the village] we have constraints, so we come here out of choice." (*Udhar, ham ko majburi hai, to idhar hum marzi se atey hain.*)

The complexities of negotiating a livelihood as a migrant worker are belied by the simplicity of this statement, which captures the essence of this book's argument in its articulation of the discursive rubric in which decisions about livelihood are made. The statement also prompts a critique of the ways in which varying, sometimes contradictory understandings of agency have been used in feminist debates on prostitution. As the project for the book developed over the course of fieldwork, agency was everywhere, but it seemed almost as elusive as the mirage of choice in understanding the ways in which women who worked as sex workers and as manual laborers in the construction industry represented their own working lives. Rather than addressing either agency or choice, it seemed the bulk of my conversations with women in all of the spaces of the project focused on the material contexts for landless SC and ST agricultural workers' migration to Mumbai, and their negotiations of a specific set of livelihood options. These conversations focused on majburi, in other words, rather than on marzi.

A crucial difference between a perspective on prostitution that gives primacy to the question of livelihood, and that enshrined in abolitionist discourses on prostitution, relates to the definition and uses of the concept of agency. Abolitionist discourses on prostitution, we may recall, conflate prostitution and trafficking by (1) excluding nonfemale sex workers (male, transgender, and *hijra* sex workers) from its analytic frame, (2) framing women doing sex work as utterly powerless victims who do not "have" agency, and (3) conflating prostitution and violence. The idea that women either do or do not "have" agency in these discourses necessitates a critique of the conflation of agency with choice, rather than using an understanding of the concept of agency as it has been defined: as an agent's *capacity to act*.

If agency is the capacity to act, then all agents "have" that capacity, whether or not they have the ability to exercise it. Choice, on the other hand, is something that individuals may or may not have (i.e., possess). If agency and choice are conflated in the abolitionist discourse on prostitution, what, then, are the effects of claiming that sex workers have no choice but to be forced to sell sexual services? If women, by definition, cannot have the agency to sell sexual services, where agency is conflated with choice, then the only explanation for their engaging in sexual commerce is that they must be forced. If they are forced, they are subject to violence, which is equivalent to prostitution within the abolitionist paradigm.

In a thoroughgoing review of anthropological formulations of agency, Laura Ahearn summarizes the problem of conflating agency with free will, which, she argues, has become commonplace. She writes, "The main weakness in treating agency as a synonym for free will is that such an approach ignores or only gives lip service to the social nature of agency and the pervasive influence of culture on human intentions, beliefs, and actions."[4] I would add that conflating free will and agency also ignores the pervasive nature of *politics* on human intentions, beliefs, and actions.

Rather than choice, a concept that is distinct from agency, agency is defined as the capacity to act and necessitates a consideration of the system or context that mediates and structures those capacities. If sex workers who refuse the category of victim are framed as immoral individuals who "choose" their fate (as opposed to moral sex workers who did not have any choice/agency), the alternative, as framed by some sex workers' rights advocates, is to reframe sex work as a moral choice. This latter perspective has also been fed into a matrix where choice and agency are read as the same, with the twist that sex workers do, in fact, "have" agency, and has been used to discuss sex workers' activism and organized resistance to abolitionist laws and policies.

This conflation of agency and resistance, while less prevalent, is also present in scholarship on sex work. For example, in an article on sex workers' AIDS prevention efforts in India, two health researchers write, "Efforts have been made to stem the tide. But most campaigns have been designed to ensure condom compliance among CSWers [commercial sex workers] by spreading awareness and increasing availability. Absent from the discursive space of such campaigns are the agency of CSWers and their ability to resist dominant social structures. The authors respond to this lacuna in health communication by foregrounding voices of CSWers participating in two HIV/AIDS interventions in India."[5]

It is clear that sex workers and sex worker advocates are forming a vibrant and sustainable movement for social change in India. It is also clear that serious scholarship on sex work must account for these movements, and the individual and organizational actors that drive them. However, the discursive effects of framing agency wholly in terms of resistance in this context are as potentially problematic as are the discursive effects of framing the lack of agency as a lack of free choice. Following on Ahearn's readings of Nancy Fraser's and Lila Abu-Lughod's work on agency from the early 1990s,[6] disaggregating agency, resistance, and choice creates an important space for theorizing action with its structural contexts. This would be agency neither as liberal individualist choice (or its lack) nor as organized resistance. It would be agency as the capacity to act— differential, context specific, and always, in some fashion, extant. In the terms of my conversation with the woman from Calcutta/Dhaka, a focus on structuring contexts for sexual commerce would pay close attention to the relationship between majburi (constraints) and marzi (choice), without reducing majburi to jabardasti (force).

A Note on the Discursive Production of Children

In addition to calling into question the effects of conflating agency with any number of descriptors for choice and subversion, this book calls into question the effects of centering agency-as-choice in the discourse on prostitution-as-trafficking. If agency stands in for free will or choice in the dominant discourse, then centering choice in that discourse gives primacy to the question of origins (how did one come to sell sex in the first place?) and locates the originary moment of engaging in prostitution within the individualized contexts of family structure and psychology, and not within a complex matrix that also includes the need to earn a living within an extremely constrained set of options. Given the extensive misuses of agency, it becomes necessary to imagine a use of agency that addresses the capacity to act, and to wonder if that capacity could be seen to include the numerous acts, large and small, required to survive while living in poverty over the course of a lifetime.

A major discursive effect of centering agency-as-choice has been the production of a slippage between the notion of women and girls. This is evidenced in the deployment of brothel raids, which are rationalized as a way to save girls from prostitution. The ways in which the rhetoric of the protection of girls drives abolitionist interventions on prostitution suggest that the idea of the child filters an understanding of women selling sexual services in these interventions. I have not addressed children directly in this book, primarily because my interactions in all three research sites were exclusively with adults. This could be considered a failing of the research, but my years of doing research in these sites and on this issue tell me otherwise. While I do not believe that there have never been any children selling sexual services in Mumbai, as confirmed by Daya in chapter 4, it is difficult to corroborate claims of the numbers of children in sexual commerce; some of these claims have been produced through conjecture, through guestimates, and, perhaps most importantly, through the discursive necessity of producing female sex workers as moral agents worthy of rescue.

Scholars contributing to the literature on the figure of the child in discourses on trafficking and prostitution have argued that the central trope of victim subjectivity in discourses of sex work and human trafficking is that of the child, and that women and children are regularly conflated in antiprostitution policy.[7] This is demonstrated in examining policies on prostitution, where the focus has generally not been on how to prevent children from working in prostitution but, rather, on how to eliminate prostitution because children are thought to be represented there in overwhelming numbers. These numbers, if they are offered, are derived from extremely disparate sources, using disparate methods, and are produced within a discursive context in which the criminalization and stigmatization of prostitution are accepted as fact. Criminality and stigmatization render prostitution extremely difficult to regulate, and even more difficult to research. Having effectively driven prostitution underground, the existence of children there becomes increasingly difficult to map, while the presupposition that children are overrepresented in sexual commerce becomes more pronounced.

Repositioning Violence

There are numerous examples of the theoretical convergence of violence, prostitution, and human trafficking in a range of South Asian discursive contexts. These convergences are important for understanding how agency, rendered as choice, is effectively produced as being incommensurate with the daily life of prostitution. The discursive convergence of prostitution and violence became evident in the early stages of my fieldwork as I attempted to speak with migrant sex workers. In the course of seeking contacts, I spoke with members of an organization that ran a free day care for the children of sex workers who lived and worked in one of Mumbai's larger red-light areas. As I explained my project, my use of the term "sex worker" elicited an immediate response about violence in the area. "You say 'sex worker' as if it is work. I know many people from the West use this expression. But there was a woman who used to come here, she was from this area, we took care of her children. She first came with a huge bruise around her eye. Her eye was even bleeding. Her pimp had done it to her. I mean . . . how can you look at that and call it work?"

While I shared the concern about the woman's injury, I disagreed that physical violence is the inevitable outcome of the exchange of money for sexual services, or that the exchange of sex and money causes violence. I pointed out that people without any power over their working conditions and lives in any number of sectors experience violence and severe injury as a result of their powerlessness, and yet we would not conflate violence and powerlessness with the work that people did in these situations, as in sweatshops or factory work. My interlocutor disagreed, claiming that these various sectors were not comparable, and that prostitution constitutes an exceptional harm.

These responses conformed closely to an argument that is at the center of abolitionist understandings of sexual commerce, that prostitution uniquely violates bodily integrity. The idea that prostitution is exceptional, that it cannot be placed within a matrix of livelihood strategies because its bodily violations are egregious beyond measure, has sustained the idea that prostitution is one of many indicators of the abject oppression of women in the Global South. This view is reflected in an article on women in Pakistan:

In South Asian countries the amalgamation of Buddhist, Confucian, Hindu, Islamic and Christian traditions have shaped the personalities of women and determined their social status. Rigid cultures and patriarchal attitudes which devalue the role of women, result in the wide spread occurrence of violence against women. The family structure, in which the man is the undisputed ruler of the household, and activities within the family are seen as private, allows violence to occur at home. As well as traditional forms of violence such as wife-battering and sexual assault, women in these countries are also exposed to dowry crimes such as bride burning, kidnapping for the purposes of prostitution, and "honor killings."[8]

This argument draws easy connections between a broad range of experiences, all framed within the rubric of violence against women. However, is this particular litany actually framed by violence, given that the axis that connects this range of phenomena is the appeal to a unitary notion of South Asian culture? Family structure and tradition, those familiar enemies of women in the Global South, frame all subsequent social ills in this passage. The argument draws classic postcolonial feminist critiques against constructing Third World women monolithically through the rubrics of tradition and culture. Feminist legal scholar Ratna Kapur has critiqued abolitionist antitrafficking initiatives by arguing that the sets of politics that conflate trafficking and prostitution reiterate culture-bound representations of women in the Global South. Of the abolitionist representation of victims of trafficking in the Global South, she writes: "The image that is produced is that of a truncated Third World woman who is sexually constrained, tradition-bound, incarcerated in the home, illiterate, and poor. It is an image that is strikingly reminiscent of the colonial construction of the Eastern woman."[9]

Drawing on these critiques, it seems that the conflation of violence, prostitution, and trafficking reiterate a historically familiar and perhaps recursive trope of the helpless Third World woman who must be saved from her Third World–ness. The familiarity of this trope is so powerful that it takes over any discussion of poverty, of rural development gone awry, or even of economic and social class in relation to sexual commerce. Rather than serving to mobilize a critique of the reasons why people living in poverty are finding it increasingly difficult to survive in rural areas in the Global South, abolitionist discourses on prostitution replace critiques of poverty with images of abused and abusive sex workers. These perspectives on sexual commerce have become mainstream, serving as the common sense of what sexual commerce is for an increasing number of people. The success of a small but influential subgenre of documentary films on sex work in India that collectively proliferate a monolithic version of victimized Third World women is a case in point.[10] However, it would be a mistake to locate the production of this view in a coherent conceptual universe, in which white Westerners produce the idea of abjected women in the Global South. The disciplinary gaze that produces abject victimization through prostitution may be resonant with the days of the "white slavery" panics and the Contagious Diseases Acts, but our analysis of this gaze must necessarily apprehend the complex and much changed set of directionalities from which it is deployed. For example, the gaze that produces the sex workers in Kamathipura as abject victims of violence will now include the middle- and upper-class Indian consumers of the shops and residences that will replace Kamathipura, who will doubtlessly laud the erasure of the brothels as a sign of progress for women.

Conclusion

Abolitionist discourses on prostitution produce the idea of violence and prostitution being inextricably intertwined in the idealized figures of victimized women and girls. This has given rise to a new era of calls to abolish sexual commerce through criminalization. However, the book shows that sexual commerce cannot be conceptualized, or acted upon, as a discrete phenomenon. Rather, understanding sexual commerce in Mumbai means examining access to water, in villages and in urban slums. It means understanding how *izzat* becomes a valence of survival for women who work in urban informal sectors. Paying close attention to poor migrants' access to public space and its relationship to sexual commerce has meant critiquing the ways in which local police are central figures in producing this space, while acknowledging that the practices of policing and the exercise of legal enforcement are often idiosyncratic, irregular, and at times negotiable. This is particularly relevant for understanding how groups of people who have little economic power, and no real electoral power, navigate the lines between legal and illegal, licit and illicit, when the systems in which they must negotiate survival operate in vastly differential ways. In this critique, selling sexual services is not without risk, but it is an important strategy of making ends meet.

My conversations with sex workers and non–sex workers in each research site, in feminist organizing spaces, and in my personal social spaces as well gave rise to the possibility of an ethnographic exploration of the intersections of sexuality and political economy. In this book, this has taken shape as an exploration of the ways in which sexual commerce is embedded within a web of negotiations for daily economic survival that poor migrants must navigate in the city of Mumbai. This analysis has entailed a particular focus on the problematics of space. The idea that the differences in spaces used for sexual commerce are rendered through their differential legibility as spaces where sexual commerce occurs is a departure from the prevailing notion that spaces for sexual commerce are spaces where prostitution-as-violence occurs, and that eradicating these spaces means eradicating this violence. Placing questions of visibility and legibility within an account of sex work in India places the aims and intents of eradicating sexual commerce in a new light, especially when prostitution eradication efforts in India are intently focused on brothels. Brothels have been subject to a heightened level of scrutiny, having become a synecdoche of all prostitution in India, rather than being understood as an aspect of a diverse range of uses of sexual commerce deployed by women working in the informal economy. Over the course of the research and writing phases of this project, the symbolic importance of eradicating brothels has become all too clear, while also revealing the ways in which red-light districts have attracted a convergence of interests, including those of policy makers, real estate developers, politicians, and prostitution abolitionists. While the erasure of red-light districts is a notable aspect of the regulation of prostitution in the late twentieth and early twenty-first centuries, the convergence of the interests of a diverse array of actors and institutions in effecting this erasure is not new. As the confluence of actors and institutions working to erase Kamathipura today agree that sex workers will ultimately benefit from this eventuality, the sundry array of actors and institutions who worked to establish Kamathipura in the late nineteenth century also agreed that a red-light district would at least succeed in sequestering prostitution and protecting the common good.

Understanding brothels as an aspect of sexual commerce in India has necessitated placing brothels in Mumbai in relation to other spaces where women working as manual laborers solicit clients for construction work and/or sex work. The spaces of the naka and the street both provide an alternate but related context for sex work to that provided by the brothel. An examination of sex work in these spaces has contributed to marshalling the idea of continua, precluding the notion that different kinds of economic activity necessarily exist in discrete and distinct urban zones, and that cities may therefore be understood as an additive agglomeration of these discrete components.

Ultimately, I have attempted to show that the conceptual terrain of sexual commerce is complex, to say the least, and that thinking of prostitution as an isolated, exceptional phenomenon erases that complexity in favor of a familiar narrative that maintains the status quo of class, mobility, and access to the city. Efforts to see sexual commerce as a livelihood strategy, and to build a juridical regime that governs sexual commerce through this optic, are new and constitute a significant departure from the discursive regimes that have governed prostitution for more than a century. This book is one of a growing number of scholarly contributions to a new way of thinking about sex work, one that accounts for the layered negotiations of survival engaged by legions of dispossessed migrant workers who exist outside of the ever-tightening circles of prosperity that have come to define economic growth. Taken together, the three spaces that have animated my analysis show that ideas about gender and sexuality as they are read through the filter of sexual commerce are imbricated within the production of space in the city. A historicized assessment of daily life in these spaces shows the dynamic nature of this production. The production of spaces in Mumbai as being for sex work or not are, in turn, components of a conceptual universe in which debates on the proper subjects of twenty-first-century Mumbai are being waged.

Preface

1. National AIDS Control Organization (NACO), *Annual Report 2010–11* (New Delhi: Ministry of Health and Family Welfare, Government of India, 2011).

Introduction

1. A growing body of work is examining "timepass" in relation to Indian modernity. See, for example, Jeffrey Craig, *Timepass: Youth, Class, and the Politics of Waiting in India* (Stanford, CA: Stanford University Press, 2010).

2. *Naka* is a term used in several north Indian languages, including those primarily spoken in Mumbai (Marathi, Hindi, and Gujarati). It refers to a day wage labor market, usually convened on a street corner or in front of a train station, that is used by manual laborers to procure paid work. Nakas constitute a space where unskilled workers (many of whom are migrant agricultural workers from rural areas) may find jobs doing manual labor, especially construction work. The concept and contexts for nakas are elaborated further in chapters 1 and 2.

3. "Scheduled Caste" and "Scheduled Tribe" are official terms that reference non-upper-caste caste categories. A more detailed discussion of caste follows in chapter 1.

4. Vinay K. Gidwani, "Subaltern Cosmopolitanism as Politics," *Antipode* 38 (2006): 12.

5. P. Sainath, "Farm Suicides Rise in Maharashtra, State Still Leads the List," *The Hindu*, July 3, 2012, accessed December 1, 2012, http://www.thehindu

.com/opinion/columns/sainath/article3595351.ece. Deepankar Basu and Amit Basole, "Food Budget Squeeze, Market Penetration and the Calorie Consumption Puzzle in India," *Sanhati* blog, December 1, 2012, accessed December 15, 2012, http://sanhati.com/excerpted/5855.

6. Naazneen Karmali, "India's 100 Richest Have Mixed Year, Eke Out Small Gain," *Forbes Asia*, November 5, 2012, accessed January 13, 2013, http://www.forbes.com/india-billionaires/list/.

7. Keith Hart, "Informal Income Opportunities and Urban Employment in Ghana," *Journal of Modern African Studies* 11 (1973): 61–89.

8. Jan Breman, *Footloose Labour: Working in India's Informal Economy* (Cambridge: Cambridge University Press, 1996).

9. Aditya Nigam, "Rethinking the Unorganised Sector," *Social Action* 47 (1997): 125–34.

10. B. Goldar, "Trade Liberalization and Manufacturing Employment: The Case of India" (Employment Paper, No. 2002/34, ILO, Geneva, 2002).

11. Keith Hart, "On the Informal Economy: The Political History of an Ethnographic Concept" (Working Paper 09/042, Centre Emile Bernheim, Brussels, 2009), accessed December 20, 2012, http://ideas.repec.org/p/sol/wpaper/09-042.html.

12. Ann Jordan, "The Annotated Guide to the Complete UN Trafficking Protocol" (Washington, DC: Global Rights, 2002), accessed January 15, 2013, http://www.globalrights.org/site/DocServer/Annotated_Protocol.pdf.

13. "Protocol to Prevent, Suppress and Punish Trafficking in Persons, Especially Women and Children 2000," Article 3 (a), United Nations Crime and Justice Information Network, Center for International Crime Prevention, Office for Drug Control and Crime Prevention, accessed May 2012, http://www.uncjin.org/Documents/.../final.../convention_%20traff_eng.pdf.

14. Center for Health and Gender Equity, "Implications of U.S. Policy Restrictions for HIV Programs Aimed at Commercial Sex Workers," August 2008, accessed December 8, 2012, http://www.genderhealth.org/files/uploads/change/publications/aplobrief.pdf (emphasis added). In June 2013, the U.S. Supreme Court struck down the "Prostitution Pledge" for groups based in the United States, including those working internationally, saying that it was unconstitutional because it violated the First Amendment. The pledge may still be applied to groups abroad who receive funding from any U.S. governmental agency. Melissa Gira Grant, "Supreme Court Strikes Down Anti-Prostitution Pledge for US Groups," *The Nation*, June 30, 2013, accessed January 28, 2014, http://www.thenation.com/blog/174910/supreme-court-strikes-down-anti-prostitution-pledge-us-groups#.

15. Kamala Kempadoo, "Introduction," in Kamala Kempadoo and Jo Doezema, eds., *Global Sex Workers: Rights, Resistance, and Redefinition* (New York: Routledge, 1998), 3.

16. In chapter 1, I reference Julia Kristeva's definition of "abjection" as "something rejected from which one does not part" in relation to migrant workers

living in Mumbai. In that chapter, I also use the past participle "abjected" to connote that which is in a state of conceptual formation, i.e., being *made* "abject," rather than *being* "abjection." My usage of "abjection" here refers to a vernacular understanding of the definition of abjection as hopeless, marginal, cast off.

17. Svati P. Shah, "Producing the Spectacle of Prostitution in India: The Politics of Red Light Visibility in Mumbai," *Cultural Dynamics* 18 (2006): 269–92.

18. *Born into Brothels* (film), dir. Zana Briski and Ross Kaufman (New York: Red Light Films, 2004).

19. Mary John and Janaki Nair, "Introduction: A Question of Silence? The Sexual Economies of Modern India," in Mary John and Janaki Nair, eds., *A Question of Silence? The Sexual Economies of Modern India* (New Delhi: Kali for Women, 1998), 1–51.

20. P. M. Nair, *A Report on Trafficking in Women and Children in India 2002–2003* (New Delhi: National Human Rights Commission, UNIFEM, Institute of Social Sciences, 2004), 332.

21. Nair, *A Report on Trafficking in Women and Children*, 361.

22. Anand Grover and Tripti Tandon, "(W)Rec(K)tifying I.T.P.A.: Proposed Amendments to the Immoral Trafficking Prevention Act: More Disaster for Prostitutes, Not Traffickers," *From the Lawyers' Collective* 21, no. 3 (2006): 7–14.

23. There is a broad consensus that laws on prostitution require revision, although there is a great deal of disagreement on what this revision would entail. One critique of laws and policies on prostitution reads, "As is clear from the circumstances of sex workers [higher rates of illiteracy and the risk of HIV] the Indian government's approach has not been very successful in protecting the rights of sex workers or improving their well-being. Yet ineffective policies of long standing, such as rehabilitation, and a legal framework that is ambiguous in its approach towards sex work but seeks to restrict entry into it continue to remain popular." Geetanjali Misra, Ajay Mahal, and Rima Shah, "Protecting the Rights of Sex Workers: The Indian Experience," *Health and Human Rights* 5 (2000): 96.

24. Other critiques of the rhetorical uses of slavery include Bridget Anderson and Rutvica Andrijasevic, "Sex, Slaves and Citizens: The Politics of Antitrafficking," *Soundings: A Journal of Politics and Culture* 40 (2008): 135–45, where the authors argue that a focus on slavery in discourses on trafficking, which already reinforce public sentiments against prostitution, also depoliticizes debates on migration.

25. Columbia University Press, "Interview with Siddharth Kara, author of *Sex Trafficking*," accessed December 1, 2012, http://cup.columbia.edu/static/siddarth-kara-interview; Siddharth Kara, *Sex Trafficking: Inside the Business of Modern Slavery* (New York: Columbia University Press, 2008).

26. Kimberly A. McCabe and Sabita Manian, eds., *Sex Trafficking: A Global Perspective* (Lanham, MD: Rowman and Littlefield, 2010), 99–100.

27. Some of these trends play out in William Dalrymple, "The Daughters of Yellamma," in *Nine Lives: In Search of the Sacred in Modern India* (New York: Vintage Books, 2011), 55–76.

28. K. K. Jordan, *From Sacred Servant to Profane Prostitute: A History of the Changing Legal Status of the Devadasis in India, 1857–1947* (New Delhi: Manohar, 2003); Lucinda Ramberg, *Given to the Goddess: South Indian Devadasis and the Sexuality of Religion* (Durham, NC: Duke University Press, 2014); V. Geetha, "Gender and the Logic of Brahminism: Periyar and the Politics of the Female Body," in K. K. Sangari and Uma Chakravarti, eds., *From Myths to Markets: Essays on Gender* (New Delhi: Manohar, 1998), 198–233.

29. Maggie Black, *Women in Ritual Slavery: Devadasi, Jogini and Mathamma in Karnataka, Andhra Pradesh, Southern India* (London: Anti-Slavery International, 2007), accessed November 10, 2012, www.antislavery.org/includes /.../women_in_ritual_slavery2007.pdf, 1.

30. Lucinda Ramberg, "When the Devi Is Your Husband: Sacred Marriage and Sexual Economy in South India," *Feminist Studies* 37 (2011): 28–33.

31. Black, *Women in Ritual Slavery*, 1.

32. Devinder Mohan Thappa, Nidhi Singh, and Sowmya Kaimal, "Prostitution in India and Its Role in the Spread of HIV Infection," *Indian Journal of Sexually Transmitted Diseases* 28 (2007): 69–75.

33. Thappa, Singh, and Kaimal, "Prostitution in India and Its Role in the Spread of HIV Infection."

34. Thappa, Singh, and Kaimal, "Prostitution in India and Its Role in the Spread of HIV Infection."

35. L. N. Rangarajan, ed. and trans., *The Arthashastra / Kautilya* (New Delhi: Penguin Books India, 1992).

36. Mary John and Janaki Nair, eds., *A Question of Silence? The Sexual Economies of Modern India* (New Delhi: Kali for Women, 1998); Partha Chatterjee, "The Nationalist Resolution of the Women's Question," in Kumkum Sangari and Sudesh Vaid, eds., *Recasting Women: Essays in Indian Colonial History* (New Delhi: Kali for Women, 1989), 233–53.

37. Rajeshwari Sunder Rajan, *The Scandal of the State: Women, Law and Citizenship in Postcolonial India* (Durham, NC: Duke University Press, 2003); Philippa Levine, *Prostitution, Race and Politics: Policing Venereal Disease in the British Empire* (New York: Routledge, 2003).

38. Kenneth Ballhatchet, *Race, Sex, and Class under the Raj: Imperial Attitudes and Policies and Their Critics, 1793–1905* (London: Weidenfeld and Nicolson, 1980); David Arnold, "Sexually Transmitted Diseases in Nineteenth- and Twentieth-Century India," *Genitourinary Medicine* 69 (1993): 3–8; Philippa Levine, "Venereal Disease, Prostitution, and the Politics of Empire: The Case of British India," *Journal of the History of Sexuality* 4 (1994): 579–602.

39. "Lock hospitals," mandated by the CD Acts, were hospitals where women believed to be sex workers were examined and treated for venereal disease. Lock hospitals were criticized because women were legally obliged to report

there for examination each month, and because they served as places of punishment, regulation. and sometimes detention for sex workers.

40. Antoinette Burton, *Burdens of History: British Feminists, Indian Women, and Imperial Culture, 1865–1915* (Chapel Hill: University of North Carolina Press, 1994).

41. Ashwini Tambe, *Codes of Misconduct: Regulating Prostitution in Late Colonial Bombay* (Minneapolis: University of Minnesota Press, 2009), 33.

42. Tambe, *Codes of Misconduct*, 17.

43. Siddharth Dube, *Sex, Lies, and AIDS* (New Delhi: HarperCollins, 2000). The gendered coding of (male) migrant and (female) sex worker echoes similarly gendered coding with respect to sex work and HIV elsewhere. See E. A. Ratliff, "Women as 'Sex Workers,' Men as 'Boyfriends': Shifting Identities in Philippine Go-Go Bars," *Anthropology and Medicine* 6 (1999): 79–101.

44. E.g., Y. N. Singh and A. N. Malaviya, "Long Distance Truck Drivers in India: HIV Infection and Their Possible Role in Disseminating HIV into Rural Areas," *International Journal of STD and AIDS* 5 (1994): 137–38; P. Pais, "HIV and India: Looking into the Abyss," *Tropical Medicine and International Health* 1 (1996): 295–304.

45. Niranjan S. Karnik, "Locating HIV/AIDS and India: Cautionary Notes on the Globalization of Categories," *Science, Technology and Human Values* 26 (2001): 326–27. The citation is to K. S. Jayaraman, "India against AIDS," *Nature* 318 (1985): 201.

46. Karnik, "Locating HIV/AIDS and India," 327.

47. Karnik, "Locating HIV/AIDS and India," 328.

48. AVERT International, "India HIV/AIDS Statistics 2013," accessed December 20, 2012, http://www.avert.org/india-hiv-aids-statistics.htm.

49. The concern of origins with respect to sex work does not extend to clients of sexual services.

50. Erica Wald, "From Begums and Bibis to Abandoned Females and Idle Women: Sexual Relationships, Venereal Disease and the Redefinition of Prostitution in Early Nineteenth-Century India," *Indian Economic Social History Review* 46 (2009): 6.

51. Wald, "From Begums and Bibis to Abandoned Females and Idle Women," 7.

52. Sarah Waheed, "Women of 'Ill Repute': Ethics and Urdu Literature in Colonial India," *Modern Asian Studies* (forthcoming).

53. Platts defines *nawab* as "viceroy, governor, or prince." *Nawabi* has a broader meaning as well, indicating a member of the nobility, an aristocrat. John T. Platts, *A Dictionary of Urdu, Classical Hindi, and English* (London: W. H. Allen, 1884).

54. Kamran Asdar Ali, "Courtesans in the Living Room," *ISIM Review* 15 (2005): 32.

55. The importance of Urdu literature in both tracing and producing the demise of courtesanship cannot be overestimated. The works of Sadat Hasan Manto, who wrote from the 1930s until his death in 1955, are paramount in

this regard. Manto's fictional characters famously included the figure of a prostitute or courtesan, as in his story "Kali Shalwar" (Black Trousers), who was folded into a narrative of breakneck and often tragic political change. See Aamir Mufti, *Enlightenment in the Colony: The Jewish Question and the Crisis of Postcolonial Culture* (Princeton, NJ: Princeton University Press, 2007); Jishna Menon, "Unimaginable Communities: Identities in Traffic in Rukhsana Ahmad's Black Shalwar," *Modern Drama* 48 (2005): 407–27.

56. Waheed, "Women of 'Ill Repute.'" See also Sumanta Banerjee, *Dangerous Outcast: The Prostitute in Nineteenth Century Bengal* (Calcutta: Seagull Books, 1998).

57. Veena Talwar Oldenburg, "Lifestyle as Resistance: The Case of the Courtesans of Lucknow, India," *Feminist Studies* 16 (1990): 259–87.

58. For regulations of prostitution after the 1857 Mutiny, also see Steve Legg, "Governing Prostitution in Colonial Delhi: From Cantonment Regulations to International Hygiene (1864–1939)," *Social History* 34 (2009): 447–67.

59. Charu Gupta, *Sexuality, Obscenity, and Community: Women, Muslims, and the Hindu Public in Colonial India* (London: Palgrave Macmillan, 2002), 110–11.

60. Tambe, *Codes of Misconduct*, 27. Here, Tambe references the mention of brothels as sites of potential public disorder in The Police Rule, Ordinance and Regulation of 1812, "a set of rules that laid the basis for police administration of the city for nearly half a century," citing S. R. Kapse, *Police Administration in Bombay 1600–1865* (Bombay: Himalaya Press, 1987).

61. Elizabeth Bernstein, "The Transformation of Sexual Commerce and Urban Space in San Francisco," *Footnotes* (January 2004), accessed December 1, 2012, http://www.asanet.org/footnotes/jan04/ indexone.html.

62. This critique is situated within a body of work on migration that aims to complicate the analytic relationship between migration and agency. Examples of this body of work include Nicholas De Genova, *Working the Boundaries: Race, Space, and "Illegality" in Mexican Chicago* (Durham, NC: Duke University Press, 2005); Alejandro Portes and Josh DeWind, eds., *Rethinking Migration: New Theoretical and Empirical Perspectives* (New York: Berghahn Books, 2007); Laura Agustín, "The Disappearing of a Migration Category: Migrants Who Sell Sex," *Journal of Ethnic and Migration Studies* 32 (2006): 29–47; Stephen Castles and Mark J. Miller, *The Age of Migration: International Population Movements in the Modern World*, 4th rev. ed. (Houndmills: Palgrave, 2008).

63. Melanie Griffiths, Ali Rogers, and Bridget Anderson, "Migration, Time and Temporalities: Review and Prospect," paper presented at the Migration, Time and Temporalities Symposium, Centre on Migration, Policy and Society, Oxford, June 29, 2012.

64. Henri Lefèbvre, *The Production of Space* (Oxford: Blackwell, 1991 [1974]), 26.

65. Lefèbvre, *The Production of Space*.

66. The idea of the spatialization of gendered hierarchies has had a long career

in feminist geography, one of the most widely cited examples being Doreen Massey's *Space, Place and Gender* (Minneapolis: University of Minnesota Press, 1994). I would include books such as Cynthia Enloe's *Bananas, Beaches and Bases: Making Feminist Sense of International Politics* (Berkeley: University of California Press, 1990) as another example of the idea of gendered space in action. These books, and scholarship deployed in this vein, have relied on theoretical frames that see spaces as gendered, particularly in articulating an understanding of public and private spaces being respectively coded as male or female. While these works are critical in defining the intellectual terrain in which we may see the imbrications of gender, space, and power, spaces are not gendered in the analysis presented here, nor are they "classed" or "caste-d"; rather, the valences of gender, class, caste, and space are mutually constituted within negotiations for survival in everyday life.

67. Janaki Nair, *The Promise of Metropolis: Bangalore's Twentieth Century* (New Delhi: Oxford University Press, 2005), 20.
68. Nair, *The Promise of Metropolis*, 26.
69. Michel Foucault, "Of Other Spaces," *Diacritics* 16 (1986): 22–27.
70. Foucault, "Of Other Spaces," 24.
71. Foucault, "Of Other Spaces," 27.
72. Foucault, "Of Other Spaces," 24.
73. Foucault, "Of Other Spaces," 22.
74. See Elzbieta Gozdziak and Frank Laczko, eds., *International Migration* 43 (2005): 5–363 (special issue on methodologies for gathering and aggregating data on trafficking by region).
75. Patty Kelly, *Lydia's Open Door: Inside Mexico's Most Modern Brothel* (Berkeley: University of California Press, 2008); Tian Tian Zheng, *Ethnographies of Prostitution in Contemporary China: Gender Relations, HIV/AIDS, and Nationalism* (New York: Palgrave Macmillan, 2009); Denise Brennan, *What's Love Got to Do with It? Transnational Desires and Sex Tourism in the Dominican Republic* (Durham, NC: Duke University Press, 2004); Pardis Mahdavi, *Gridlock: Labor, Migration and Human Trafficking in Dubai* (Stanford, CA: Stanford University Press, 2011); Rhacel Parreñas, *Illicit Flirtations: Labor, Migration, and Sex Trafficking in Tokyo* (Stanford, CA: Stanford University Press, 2011); Mark Padilla, *Caribbean Pleasure Industry: Tourism, Sexuality, and AIDS in the Dominican Republic* (Chicago: University of Chicago Press, 2007); Sealing Cheng, *On the Move for Love: Migrant Entertainers and the U.S. Military in South Korea* (Philadelphia: University of Pennsylvania Press, 2010); Fouzia Saeed, *Taboo: A Ph.D. Girl in the Red Light Area* (Oxford: Oxford University Press, 2002).
76. William Foote Whyte, *Street Corner Society: The Social Structure of an Italian Slum* (Chicago: University of Chicago Press, 1943).
77. Foucault, "Of Other Spaces," 24.
78. This is a broad statement, meant to highlight an emblematicity in much of

the research on sexual commerce that is supported by universities, research institutes, and governments. This is not a comment on the growing body of work being produced by community-based organizations and current and former sex workers who are aiming to produce research on communities and networks of sex workers of which they are a part.

79. Sharad Chari and Vinay Gidwani, "Introduction: Grounds for a Spatial Ethnography of Labor," *Ethnography* 6 (2005): 268.

1. Day Wage Labor and Migration

1. "Scheduled Caste" and "Scheduled Tribe" (SC/ST) refer to all caste and tribal community categories that are eligible for quotas in state and national parliamentary representation, in higher education, and for government services that are instituted specifically for lower-caste and tribal communities. These are official categories for non-upper-caste groups, where "upper caste" broadly refers to Brahmins, Kshatriyas, and Vaishyas. Many of the workers with whom I spoke were converts to Buddhism, as part of an anti-caste set of politics practiced by those most marginalized by the caste system. The relationship between SC/ST-based categories and the politics of dalit identity are discussed further in this chapter.

2. While Mumbai's caste politics differ from those in villages where workers originated, the city is not free of caste-based violence and geographic segregation based on caste and community. Anand Patwardhan details the politics of caste in Mumbai over the course of the late 1990s and early 2000s in his film *Jai Bhim Comrade* (Mumbai, 2012).

3. Keith Hart, "Informal Income Opportunities and Urban Employment in Ghana," *Journal of Modern African Studies* 11 (1973): 61–89.

4. Daryl D'Monte, *Ripping the Fabric: The Decline of Mumbai and Its Mills* (New Delhi: Oxford University Press, 2002).

5. John T. Platts, *A Dictionary of Urdu, Classical Hindi, and English* (London: W. H. Allen, 1884).

6. Neetha N. Pillai, "Women's Work in the Post Reform Period: An Exploration of Macro Data" (Occasional Paper No. 52, Center for Women's Development Studies, 2009), accessed December 12, 2012, http://www.cwds.ac.in/OCPaper /OccassionalPaperNeetha.pdf.

7. While a discussion of rural land distribution policies is beyond the scope of this book, I flag it here to note that "landlessness" was not a natural state of being for SC and ST peasants but was produced historically through feudal relations of power and colonial management of arable land, modified through postindependence land reforms and access that did not significantly alter the balance of power with respect to control and ownership of agricultural tracts for the workers I discuss here.

8. India's autonomous women's movement consists of a network of organiza-

tions that consider themselves autonomous because they do not take any regular funding, are not affiliated with a political party, and are not nongovernmental organizations.

9. *Tai* in Marathi means "aunt" and, like *didi* (older sister), was a common mode of address for social workers and other middle-class NGO workers in their interactions with laborers in this space.

10. Michel Foucault, "Of Other Spaces," *Diacritics* 16 (1986): 26.

11. Hannah Arendt, *The Human Condition* (Chicago: University of Chicago Press, 1958), 50–52.

12. Carole Pateman, "Feminist Critiques of the Public/Private Dichotomy," in S. I. Benn and G. F. Gaus, eds., *Public and Private in Social Life* (New York: St. Martin's, 1983), 281–303; Morton J. Horwitz, "The History of the Public/Private Distinction," *University of Pennsylvania Law Review* 130 (1982): 1423–28.

13. Respectively, Nancy Frasier, "What's Critical about Critical Theory? The Case of Habermas and Gender," *New German Critique* 35 (1985): 97–131; and Michael Warner, *Publics and Counterpublics* (Brooklyn: Zone Books, 2002).

14. Matias Echanove and Rahul Srivastava, "Urban Journal: The Vanishing Public of the 'World Class City,'" *Wall Street Journal*, March 29, 2011, accessed July 15, 2011, http://blogs.wsj.com/indiarealtime/2011/03/29/urban-journal-the-vanishing-public-of-the-world-class-city/.

15. Will Glover, "Construing Urban Space as 'Public' in Colonial India: Some Notes from Punjab," *Journal of Punjab Studies* 14 (2007): 211.

16. Glover, "Construing Urban Space as 'Public' in Colonial India," 212.

17. Sunil Khilnani, *The Idea of India* (New York: Farrar, Straus and Giroux, 1997); Bernard Cohn, *Colonialism and Its Forms of Knowledge: The British in India* (Princeton, NJ: Princeton University Press, 1996); Sugata Bose and Ayesha Jalal, *Modern South Asia: History, Culture, Political Economy* (New York: Routledge, 1998).

18. E.g., Section 372, which outlaws selling a minor for the purposes of prostitution; Section 373, which outlaws purchasing a minor for the purposes of prostitution; and numerous other laws codified in the Indian Penal Code that prohibit abduction, kidnapping, and profiting from abduction and kidnapping in any way.

19. Phillipa Levine, *Prostitution, Race and Politics: Policing Venereal Disease in the British Empire* (New York: Routledge, 2003); Geetanjali Gangoli and Nicole Westmarland, *International Approaches to Prostitution: Law and Policy in Europe and Asia* (Bristol: Policy Press, 2006).

20. Rabindranath Tagore, *The Home and the World* (New York: Macmillan, 1919); Partha Chatterjee, "The Nationalist Resolution of the 'Women's' Question," in Kumkum Sangari and Sudesh Vaid, eds., *Recasting Women: Essays in Indian Colonial History* (New Delhi: Kali for Women, 1989), 233–53; Durba

Ghosh, *Sex and the Family in Colonial India: The Making of Empire* (Cambridge: Cambridge University Press, 2006). This is discussed further in chapter 3, in the context of street-based prostitution.

21. Nicholas De Genova, "The Queer Politics of Migration: Reflections on 'Illegality' and Incorrigibility," *Studies in Social Justice* 4, no. 2 (2010): 104. The citation is Nicholas De Genova, "The Production of Culprits: From Deportability to Detainability in the Aftermath of 'Homeland Security,'" *Citizenship Studies* 11, no. 5 (2007): 421–48. De Genova quotes Julia Kristeva, *Powers of Horror: An Essay on Abjection*, trans. Leon S. Roudiez (1980; New York: Columbia University Press, 1982), 1–4.

22. *Dalit* is a term that emerges from the anti-caste movement in India, of which Dr. B. R. Ambedkar and E. V. R. Periyar are important progenitors. *Dalit* is technically used to describe people who are classified as "untouchable" within the Hindu caste system, although it is a term that has been taken up by a range of non-upper-caste groups. The word literally means "oppressed group" and is used as a rallying point for ending caste-based discrimination in both Indian and international venues, such as the 2001 World Conference against Racism in Durban, South Africa.

23. S. Srinivasan, "Marathwada: Will Someone Please Pay Attention Here?," *Rediff.com*, October 6, 2004, accessed June 15, 2010, http://www.rediff.com /election/2004/oct/06maha1.htm.

24. United Nations Development Programme, *Human Development Report Maharashtra 2002*, accessed June 2010, http://hdrc.undp.org.in/shdr/mhdr/.

25. Nearly 20 percent of Marathwada's population is from SC or ST communities; nearly 25 percent is Muslim. S. Srinivasan, "Marathwada."

26. Eric Lewis Beverley, "Muslim Modern: Hyderabad State, 1883–1948" (PhD diss., Harvard University, 2007).

27. Beverley, "Muslim Modern."

28. Dipankar Gupta, "Understanding the Marathwada Riots: A Repudiation of Eclectic Marxism," *Social Scientist* 7 (1979): 3–22; Gail Omvedt, "Marathwada: Reply to Dipankar Gupta," *Social Scientist* 8 (1979): 51–58.

29. T. R. K. Chetty and M. N. Rao, "Latur Earthquake," *Geological Society of India Memoirs* 35 (1994): 65–73.

30. Anupama Katakam, "A State of Disparity," *Frontline* 19 (June 22–July 5, 2002), accessed June 15, 2010, http://www.frontlineonnet.com/fl1913 /19130810.htm.

31. Amita Bhaviskar, "Introduction," in Amita Bhaviskar, ed., *Waterscapes: The Cultural Politics of a Natural Resource* (New Delhi: Permanent Black, 2007), 6.

32. One lakh = 100,000; 400,000 rupees = US$8,333.

33. This issue is the subject of both national and international debate. In India, the issue of water scarcity is being addressed in many different venues, including the film industry. Director Dev Benegal's film *Split Wide Open* (Mumbai: Adlabs Films, 1999) tells the story of a member of the "water

mafia" in Mumbai and the politics of water privatization. The movement against the Narmada dam project, organized under the aegis of the Narmada Bachao Andolan, agitated around issues of access to water and electricity, the displacement of nearly 200,000 tribal villagers living in the region, and the concern that the river's resources would be allocated to a few wealthy farmers who would profit through the increased cash-cropping made possible by redirecting the river from its natural course. See Friends of the Narmada, accessed June 15, 2010, http://www.narmada.org; Arundhati Roy, *The Cost of Living* (New York: Modern Library, 1999).

34. Maxine Margolis, "We Are Not Immigrants! A Contested Category among Brazilians in New York City and Rio de Janeiro," in Carole A. Mortland, ed., *Diasporic Identity: Selected Papers on Refugees and Immigrants VI* (Arlington, VA: American Anthropological Association, 1998), 30–50; Akhil Gupta, "The Song of the Nonaligned World: Transnational Identities and the Reinscription of Space in Late Capitalism," *Cultural Anthropology* 7 (1992): 63–79; Priya Deshingkar and John Farrington, eds., *Circular Migration and Multilocational Livelihood Strategies in Rural India* (New Delhi: Oxford University Press, 2009).

35. *Basti* literally means a settlement and is used here to differentiate between the temporary huts and shacks in the hillside slums and the solid, concrete rooms that formed the area in which Shubha lived.

36. Sharmila Rege, *Writing Caste, Writing Gender: Reading Dalit Women's Testimonios* (New Delhi: Zubaan, 2006), 24.

37. The advent of skin-lightening and fairness creams in India marks the social and cultural capital associated with light and "white" skin, to be sure, and has been folded into South Asian discourses of appearance as a marker of physical beauty. It bears noting that, in this particular context, a wedding, the use of a skin-lightening cosmetic product was part of being dressed for a special occasion. People who worked at the naka and lived in the surrounding areas did not use cosmetics, including these creams, day to day.

38. Sapana Doshi, "The Politics of Persuasion: Gendered Slum Citizenship in Neoliberal Mumbai," in Renu Desai and Romola Sanyal, eds., *Urban India: Emerging Citizenships and Contested Spaces* (New Delhi: Sage India, 2010), 82–108; Jonathan Shapiro Anjaria, "Street Hawkers and Public Space in Mumbai," *Economic and Political Weekly* 41 (2006): 2140–46.

39. Indian People's Human Rights Tribunal, "Summary of the Interim Report of the Tribunal Set Up by IPHRC to Study the Impact of the Demolitions in the Sanjay Gandhi National Park," April 12, 2001, accessed October 15, 2008, http://www.cscsarchive.org:8081/MediaArchive/liberty.nsf/%28docid%29/8E378F6D378D1AC1E5256B19001BC6C6.

40. Rahul Wadke, "Maharashtra May Repeal Urban Land Ceiling Act," *Hindu Business Line*, January 21, 2006, accessed October 15, 2008, http://www.thehindubusinessline.in/2006/01/21/stories/2006012103480100.htm.

41. Asian Development Bank, "Support for the Jawaharlal Nehru National Urban Renewal Mission Project," February 2006, accessed October 15, 2010, http://www.adb.org/documents/tars/ind/39645-ind-tar.pdf.
42. Aditya Nigam, "'Molecular Economies': Is There an 'Outside' to Capital?," in Nivedita Menon, Aditya Nigam, and Sanjay Palshikar, eds., *Critical Studies in Politics: Exploring Sites, Selves, Power* (New Delhi: Indian Institute of Advanced Study and Orient Blackswan, 2013), 548.
43. Neeta Deshpande, "A New Home, but in a Nala!," *India Together*, February 5, 2010, accessed June 20, 2011, http://www.indiatogether.org/2010/feb/hrt-nala.htm.
44. Veena Talwar Oldenburg, *Dowry Murder: The Imperial Origins of a Cultural Crime* (New York: Oxford University Press, 2002), 27.
45. M. N. Srinivas, "Some Reflections on Dowry" (New Delhi: Centre for Women's Development Studies, 1984), 6, accessed December 14, 2012, http://www.womenstudies.in/elib/dowry/dw_some_reflections.pdf.
46. Uma Chakravarti, *Beyond the Kings and Brahmans of "Ancient" India* (New Delhi: Tulika Press, 2006); V. Geetha and Nalini Rajan, *Religious Faith, Ideology, Citizenship: The View from Below* (New Delhi: Routledge India, 2011); Veena Talwar Oldenburg, *Dowry Murder: The Imperial Origins of a Cultural Crime* (New York: Oxford University Press, 2002); Srimati Basu, ed., *Dowry and Inheritance: Issues in Contemporary Feminism* (New Delhi: Women Unlimited, 2005); Bina Agarwal, *A Field of One's Own: Gender and Land Rights in South Asia* (Cambridge: Cambridge University Press, 1994); Sharmila Rege, *Writing Caste, Writing Gender: Reading Dalit Women's Testimonios* (New Delhi: Zubaan, 2006). Lata Mani, "Contentious Traditions: The Debate on Sati in Colonial India," in Kumkum Sangari, ed., *Recasting Women: Essays in Indian Colonial History* (New Delhi: Kali for Women, 1989), 88–126.

2. Sex, Work, and Silence

1. Michel Foucault, *Discipline and Punish: The Birth of the Prison* (New York: Vintage Books, 1995 [1977]), 184.
2. Keith Hart, "Informal Income Opportunities and Urban Employment in Ghana," *Journal of Modern African Studies* 11 (1973): 61–89.
3. Keith Hart, "Informal Economy," accessed December 20, 2012, http://the memorybank.co.uk/papers/informal-economy/.
4. Geert de Neve, *The Everyday Politics of Labour: Working Lives in India's Informal Economy* (New Delhi: Social Science Press, 2005), 8, quoting Barbara Harriss-White, *India Working: Essays on Society and Economy* (Cambridge: Cambridge University Press, 2003), 4.
5. Jan Breman discusses "casualization" in his classic book *Footloose Labour: Working in India's Informal Economy* (Cambridge: Cambridge University Press, 1996), 10. On "informalization" of the economy as a whole, see Nandini Gooptu, *The Politics of the Urban Poor in Early Twentieth-Century India*

(Cambridge: Cambridge University Press, 2001); Barbara Harriss-White and Nandini Gooptu, "Mapping India's World of Unorganised Labour," *Socialist Register* 37 (2001): 89–118; and Harriss-White, *India Working*.

6. Numerous scholars have commented on the blurred boundaries between formal and informal sectors; see Breman, *Footloose Labour*; Harriss-White, *India Working*; and de Neve, *The Everyday Politics of Labour*.

7. Hart, "Informal Economy."

8. National Sample Survey Office, National Statistical Organisation, Ministry of Statistics and Programme Implementation, Government of India, "Informal Sector and Conditions of Employment in India: NSS 66th ROUND (July 2009–June 2010)," accessed January 10, 2013, http://www.indiaenviron mentportal.org.in/reports-documents/informal-sector-and-conditions -employment-india-july-2009-%E2%80%93-june-2010.

9. Satyabrata Chakrabarti, "Gender Dimensions of the Informal Sector and Informal Employment in India," paper presented at the Global Forum on Gender Statistics, January 26–28, 2009, accessed December 20, 2012, http://unstats.un.org/unsd/gender/Ghana_Jan2009/Doc41.pdf.

10. Aditya Nigam, "Rethinking the Unorganised Sector," *Social Action* 47 (1997): 128.

11. Nigam, "Rethinking the Unorganised Sector," 129.

12. Aditya Nigam, "'Molecular Economies': Is There an 'Outside' to Capital?," in Nivedita Menon, Aditya Nigam, and Sanjay Palshikar, eds., *Critical Studies in Politics: Exploring Sites, Selves, Power* (New Delhi: Indian Institute of Advanced Study and Orient Blackswan, 2013), 548.

13. Hart, "Informal Economy."

14. Michael Denning, "Wageless Life," *New Left Review* 66 (2010), accessed December 20, 2012, http://newleftreview.org/II/66/michael-denning -wageless-life.

15. Hart, "Informal Economy."

16. Shubha's way of pronouncing my name, rendered phonetically.

17. Sharmila Rege, *Writing Caste, Writing Gender: Reading Dalit Women's Testimonios* (New Delhi: Zubaan, 2006), 14.

18. Uma Chakravarti, *Rewriting History: The Life and Times of Pandita Ramabai* (New Delhi: Kali for Women, 1998), 17, cited in Rege, *Writing Caste, Writing Gender*, 16. In the previous chapter, I use caste and community markers such as Nav Buddho and Lambadi to identify groups of laborers at the naka, terms that workers used to express their caste affiliations. I use the official labels "Scheduled Caste" (SC) and "Scheduled Tribe" (ST) here as shorthand terms that also indicate the biopolitical production of these communities via state-level enumeration and nomination, policing, educational practices, and economic policies.

19. Rege, *Writing Caste, Writing Gender*, 51.

20. Babasaheb Ambedkar, "Castes in India," in Vasant Moon, comp., *Dr. Ba-*

basaheb Ambedkar's Writings and Speeches, vol. 1 (Bombay: Government of Maharashtra, Education Department, 1979–97), 5–22, cited in Rege, *Writing Caste, Writing Gender*, 57.

21. The Mandal Commission's 1980 report on caste recommended reservations for lower-caste students in higher education. When the V. P. Singh government attempted to implement the recommendations, massive riots by upper-caste students ensued. See Uma Chakravarti, *Gendering Caste: Through a Feminist Lens* (New Delhi: Stree, 2003).

22. Rege, *Writing Caste, Writing Gender*, 31.

23. Rege, *Writing Caste, Writing Gender*, 27, quoting Sanjay Joshi, *Fractured Modernity: Making of a Middle Class in Colonial North India* (New Delhi: Oxford University Press, 2001).

24. "Garibi hatao!" is a famous slogan used by Indira Gandhi in her election campaigns; it is often juxtaposed against the negative impacts her administration on both rural and urban poor communities, especially during the Emergency (1975–77), during which time Gandhi declared martial law, suspended civil liberties, enforced compulsory sterilization, and targeted political opponents.

25. Sonia Gandhi, wife of the late Rajiv Gandhi, son of Indira Gandhi and prime minister of India from 1984 until his assassination in 1989, is head of the Indian Congress Party and abdicated her right to assume the role of prime minister of India following her party's victory in the 2004 national elections, perhaps prompting this comment.

26. The description "had to wear a vessel [*lota*] on their front, with a broom [*jhadu*] hanging behind" refers to the historically caste-based occupation of cleaning human waste with a vessel and a broom barehanded. The Human Rights Watch report on caste-based discrimination *Broken People* documents places in which this practice continues. The abolition of the practice is a key demand of the *dalit* rights movement. Human Rights Watch, *Broken People: Caste Violence against India's "Untouchables"* (New York: Human Rights Watch, 1999), accessed January 20, 2008, http://www.hrw.org/reports/1999/india/.

27. This event is seen as the formal inception of the contemporary Hindu fundamentalist movement in India. Naunidhi Kaur, "Mumbai: A Decade after Riots," *Frontline* 20 (July 5–18, 2003), accessed January 30, 2013, http://www.hindu.com/thehindu/thscrip/print.pl?file=20030718002704100.htm&date=fl2014/&prd=fline&.

28. Mangalsutras were also worn by sex workers in the red-light area, regardless of marital status or religion. Meena Seshu, a sex workers' rights activist in southern Maharashtra, proposed an explanation for this to a crowd of sex workers at the national sex workers' rights conference in 2003: "Why is it that all women in prostitution [*dhandhe-walis*] wear the *mangalsutra*? Is it because they are all married? Is it because they want to be married? Or is it

because they are showing that they have a license to have sex??" The crowd responded to Seshu's query with raucous laughter and applause.

29. Marshall Berman, *Adventures in Marxism* (London: Verso, 1999), 167–69, cited in Sharad Chari and Vinay Gidwani, "Introduction: Grounds for a Spatial Ethnography of Labor," *Ethnography* 6 (2005): 269.

30. Chari and Gidwani, "Introduction," 268.

31. Chari and Gidwani, "Introduction," 270; Henri Lefèbvre, *The Production of Space* (Oxford: Blackwell, 1991 [1974]).

32. Eve Kosofsky Sedgwick, *Epistemology of the Closet* (Berkeley: University of California Press), 8.

3. Sex Work and the Street

1. Dance bars where women danced fully clothed for tips from primarily male customers were not uncommon in Mumbai until 2005, when they were the subject of an intense public debate. The debate resulted in the legal status of female dancers at the bars being pushed into a legal limbo. See Research Centre for Women's Studies and Forum against the Oppression of Women, *Working Conditions and Backgrounds of Women Working as Dancers in Dance Bars* (Mumbai: SNDT University, 2005); and Flavia Agnes, "Hypocritical Morality," *India Together* (October 2005), reprinted from *Manushi* 149, accessed January 15, 2013, http://www.indiatogether.org/manushi/issue149 /bardance.htm.

2. "Street-based sex worker" is part of a growing set of terms, stemming largely from discourses on HIV prevention, that identify different categories of sex workers. It refers to people who are not based in a brothel and who instead use the street to solicit clients for sexual services.

3. Most information collected on remittances to countries in the Global South has focused on international migrants. The available data on internal migrants are growing but far from comprehensive. Geographer Priya Deshingkar writes, "India is one such country where internal migration is more important than international migration in terms of the numbers of people involved and possibly even the volume of remittances." Priya Deshingkar, "Circular Internal Migration and Development in India," in International Organization for Migration, ed., *Migration and Development within and across Borders: Research and Policy Perspectives on Internal and International Migration* (Geneva: International Organization for Migration, 2008), 163.

4. The suffix "bai" means "woman," literally, and may be used as a form of address among and for Marathi-speaking women. The names "Radha" and "Radhabai" refer to the same person.

5. *Majburi* is a word used often by people at all three ethnographic sites to describe their own situations and was usually used in reference to things that had to be done for the sake of survival. John T. Platts defines *majburi* as "compulsion, constraint; powerlessness, helplessness . . . *majburi-se*, adv. In

consequence of compulsion or constraint; from helplessness; of necessity."
John T. Platts, *A Dictionary of Urdu, Classical Hindi, and English* (London:
W. H. Allen, 1884). I choose the term "constraint" in translation to approx-
imate the closest sense of this word used during these interviews. My understanding of this sense includes the notion of a context with few options,
which compelled survival in extreme hardship.

6. See the conclusion for a more detailed discussion of *marzi, majburi,* and
jabardasti.

7. This perspective on police, that physical violence in the course of soliciting
clients is particularly egregious because it is being done "for the stomach,"
also appears in a study conducted in Andhra Pradesh among sex workers
who solicited clients from the highway near their village. In that case, prior
to an intervention that facilitated a better working relationship with local
police, women accepted being arrested but could not understand being
beaten. Monica Biradavolu, Scott Burris, Annie George, Asima Jena, and
Kim Blakenship, "Can Sex Workers Regulate Police? Learning from an HIV
Prevention Project for Sex Workers in Southern India," *Social Science and
Medicine* 68 (2009): 1541–47.

8. My engagement with LGBTQ activists in India informs this argument, as
well as an extensive and growing literature on Section 377. A few examples
of this literature include Gautam Bhan and Arvind Narrain, eds., *Because
I Have a Voice: Queer Politics in India* (New Delhi: Yoda Press, 2005); Ruth
Vanita, ed., *Queering India: Same Sex Love and Eroticism in Indian Culture
and Society* (New York: Routledge, 2002); Animesh Sharma, "Section 377:
No Jurisprudential Basis," *Economic and Political Weekly* 43, no. 46 (2008):
12–14; Alok Gupta, *This Alien Legacy: The Origins of "Sodomy" Laws in British
Colonialism* (New York: Human Rights Watch, 2008); and the 2009 New
Delhi High Court judgment itself, *Government of NCT of Delhi and Others v.
Naz Foundation*, No. 7455/2001, Delhi High Court, India, July 2, 2009, pp.
1–105, accessed June 4, 2011, http://timesofindia.indiatimes.com/photo
.cms?msid=4728348.

9. Feminists have critiqued a juridical focus in the question of human freedom,
arguing that a focus on *legal* transformation, instead of transformations in
other social or economic registers, ultimately reifies the law, as well as the
identitarian, stable categories that the law necessitates. Several key works
from this literature that have informed my argument here include Nivedita
Menon, *Recovering Subversion: Feminist Politics beyond the Law* (New Delhi:
Permanent Black, 2004); Wendy Brown, *States of Injury: Power and Freedom
in Late Modernity* (Princeton, NJ: Princeton University Press, 2005); Wendy
Brown and Janet Halley, eds., *Left Legalism / Left Critique* (Durham, NC:
Duke University Press, 2002).

10. Eithne Luibheid, "A Blueprint for Exclusion: The Page Law, Prostitution and
Discrimination against Chinese Women," in *Entry Denied: Controlling Sexuality at the Border* (Minneapolis: University of Minnesota Press, 2002), 31–54.

11. Thomas Blom Hansen, *Wages of Violence: Naming and Identity in Postcolonial Bombay* (Princeton, NJ: Princeton University Press, 2001); Sujata Patel and Jim Masselos, eds., *Bombay and Mumbai: The City in Transition* (New Delhi: Oxford University Press, 2005); Sujata Patel and Alice Thorner, eds., *Bombay: Metaphor for Modern India* (New Delhi: Oxford University Press, 1996).
12. David Arnold, "The Police and Colonial Control in South India," *Social Scientist* 4 (1976): 3–16.
13. Arnold, "The Police and Colonial Control in South India," 3.
14. Arnold, "The Police and Colonial Control in South India," 4.
15. Arnold, "The Police and Colonial Control in South India."
16. Arnold, "The Police and Colonial Control in South India," 8.
17. Arnold, "The Police and Colonial Control in South India," 10.
18. This statement belies a complex discourse on the ways in which Indian cities evince the lasting effects of events that reinscribe segregation, events that include the upheavals wrought by communal violence, as well as slum demolitions undertaken throughout Indian cities. See *Ramola Naik-Singru, "Mumbai:* Spatial *Segregation* in a 'Globalizing' City," in R. S. Sandhu and Jasmeet Sandhu, eds., *Globalizing Cities: Inequality and Segregation in Developing Countries* (Jaipur: Rawat, 2007), 131–70; Aditi Nargundkar Pathak, "Sociospatial Exclusion in Urban Spaces: Mumbai City," *The Urban Vision: Expert Diary*, October 10, 2009, accessed January 30, 2013, http://www.theurban vision.com/blogs/?p=275; Bombay Ki Kahani, Mumbai Ki Zubani, December 14, 2012–January 13, 2013, accessed January 30, 2013, http://bombay kikahani.wordpress.com/; Leela Fernandes, "The Politics of Forgetting: Class, Politics, State Power and the Restructuring of Urban Space in India," *Urban Studies* 41 (2004): 2415–30; Arvind Rajagopal, "Special Political Zone: Urban Planning, Spatial Segregation and the Infrastructure of Violence in Ahmedabad," *South Asian History and Culture* 1 (2010): 529–56; Hans Schenk, "Towards Apartheid? Policies of Segregation and Deprivation in Delhi," in K. R. Gupta, ed., *Urban Development Debates in the New Millennium*, vol. 1 (Delhi: Atlantic, 2004), 96–114.
19. The United Nations Global Commission on HIV/AIDS conducted a series of public meetings on the intersections of criminality and HIV in 2011 in every region of the world, taking testimony from many categories of sex workers, including street-based sex workers, and from LGBTQ people and drug users, who all spoke about the effects of criminal law and policing practices on their daily existence. See Global Commission on HIV and the Law, "HIV and the Law: Risks, Rights and Health," accessed June 1, 2012, http://www .hivlawcommission.org/.
20. Coalition Against Trafficking in Women, "India Fact Sheet," accessed September 2011, http://www.catwinternational.org/factbook/india.php.
21. This is now less true of this theater, with the advent of a growing number of multiplex cinemas.
22. Aditya Nigam, "Politics, Political Society, and the Everyday," *Kafila*, March

31, 2012, accessed January 20, 2013, http://kafila.org/2012/03/31/politics
-political-society-and-the-everyday/, quoting Partha Chatterjee, *The Politics
of the Governed: Reflections on Popular Politics in Most of the World* (New York:
Columbia University Press, 2006). See also Partha Chatterjee, *Lineages
of Political Society* (Ranikhet: Permanent Black, 2011); Nivedita Menon,
"Introduction," in Partha Chatterjee, ed., *Empire and Nation: Selected Essays,
1985–2005* (Ranikhet: Permanent Black, 2010), 1–22; Stuart Corbridge, Glyn
Williams, Manoj Srivastava, and René Veron, *Seeing the State: Governance
and Governmentality in India* (Cambridge: Cambridge University Press,
2005).

23. Chatterjee, *The Politics of the Governed*, 23.
24. Chatterjee, *The Politics of the Governed*, 39–40.
25. Chatterjee, *The Politics of the Governed*, 50–51.
26. Chatterjee, *The Politics of the Governed*, 34.
27. On India's Unique Identification scheme, see Unique Identification Authority of India, accessed January 15, 2012, http://uidai.gov.in/, as well as critique and commentary on the scheme, e.g., Lawrence Cohen, "1," paper presented at the Annual Conference on South Asia, Madison, Wisconsin, October 11–14, 2012, accessed December 15, 2012, http://followuidai.word press.com/.
28. Chatterjee, *The Politics of the Governed*, 36–37.
29. Chatterjee, *The Politics of the Governed*, 76.
30. Chatterjee, *The Politics of the Governed*, 40.
31. Sunil Khilnani, "The Development of Civil Society," in S. Kaviraj and S. Khilnani, eds., *Civil Society: History and Possibilities* (Cambridge: Cambridge University Press, 2001), 11–32. Also see Karl Marx, *Critique of Hegel's Philosophy of Right*, trans. John O'Malley (Cambridge: Cambridge University Press, 1970 [1843]).
32. Khilnani, "The Development of Civil Society," 27.
33. Ashutosh Varshney, "Ethnic Conflict and Civil Society: India and Beyond," *World Politics* 53 (2001): 362–98.

4. Red-Light Districts

1. A widely cited example of organized brothel-based sex work is that of red-light areas in Calcutta, where condom use can be negotiated more easily, where brothels agree to maintain condom use as an area-wide policy, and where sex workers have formed antitrafficking initiatives in the red-light districts where they live and work. See Swati Ghosh, "The Shadow Lines of Citizenship," *Identity, Culture and Politics* 5 (2004): 105–23; Durbar Mahila Samanwaya Committee, "The 'Fallen' Learn to Rise: The Social Impact of STD/HIV Intervention Programme," Calcutta: Durbar, 1998, accessed January 15, 2013, http://www.durbar.org/html/activities.asp; Nandinee Bandyopadhyay, Durbar Mahila Samanwaya Committee, University of Sussex Institute of Development Studies, "Streetwalkers Show the Way:

Reframing the Global Debate on Trafficking from Sex Workers' Perspectives" (IDS Working Paper, Institute of Development Studies at the University of Sussex, Brighton, 2008).

2. In addition to works cited in the previous chapter on this issue (Fernandes, Schenk, Rajagopal, Pathak, Naik-Singru), see Jan Nijman, "Against the Odds: Slum Rehabilitation in Neoliberal Mumbai," *Cities* 25 (2008): 73–85; Amita Bhide, "Shifting Terrains of Communities and Community Organization: Reflections on Organizing for Housing Rights in Mumbai," *Community Development Journal* 44 (2009): 367–81; Liza Weinstein and Xuefei Ren, "The Changing Right to the City: Urban Renewal and Housing Rights in Globalizing Shanghai and Mumbai," *City and Community* 8 (2009): 407–32.

3. Svati P. Shah, "Producing the Spectacle of Prostitution in India: The Politics of Red Light Visibility in Mumbai," *Cultural Dynamics* 18 (2006): 269–92.

4. I retain the convention throughout this chapter of referring to the city as Bombay when discussing events prior to 1995, when the Hindu fundamentalist Shiv Sena Party changed the city's official name in English to Mumbai. The late eighteenth century is politically significant for the migration of the Kamathis from an area that would have been controlled by the nizam of Hyderabad until his defeat by the Maratha army in 1795. The migration of the Kamathis to Bombay was part of a widespread set of migrations undertaken all over South Asia at the time, especially from and between regions where political alignments were changing. See G. S. Chhabra, *Advanced Study in the History of Modern India*, vol. 1 (1707–1813) (Delhi: Lotus Press, 2005).

5. Sujata Patel and Alice Thorner, eds., *Mumbai: Mosaic of Modern Culture* (New Delhi: Oxford University Press, 1995); Gillian Tindall, *City of Gold: The Biography of Mumbai* (London: Temple Smith, 1982).

6. Hubert van Wersch, *The Mumbai Textile Strike* (New Delhi: Oxford University Press, 1991).

7. Stephen Legg, "Governing Prostitution in Colonial Delhi: From Cantonment Regulations to International Hygiene," *Social History* 34 (2009): 448–67; Philippa Levine, "Rereading the 1890s: Venereal Disease as 'Constitutional Crisis,'" *Journal of Asian Studies* 55 (1996): 586–12.

8. Philippa Levine, *Prostitution, Race and Politics: Policing Venereal Disease in the British Empire* (New York: Routledge, 2003), 179.

9. Ashwini Tambe, "The Elusive Ingénue: A Transnational Feminist Analysis of European Prostitution in Colonial Bombay," *Gender and Society* 19 (2005): 165, quoting Stephen Edwardes, *Crime in British India* (New Delhi: ABC, 1983 [1924]), and Stephen Edwardes, *Bombay City Police: A Historical Sketch* (London: Oxford University Press, 1923).

10. Shah, "Producing the Spectacle of Prostitution in India," 287.

11. Svati P. Shah, "Brothels and Big Screen Rescues: Producing 'Prostitution in India' through Documentary Film," *Interventions: Journal of Postcolonial Studies* 15 (2013): 549–66.

12. *Harishchandrachi Factory* (film), dir. Paresh Mokashi (Mumbai: Mayasabha Productions, 2009).

13. Deepak Sakunde, "Kareena and Rani to Play Sex Workers in Kamathipura," *Zimbio*, January 9, 2011, accessed January 2012, http://www.zimbio.com /Bollywood+Movies/articles/CCI10Zta6bM/Kareena+Rani+play+sex +workers+Kamathipura.

14. Teena Thacker, "Bill Gates Foundation to Stop Funding HIV Programs," *Indian Express*, March 25, 2011, accessed February 15, 2012, http://www .indianexpress.com/news/bill-gates-foundation-to-stop-funding-hiv -programmes/767166/0.

15. While applying for permission to receive foreign funds had been an elaborate process, comparable to but more difficult than applying for tax-free, not-for-profit status in the United States, amendments in 2010 to the Indian Foreign Contribution Regulation Act (FCRA) have made the process much more difficult. Several commentators have suggested that the new FCRA regime may be aimed at controlling and restricting activists and social movements. Praful Bidwai, "How the Government Suppresses Dissent," *Rediff.com*, May 30, 2013, accessed February 1, 2014, http://www.rediff.com /news/report/column-how-the-government-suppresses-dissent/20130530 .htm.

16. *Dhandha* here, as in previous chapters, means "business" or "profession"; used in this context, it refers to sex work.

17. Avid fans of Hindi cinema will recognize the resonances between this exchange and the scene in the film *Chameli* (2004), in which the main character, a sex worker played by Kareena Kapoor, tells several versions of a story of violent induction into the sex trade to the male protagonist, before laughing and saying that her real story is none of these.

18. A *chawl* is usually four to five stories high, and has ten to twenty rooms that open onto a shared balcony that leads to the staircase connecting the floors. People use shared latrines in chawls, usually one or two per floor. Chawls were built in numbers in Mumbai in the early and mid-nineteenth century to house workers coming to the city to work in the textile mills. The existence of chawls in Kamathipura references the existence of migrant workers in the area since its beginnings, as discussed earlier in the chapter. See Neera Adarkar, *The Chawls of Mumbai: Galleries of Life* (New Delhi: Imprint-One, 2011).

19. *Vada pav*, an inexpensive and filling snack, is a lentil fritter sandwich on a roll spread with chutney. It is available from almost any roadside stall, and is often a mainstay for people living on extremely limited income, although it holds pride of place as Mumbai's unofficial street food delicacy and is enjoyed by all.

20. See the discussion of majburi in chapter 3.

21. Hina referred specifically to the Maharashtra Industrial Development Corporation (MIDC).

22. Ganesh Chaturthi is a festival celebrating the (re)birth of the Hindu god Ganesh. It takes place between late August and late September and is observed with processions and music throughout Mumbai.
23. P. K. Navya, "Hundreds of Ejipura Slum Residents Thrown Out of Homes," *Citizen Matters, Bangalore*, January 19, 2013, accessed February 15, 2013, http://bangalore.citizenmatters.in/articles/view/4828-hundreds-of -ejipura-ews-residents-thrown-out-of-homes.
24. Sunainaa Chadha, "Why Bullishness on Indian Real Estate Is Misplaced," *Firstpost*, December 4, 2012, accessed January 20, 2013, http://www.first post.com/real-estate/why-bullishness-on-indian-real-estate-is-misplaced -544459.html; Wayne Arnold, "Monuments to the Thai Debt; Real Estate Fiascoes Rear Their Heads on Bangkok Skyline," *New York Times*, February 25, 2000, accessed January 20, 2013, http://www.nytimes.com/2000/02/25 /business/monuments-thai-debt-real-estate-fiascoes-rear-their-heads -bangkok-skyline.html?pagewanted=all&src=pm; Eliot Brown, "Demand for Office Space Still Sluggish," *Wall Street Journal*, January 7, 2013, accessed January 20, 2013, http://online.wsj.com/article/SB100014241278873236896 04578222192171334314.html.
25. E.g., Nauzer K. Bharucha, "Despite Opposition, Slum Rehabilitation Authority Clears Prime Plot for Redevelopment," *Times of India*, January 29, 2013, accessed February 5, 2013, http://articles.timesofindia.indiatimes .com/2013-01-29/mumbai/36615544_1_lokhandwala-infrastructure-mata -ramabai-nagar-worli-land.
26. "Violent Reactions to Delhi Demolitions," *Business Standard*, December 20, 2005, accessed March 3, 2013, http://www.business-standard.com/article /Economy-Policy/Violent-reactions-to-Delhi-demolitions-105122001125_1 .html; "Citizens Vent Ire at Demolitions in Pune," *Daily News and Analysis (DNA), India*, August 24, 2012, accessed March 3, 2013, http://www.dnaindia .com/pune/report_citizens-vent-ire-at-demolitions-in-pune_1732155; "Court Clears Way for Demolitions in Ahmedabad," *Sify News*, January 25, 2011, accessed March 3, 2013, http://www.sify.com/news/court-clears-way -for-demolitions-in-ahmedabad-news-national-lbzaFafdjcf.html; Housing and Land Rights Network (Delhi) and People's Union of Civil Liberties (Karnataka), *Governance by Denial: Forced Eviction and Demolition of Homes in Koramangala (Ejipura) Bangalore* (Bangalore: HLRN and PUCL, 2013), accessed March 3, 2013, http://www.hic-sarp.org/documents/Interim _Report_Fact-finding_Koramangala.pdf.
27. Neeta Kolhatkar, "Builders Eye Red Light Area," *Daily News and Analysis (DNA), India*, April 14, 2008, accessed January 20, 2012, http://www .dnaindia.com/mumbai/report_builders-eye-red-light-area_1159675.
28. Clara Lewis, "Red Light District Swaps Sin for Skyscrapers," *Times of India*, November 6, 2010, accessed January 20, 2012, http://articles.timesofindia .indiatimes.com/2010-11-06/mumbai/28263687_1_prostitutes-kamathipura -mira-road.

29. J. Dey, "Kamathipura Seduces Land Sharks," *Mid-Day*, March 22, 2009, accessed January 20, 2012, http://www.mid-day.com/news/2009/mar/220309 -Kamathipura-sex-workers-brothels-Grant-Road-Byculla-Mazagaon-Loan -Sharks-Mumbai-news.htm.

30. *Gorey lok* could also reference people with privilege, where lighter skin was associated with higher social status, derived from the idea of a racialized color line that is seen to mark caste.

31. "Remand" literally means "to return to custody pending trial or for further detention"; used in this context, "remand homes" are detention facilities where teenagers and women, primarily, who were living on the streets and/or surviving through illegal means are kept until they were "fully rehabilitated."

32. Chinki Sinha, "The Fading Red Light," *Open Magazine*, September 15, 2012, accessed January 15, 2013, http://www.openthemagazine.com/article /nation/the-fading-red-light.

33. Gayatri Jayaraman, "Kamathipura: Bought and Sold," *Live Mint*, June 9, 2012, accessed February 1, 2014, http://www.livemint.com/Leisure /FL9q0QjrzIdtsYshID8McP/Kamathipura-bought-and-sold.html.

34. Ajay Bailey, Inge Hutter, and Paulus P. P. Huigen, "The Spatial-Cultural Configuration of Sex Work in Goa India," *Tijdschrift voor Economische en Sociale Geografie* 102 (2011): 167; Sanjay Banerjee, "Goa CM Cracks Down on Red Light Area," *Times of India*, June 14, 2004, accessed January 20, 2011, http://timesofindia.indiatimes.com/city/Goa-CM-cracks-down-on-red -light-area/articleshow/738920.cms.

35. Harit Mehta, "Red Lights May Go Out of Surat's Chakla Bazaar," *Times of India*, September 13, 2003, accessed January 20, 2012, http://articles.time sofindia.indiatimes.com/2003-09-13/ahmedabad/27186097_1_workers -red-light-area-rehabilitation-package.

36. Mehta, "Red Lights May Go Out of Surat's Chakla Bazaar."

37. Sinha, "The Fading Red Light."

Conclusion

1. *Kotha* is a word that is sometimes used to mean "brothel," and which is associated with the spaces where courtesans lived and worked during the Mughal era in India.

2. Of course, the ultimate and central trope of victim subjectivity in discourses of sex work and human trafficking is that of the child. I address the subject of children directly at the end of this conclusion. For an explication of the dilemmas that inhere in critically examining children in prostitution in the Global South, see Heather Montgomery, "Working with Child Prostitutes in Thailand: Problems of Practice and Interpretation," *Childhood: A Global Journal of Child Research* 14 (2007): 415–30.

3. Eve Kosofsky Sedgwick, *Epistemology of the Closet* (Berkeley: University of California Press, 1990), 4.

4. Laura Ahearn, "Language and Agency," *Annual Review of Anthropology* 30 (2001): 114.
5. Ambar Basu and Mohan Dutta, "Participatory Change in a Campaign Led by Sex Workers: Connecting Resistance to Action-Oriented Agency," *Qualitative Health Research* 18 (2008): 106.
6. Ahearn, "Language and Agency," 109–37.
7. In addition to Heather Montgomery's work on children in the discourse of sex work, cited earlier, this includes Julia O'Connell-Davidson, *Children in the Global Sex Trade* (Cambridge: Polity, 2005).
8. U. Niaz, "Violence against Women in South Asian Countries," *Archives of Women's Mental Health* 6 (2003): 173.
9. Ratna Kapur, "The Tragedy of Victimization Rhetoric: Resurrecting the Native Subject in International/Postcolonial Feminist Legal Politics," *Harvard Human Rights Law Journal* 15 (2002): 18–19.
10. Svati P. Shah, "Brothels and Big Screen Rescues: Producing 'Prostitution in India' through Documentary Film," *Interventions: Journal of Postcolonial Studies* 15 (2013): 549–66.

Adarkar, Neera. *The Chawls of Mumbai: Galleries of Life*. New Delhi: ImprintOne, 2011.

Agarwal, Bina. *A Field of One's Own: Gender and Land Rights in South Asia*. Cambridge: Cambridge University Press, 1994.

Agnes, Flavia. "Hypocritical Morality." *India Together*, October 2005. Reprinted from *Manushi* 149. Accessed January 15, 2013. http://www.indiatogether.org /manushi/issue149/bardance.htm.

Agustín, Laura. "The Disappearing of a Migration Category: Migrants Who Sell Sex." *Journal of Ethnic and Migration Studies* 32 (2006): 29–47.

Ahearn, Laura. "Language and Agency." *Annual Review of Anthropology* 30 (2001): 109–37.

Ali, Kamran Asdar. "Courtesans in the Living Room." *ISIM Review* 15 (2005): 32–33.

Ambedkar, Babasaheb. "Castes in India." In Vasant Moon, comp., *Dr. Babasaheb Ambedkar's Writings and Speeches*. 15 vols. Bombay: Government of Maharashtra, Education Department, 1979–97.

Amin, Avni. "Risk, Morality, and Blame: A Critical Analysis of Government and US Donor Responses to HIV Infections among Sex Workers in India." Washington, DC: Center for Health and Gender Equity, 2004. Accessed January 30, 2013. http://www.hivpolicy.org/Library/HPP000864.pdf.

Anderson, Bridget, and Rutvica Andrijasevic. "Sex, Slaves and Citizens: The

Politics of Anti-trafficking." *Soundings: A Journal of Politics and Culture* 40 (2008): 135–45.

Anjaria, Jonathan Shapiro. "Street Hawkers and Public Space in Mumbai." *Economic and Political Weekly* 41 (2006): 2140–46.

Arendt, Hannah. *The Human Condition.* Chicago: University of Chicago Press, 1958.

Arnold, David. "The Police and Colonial Control in South India." *Social Scientist* 4 (1976): 3–16.

———. "Sexually Transmitted Diseases in Nineteenth- and Twentieth-Century India." *Genitourinary Medicine* 69 (1993): 3–8.

Arnold, Wayne. "Monuments to the Thai Debt; Real Estate Fiascoes Rear Their Heads on Bangkok Skyline." *New York Times*, February 25, 2000. Accessed January 20, 2013. http://www.nytimes.com/2000/02/25/business /monuments-thai-debt-real-estate-fiascoes-rear-their-heads-bangkok -skyline.html?pagewanted=all&src=pm.

Asian Development Bank. "Support for the Jawaharlal Nehru National Urban Renewal Mission Project." February 2006. Accessed October 15, 2010. http://www.adb.org/documents/tars/ind/39645-ind-tar.pdf.

AVERT International. "India HIV/AIDS Statistics 2013." Accessed December 20, 2012. http://www.avert.org/india-hiv-aids-statistics.htm.

Bailey, Ajay, Inge Hutter, and Paulus P. P. Huigen. "The Spatial-Cultural Con-figuration of Sex Work in Goa India." *Tijdschrift voor Economische en Sociale Geografie* 102 (2011): 162–75.

Ballhatchet, Kenneth. *Race, Sex, and Class under the Raj: Imperial Attitudes and Policies and Their Critics, 1793–1905.* London: Weidenfeld and Nicolson, 1980.

Bandyopadhyay, Nandinee, Durbar Mahila Samanwaya Committee, University of Sussex Institute of Development Studies. "Streetwalkers Show the Way: Reframing the Global Debate on Trafficking from Sex Workers' Perspectives." IDS Working Paper, Institute of Development Studies at the University of Sussex, Brighton, 2008.

Banerjee, Sanjay. "Goa CM Cracks Down on Red Light Area." *Times of India*, June 14, 2004. Accessed January 20, 2011. http://timesofindia.indiatimes.com /city/Goa-CM-cracks-down-on-red-light-area/articleshow/738920.cms.

Banerjee, Sumanta. *Dangerous Outcast: The Prostitute in Nineteenth Century Bengal.* Calcutta: Seagull Books, 1998.

Basu, Ambar, and Mohan Dutta. "Participatory Change in a Campaign Led by Sex Workers: Connecting Resistance to Action-Oriented Agency." *Qualitative Health Research* 18 (2008): 106–19.

Basu, Deepankar, and Amit Basole. "Food Budget Squeeze, Market Penetration and the Calorie Consumption Puzzle in India." *Sanhati* blog, December 1, 2012. Accessed December 15, 2012. http://sanhati.com/excerpted/5855.

Basu, Srimati, ed. *Dowry and Inheritance: Issues in Contemporary Feminism.* New Delhi: Women Unlimited, 2005.

Berman, Marshall. *Adventures in Marxism.* London: Verso, 1999.

Bernstein, Elizabeth. *Temporarily Yours: Intimacy, Authenticity, and the Commerce of Sex*. Chicago: University of Chicago Press, 2007.

———. "The Transformation of Sexual Commerce and Urban Space in San Francisco." *Footnotes*, January 2004. Accessed December 1, 2012. http://www.asanet.org/footnotes/jan04/ indexone.html.

Beverley, Eric Lewis. "Muslim Modern: Hyderabad State, 1883–1948." PhD diss., Harvard University, 2007.

Bhan, Gautam, and Arvind Narrain, eds. *Because I Have a Voice: Queer Politics in India*. New Delhi: Yoda Press, 2005.

Bharucha, Nauzer K. "Despite Opposition, Slum Rehabilitation Authority Clears Prime Plot for Redevelopment." *Times of India,* January 29, 2013. Accessed February 5, 2013. http://articles.timesofindia.indiatimes.com/2013 –01–29/mumbai/36615544_1_lokhandwala-infrastructure-mata-ramabai-nagar-worli-land.

Bhaviskar, Amita. "Introduction." In Amita Bhaviskar, ed., *Waterscapes: The Cultural Politics of a Natural Resource*, 1–10. New Delhi: Permanent Black, 2007.

Bhide, Amita. "Shifting Terrains of Communities and Community Organization: Reflections on Organizing for Housing Rights in Mumbai." *Community Development Journal 44* (2009): 367–81.

Bidwai, Praful. "How the Government Suppresses Dissent." *Rediff.com*, May 30, 2013. Accessed February 1, 2014. http://www.rediff.com/news/report /column-how-the-government-suppresses-dissent/20130530.htm.

Biradavolu, M., S. Burris, A. George, A. Jena, and K. Blankenship. "Can Sex Workers Regulate Police? Learning from an HIV Prevention Project for Sex Workers in Southern India." *Social Science and Medicine* 68 (2009): 1541–47.

Black, Maggie. *Women in Ritual Slavery: Devadasi, Jogini and Mathamma in Karnataka, Andhra Pradesh, Southern India*. London: Anti-Slavery International, 2007. Accessed November 10, 2012. http://www.antislavery.org/includes /documents/cm_docs/2009/w/women_in_ritual_slavery2007.pdf.

Bombay Ki Kahani, Mumbai Ki Zubaani, December 14, 2012–January 13, 2013. Accessed January 30, 2013. http://bombaykikahani.wordpress.com/.

Bose, Sugata, and Ayesha Jalal, eds. *Modern South Asia: History, Culture, Political Economy*. New York: Routledge, 1998.

———. *Nationalism, Democracy, and Development: State and Politics in India*. New Delhi: Oxford University Press, 1997.

Breman, Jan. *Footloose Labour: Working in India's Informal Economy*. Cambridge: Cambridge University Press, 1996.

Brennan, Denise. *What's Love Got to Do with It? Transnational Desires and Sex Tourism in the Dominican Republic*. Durham, NC: Duke University Press, 2004.

Brown, Eliot. "Demand for Office Space Still Sluggish." *Wall Street Journal*, January 7, 2013. Accessed January 20, 2013. http://online.wsj.com/article /SB10001424127887323689604578222192171334314.html.

Brown, Wendy. *States of Injury: Power and Freedom in Late Modernity*. Princeton, NJ: Princeton University Press, 2005.

Brown, Wendy, and Janet Halley, eds. *Left Legalism / Left Critique*. Durham, NC: Duke University Press, 2002.

Burton, Antoinette. *Burdens of History: British Feminists, Indian Women, and Imperial Culture, 1865–1915*. Chapel Hill : University of North Carolina Press, 1994.

Castles, Stephen, and Mark J. Miller. *The Age of Migration: International Population Movements in the Modern World*. 4th rev. ed. Houndmills: Palgrave, 2008.

Center for Health and Gender Equity. "Implications of U.S. Policy Restrictions for HIV Programs Aimed at Commercial Sex Workers." August 2008. Accessed December 8, 2012. http://www.genderhealth.org/files/uploads/change /publications/aplobrief.pdf.

Chadha, Sunainaa. "Why Bullishness on Indian Real Estate Is Misplaced." *Firstpost*, December 4, 2012. Accessed January 20, 2013. http://www.firstpost .com/real-estate/why-bullishness-on-indian-real-estate-is-misplaced-544459 .html.

Chakrabarti, Satyabrata. "Gender Dimensions of the Informal Sector and Informal Employment in India." Paper prepared for the Global Forum on Gender Statistics, January 26–28, 2009. Accessed December 20, 2012. http://unstats .un.org/unsd/gender/Ghana_Jan2009/Doc41.pdf.

Chakravarti, Uma. *Beyond the Kings and Brahmans of "Ancient" India*. New Delhi: Tulika Press, 2006.

———. *Gendering Caste: Through a Feminist Lens*. New Delhi: Stree, 2003.

———. *Rewriting History: The Life and Times of Pandita Ramabai*. New Delhi: Kali for Women, 1998.

Chari, Sharad, and Vinay Gidwani. "Introduction: Grounds for a Spatial Ethnography of Labor." *Ethnography* 6 (2005): 267–81.

Chatterjee, Partha. *Lineages of Political Society*. Ranikhet: Permanent Black, 2011.

———. "The Nationalist Resolution of the Women's Question." In Kumkum Sangari and Sudesh Vaid, eds., *Recasting Women: Essays in Indian Colonial History*, 233–53. New Delhi: Kali for Women, 1989.

———. *The Politics of the Governed: Reflections on Popular Politics in Most of the World*. New York: Columbia University Press, 2006.

Cheng, Sealing. *On the Move for Love: Migrant Entertainers and the U.S. Military in South Korea*. Philadelphia: University of Pennsylvania Press, 2010.

Chetty, T. R. K., and M. N. Rao. "Latur Earthquake." *Geological Society of India Memoirs* 35 (1994): 65–73.

Chhabra, G. S. *Advanced Study in the History of Modern India*, vol. 1 (1707–1813). Delhi: Lotus Press, 2005.

"Citizens Vent Ire at Demolitions in Pune." *Daily News and Analysis (DNA), India*, August 24, 2012. Accessed March 3, 2013. http://www.dnaindia.com/pune /report_citizens-vent-ire-at-demolitions-in-pune_1732155.

Coalition Against Trafficking in Women. "India Fact Sheet." Accessed September 2011. http://www.catwinternational.org/factbook/india.php.

Cohen, Lawrence. "1." Paper presented at the annual conference on South Asia, Madison, Wisconsin, October 11–14, 2012. Accessed December 15, 2012. http://followuidai.wordpress.com/.

Cohn, Bernard. *Colonialism and Its Forms of Knowledge: The British in India.* Princeton, NJ: Princeton University Press, 1996.

Columbia University Press. "Interview with Siddharth Kara, author of *Sex Trafficking.*" Accessed December 1, 2012. http://cup.columbia.edu/static /siddarth-kara-interview.

Corbridge, Stuart, Glyn Williams, Manoj Srivastava, and René Veron. *Seeing the State: Governance and Governmentality in India.* Cambridge: Cambridge University Press, 2005.

"Court Clears Way for Demolitions in Ahmedabad." *Sify News*, January 25, 2011. Accessed March 3, 2013. http://www.sify.com/news/court-clears-way-for -demolitions-in-ahmedabad-news-national-lbzaFafdjcf.html.

Craig, Jeffrey. *Timepass: Youth, Class, and the Politics of Waiting in India.* Stanford, CA: Stanford University Press, 2010.

Cummings, Scott. "Litigation at Work: Defending Day Labor in Los Angeles." August 2009. UCLA School of Law Research Paper, No. 11-25, 2011. Accessed December 20, 2012. http://papers.ssrn.com/sol3/papers.cfm?abstract_id =1907315.

Dalrymple, William. "The Daughters of Yellamma." In *Nine Lives: In Search of the Sacred in Modern India*, 55–76. New York: Vintage Books, 2011.

D'Cunha, Jean. *The Legalization of Prostitution: A Sociological Inquiry into the Laws Relating to Prostitution in India and the West.* Bangalore: Wordmakers for the Christian Institute for the Study of Religion and Society, 1991.

De Genova, Nicholas. "The Production of Culprits: From Deportability to Detainability in the Aftermath of 'Homeland Security.'" *Citizenship Studies* 11 (2007): 421–48.

———. "The Queer Politics of Migration: Reflections on 'Illegality' and Incorrigibility." *Studies in Social Justice* 4 (2010): 101–26.

———. *Working the Boundaries: Race, Space, and "Illegality" in Mexican Chicago.* Durham, NC: Duke University Press, 2005.

Denning, Michael. "Wageless Life." *New Left Review* 66 (2010). Accessed December 20, 2012. http://newleftreview.org/II/66/michael-denning-wageless-life.

Deshingkar, Priya. "Circular Internal Migration and Development in India." In International Organization for Migration, ed., *Migration and Development within and across Borders: Research and Policy Perspectives on Internal and International Migration*, 161–87. Geneva: International Organization for Migration, 2008.

Deshingkar, Priya, and John Farrington, eds. *Circular Migration and Multilocational Livelihood Strategies in Rural India.* New York: Oxford University Press, 2009.

Deshpande, Neeta. "A New Home, but in a Nala!" *India Together*, February 5, 2010. Accessed June 20, 2011. http://www.indiatogether.org/2010/feb /hrt-nala.htm.

Dey, J. "Kamathipura Seduces Land Sharks," *Mid-Day*, March 22, 2009. Accessed January 20, 2012. http://www.mid-day.com/news/2009/mar/220309 -Kamathipura-sex-workers-brothels-Grant-Road-Byculla-Mazagaon-Loan -Sharks-Mumbai-news.htm.

D'Monte, Daryl. *Ripping the Fabric: The Decline of Mumbai and Its Mills*. New Delhi: Oxford University Press, 2002.

Doshi, Sapana. "The Politics of Persuasion: Gendered Slum Citizenship in Neo-liberal Mumbai." In Renu Desai and Romola Sanyal, eds., *Urban India: Emerging Citizenships and Contested Spaces*, 82–108. New Delhi: Sage India, 2010.

Dube, Siddharth. *Sex, Lies, and AIDS*. New Delhi: HarperCollins, 2000.

Durbar Mahila Samanwaya Committee. "The 'Fallen' Learn to Rise: The Social Impact of STD/HIV Intervention Programme." Calcutta: Durbar, 1998. Accessed January 15, 2013. http://www.durbar.org/html/activities.asp.

Echanove, Matias, and Rahul Srivastava. "Urban Journal: The Vanishing Public of the 'World Class City.'" *Wall Street Journal*, March 29, 2011. Accessed July 15, 2011. http://blogs.wsj.com/indiarealtime/2011/03/29/urban -journal-the-vanishing-public-of-the-world-class-city/.

Edwardes, Stephen. *Bombay City Police: A Historical Sketch*. London: Oxford University Press, 1923.

———. *Crime in British India*. New Delhi: ABC, 1983 [1924].

Enloe, Cynthia. *Bananas, Beaches and Bases: Making Feminist Sense of International Politics*. Berkeley: University of California Press, 1990.

Fernandes, Leela. "The Politics of Forgetting: Class, Politics, State Power and the Restructuring of Urban Space in India." *Urban Studies* 41 (2004): 2415–30.

Foucault, Michel. *Discipline and Punish: The Birth of the Prison*. New York: Vintage Books, 1995 [1977].

———. *History of Sexuality*, vol. 1, *An Introduction*. New York: Random House, 1978.

———. "Of Other Spaces." *Diacritics* 16 (1986): 22–27.

Frasier, Nancy. "What's Critical about Critical Theory? The Case of Habermas and Gender." *New German Critique* 35 (1985): 97–131.

Gangoli, Geetanjali. "Prostitution, Legalization and Decriminalization—Recent Debates." *Economic and Political Weekly* 33 (1998): 504–5.

Gangoli, Geetanjali, and Nicole Westmarland. *International Approaches to Prostitution: Law and Policy in Europe and Asia*. Bristol: Policy Press, 2006.

Geetha, V. "Gender and the Logic of Brahminism: Periyar and the Politics of the Female Body." In K. K. Sangari and Uma Chakravarti, eds., *From Myths to Markets: Essays on Gender*, 198–233. New Delhi: Manohar, 1998.

Geetha, V., and Nalini Rajan. *Religious Faith, Ideology, Citizenship: The View from Below*. New Delhi: Routledge India, 2011.

Ghosh, Durba. *Sex and the Family in Colonial India: The Making of Empire*. Cambridge: Cambridge University Press, 2006.

Ghosh, Swati. "The Shadow Lines of Citizenship." *Identity, Culture and Politics* 5 (2004): 105–23.

Gidwani, Vinay K. "Subaltern Cosmopolitanism as Politics." *Antipode* 38 (2006): 7–21.

Global Commission on HIV and the Law. "HIV and the Law: Risks, Rights and Health." Accessed June 1, 2012. http://www.hivlawcommission.org/.

Glover, Will. "Construing Urban Space as 'Public' in Colonial India: Some Notes from Punjab." *Journal of Punjab Studies* 14 (2007): 211–24.

Goldar, B. "Trade Liberalization and Manufacturing Employment: The Case of India." Employment Paper, No. 2002/34, ILO, Geneva, 2002.

Gooptu, Nandini. *The Politics of the Urban Poor in Early Twentieth-Century India.* Cambridge: Cambridge University Press, 2001.

Gooptu, Nandini, and Nandinee Bandopadhyay. "'Rights to Stop the Wrong': Cultural Change and Collective Mobilization—The Case of Kolkota Sex Workers." *Oxford Development Studies* 35 (2007): 251–72.

Government of NCT of Delhi and Others v. Naz Foundation, No. 7455/2001, Delhi High Court, India, July 2, 2009, pp. 1–105. Accessed June 4, 2011. http://timesofindia.indiatimes.com/photo.cms?msid=4728348.

Gozdziak, Elzbieta, and Frank Laczko, eds. *International Migration* 43 (2005): 5–363.

Griffiths, Melanie, Ali Rogers, and Bridget Anderson. "Migration, Time and Temporalities: Review and Prospect." Paper presented at the Migration, Time and Temporalities Symposium, Centre on Migration, Policy and Society, Oxford, June 29, 2012.

Grover, Anand, and Tripti Tandon. "(W)Rec(K)tifying I.T.P.A.: Proposed Amendments to the Immoral Trafficking Prevention Act: More Disaster for Prostitutes, Not Traffickers." *From the Lawyers' Collective* 21, no. 3 (2006): 7–14.

Gupta, Akhil. "The Song of the Nonaligned World: Transnational Identities and the Reinscription of Space in Late Capitalism." *Cultural Anthropology* 7 (1992): 63–79.

Gupta, Alok. *This Alien Legacy: The Origins of "Sodomy" Laws in British Colonialism.* New York: Human Rights Watch, 2008.

Gupta, Charu. *Sexuality, Obscenity, and Community: Women, Muslims, and the Hindu Public in Colonial India.* London: Palgrave Macmillan, 2002.

Gupta, Dipankar. "Understanding the Marathwada Riots: A Repudiation of Eclectic Marxism." *Social Scientist* 7 (1979): 3–22.

Hansen, Thomas Blom. *Wages of Violence: Naming and Identity in Postcolonial Bombay.* Princeton, NJ: Princeton University Press, 2001.

Harriss-White, Barbara. *India Working: Essays on Society and Economy.* Cambridge: Cambridge University Press, 2003.

Harriss-White, Barbara, and Nandini Gooptu. "Mapping India's World of Unorganised Labour." *Socialist Register* 37 (2001): 89–118.

Hart, Keith. "Informal Economy." Accessed December 20, 2012. http://thememorybank.co.uk/papers/informal-economy/.

———. "Informal Income Opportunities and Urban Employment in Ghana." *Journal of Modern African Studies* 11 (1973): 61–89.

————. "On the Informal Economy: The Political History of an Ethnographic Concept." Working Paper 09/042, Centre Emile Bernheim, Brussels, 2009. Accessed December 20, 2012. http://ideas.repec.org/p/sol/wpaper/09-042.html.

Hoang, Kimberly. "She's Not a Low-Class Dirty Girl! Sex Work in Ho Chi Minh City, Vietnam." *Journal of Contemporary Ethnography* 40 (2011): 367–96.

Horwitz, Morton J. "The History of the Public/Private Distinction." *University of Pennsylvania Law Review* 130 (1982): 1423–28.

Housing and Land Rights Network (Delhi) and People's Union of Civil Liberties (Karnataka). *Governance by Denial: Forced Eviction and Demolition of Homes in Koramangala (Ejipura) Bangalore.* Bangalore: HLRN and PUCL, 2013. Accessed March 3, 2013. http://www.hic-sarp.org/documents/Interim_Report_Fact -finding_Koramangala.pdf.

Human Rights Watch. *Broken People: Caste Violence against India's "Untouchables."* New York: Human Rights Watch, 1999. Accessed January 20, 2008, http://www.hrw.org/reports/1999/india/.

Indian People's Human Rights Tribunal. "Summary of the Interim Report of the Tribunal Set Up by IPHRC to Study the Impact of the Demolitions in the Sanjay Gandhi National Park." April 12, 2001. Accessed October 15, 2008. http://www.cscsarchive.org:8081/MediaArchive/liberty.nsf/%28 docid%29/8E378F6D378D1AC1E5256B19001BC6C6.

Jayaraman, Gayatri. "Kamathipura: Bought and Sold." *Live Mint*, June 9, 2012. Accessed February 1, 2014. http://www.livemint.com/Leisure/FL9qoQjrzIdts YshID8McP/Kamathipura-bought-and-sold.html.

Jayaraman, K. S. "India against AIDS." *Nature* 318 (1985): 201.

John, Mary, and Janaki Nair, eds. *A Question of Silence? The Sexual Economies of Modern India.* New Delhi: Kali for Women, 1998.

Jordan, Ann. "The Annotated Guide to the Complete UN Trafficking Protocol." Washington, DC: Global Rights, 2002. Accessed January 15, 2013. http:// www.globalrights.org/site/DocServer/Annotated_Protocol.pdf.

Jordan, K. K. *From Sacred Servant to Profane Prostitute: A History of the Changing Legal Status of the Devadasis in India, 1857–1947.* New Delhi: Manohar, 2003.

Joshi, Sanjay. *Fractured Modernity: Making of a Middle Class in Colonial North India.* New Delhi: Oxford University Press, 2001.

Kamala Kempadoo. "Introduction." In Kamala Kempadoo and Jo Doezema, eds., *Global Sex Workers: Rights, Resistance, and Redefinition*, 1–29. New York: Routledge, 1998.

Kapse, S. R. *Police Administration in Bombay, 1600–1865.* Bombay: Himalaya Press, 1987.

Kapur, Ratna. *Erotic Justice: Law and the New Politics of Postcolonialism.* London: Glass House, 2005.

————. "The Tragedy of Victimization Rhetoric: Resurrecting the Native Subject in International/Postcolonial Feminist Legal Politics." *Harvard Human Rights Law Journal* 15 (2002): 1–37.

Kara, Siddharth. *Sex Trafficking: Inside the Business of Modern Slavery*. New York: Columbia University Press, 2008.

Karmali, Naazneen. "India's 100 Richest Have Mixed Year, Eke Out Small Gain." *Forbes Asia*, November 5, 2012. Accessed January 13, 2013. http://www.forbes.com/india-billionaires/list/.

Karnik, Niranjan S. "Locating HIV/AIDS and India: Cautionary Notes on the Globalization of Categories." *Science, Technology and Human Values* 26 (2001): 322–48.

Katakam, Anupama. "A State of Disparity." *Frontline* 19 (June 22–July 5, 2002). Accessed June 15, 2010. http://www.frontlineonnet.com/fl1913/19130810.htm.

Kaur, Naunidhi. "Mumbai: A Decade after Riots." *Frontline* 20 (July 5–18, 2003). Accessed January 30, 2013. http://www.frontlineonnet.com/fl2014/stories/20030718002704100.htm.

Kelly, Patty. *Lydia's Open Door: Inside Mexico's Most Modern Brothel*. Berkeley: University of California Press, 2008.

Kettles, Gregg W. "Day Labor Markets and Public Space." February 2009. Mississippi College School of Law Research Paper No. 2009-05; Loyola-LA Legal Studies Paper No. 2009-5. Accessed December 20, 2012. http://ssrn.com/abstract=1332832 or http://dx.doi.org/10.2139/ssrn.1332832.

Khilnani, Sunil. "The Development of Civil Society." In S. Kaviraj and S. Khilnani, eds., *Civil Society: History and Possibilities*, 11–32. Cambridge: Cambridge University Press, 2001.

———. *The Idea of India*. New York: Farrar, Straus and Giroux, 1997.

Kolhatkar, Neeta. "Builders Eye Red Light Area." *Daily News and Analysis (DNA), India*, April 14, 2008. Accessed January 20, 2012. http://www.dnaindia.com/mumbai/report_builders-eye-red-light-area_1159675.

Lefèbvre, Henri. *The Production of Space*. Oxford: Blackwell, 1991 [1974].

Legg, Steve. "Governing Prostitution in Colonial Delhi: From Cantonment Regulations to International Hygiene (1864–1939)." *Social History* 34 (2009): 447–67.

Levine, Philippa. *Prostitution, Race and Politics: Policing Venereal Disease in the British Empire*. New York: Routledge, 2003.

———. "Rereading the 1890s: Venereal Disease as 'Constitutional Crisis.'" *Journal of Asian Studies* 55 (1996): 586–12.

———. "Venereal Disease, Prostitution, and the Politics of Empire: The Case of British India." *Journal of the History of Sexuality* 4 (1994): 579–602.

Lewis, Clara. "Red Light District Swaps Sin for Skyscrapers." *Times of India*, November 6, 2010. Accessed January 20, 2012. http://articles.timesofindia.indiatimes.com/2010-11-06/mumbai/28263687_1_prostitutes-kamathipura-mira-road.

Luibheid, Eithne. "A Blueprint for Exclusion: The Page Law, Prostitution and Discrimination against Chinese Women." In *Entry Denied: Controlling Sexuality at the Border*, 31–54. Minneapolis: University of Minnesota Press, 2002.

Mahdavi, Pardis. *Gridlock: Labor, Migration and Human Trafficking in Dubai*. Stanford, CA: Stanford University Press, 2011.

Mani, Lata. "Contentious Traditions: The Debate on Sati in Colonial India." In Kumkum Sangari, ed., *Recasting Women: Essays in Indian Colonial History*, 88–126. New Delhi: Kali for Women, 1989.

Manto, Sadat Hasan. *Kali Shalwar*. London: Indian Bookshelf, 2007.

Margolis, Maxine. "We Are Not Immigrants! A Contested Category among Brazilians in New York City and Rio de Janeiro." In Carole A. Mortland, ed., *Diasporic Identity: Selected Papers on Refugees and Immigrants VI*, 30–50. Arlington, VA: American Anthropological Association, 1998.

Marx, Karl. *Critique of Hegel's Philosophy of Right*. Trans. John O'Malley. Cambridge: Cambridge University Press, 1970 [1843].

Massey, Doreen. *Space, Place and Gender*. Minneapolis: University of Minnesota Press, 1994.

McCabe, Kimberly A., and Sabita Manian, eds. *Sex Trafficking: A Global Perspective*. Lanham, MD: Rowman and Littlefield, 2010.

Mehta, Harit. "Red Lights May Go Out of Surat's Chakla Bazaar." *Times of India*, September 13, 2003. Accessed January 20, 2012. http://articles.timesofindia .indiatimes.com/2003-09-13/ahmedabad/27186097_1_workers-red-light -area-rehabilitation-package.

Menon, Jishna. "Unimaginable Communities: Identities in Traffic in Rukhsana Ahmad's Black Shalwar." *Modern Drama* 48 (2005): 407–27.

Menon, Nivedita. "Introduction." In Partha Chatterjee, ed., *Empire and Nation: Selected Essays, 1985–2005*, 1–22. Ranikhet: Permanent Black, 2010.

———. *Recovering Subversion: Feminist Politics beyond the Law*. New Delhi: Permanent Black, 2004.

Misra, Geetanjali, Ajay Mahal, and Rima Shah. "Protecting the Rights of Sex Workers: The Indian Experience." *Health and Human Rights* 5 (2000): 88–115.

Montgomery, Heather. "Working with Child Prostitutes in Thailand: Problems of Practice and Interpretation." *Childhood: A Global Journal of Child Research* 14 (2007): 415–30.

Mufti, Aamir. *Enlightenment in the Colony: The Jewish Question and the Crisis of Postcolonial Culture*. Princeton, NJ: Princeton University Press, 2007.

Naik-Singru, Ramola. "Mumbai: Spatial *Segregation* in a 'Globalizing' City." In R. S. Sandhu and Jasmeet Sandhu, eds., *Globalizing Cities: Inequality and Segregation in Developing Countries*, 131–70. Jaipur: Rawat, 2007.

Nair, Janaki. *The Promise of Metropolis: Bangalore's Twentieth Century*. New Delhi: Oxford University Press, 2005.

Nair, P. M. *A Report on Trafficking in Women and Children in India 2002–2003*. New Delhi: National Human Rights Commission, UNIFEM, Institute of Social Sciences, 2004.

National Sample Survey Office, National Statistical Organisation, Ministry of Statistics and Programme Implementation, Government of India. "Informal Sector and Conditions of Employment in India: NSS 66th ROUND (July

2009–June 2010)." Accessed January 10, 2013. http://www.indiaenvironment portal.org.in/reports-documents/informal-sector-and-conditions-employ ment-india-july-2009-%E2%80%93-june-2010.

Navya, P. K., "Hundreds of Ejipura Slum Residents Thrown Out of Homes." *Citizen Matters, Bangalore*, January 19, 2013. Accessed February 15, 2013. http:// bangalore.citizenmatters.in/articles/view/4828-hundreds-of-ejipura -ews-residents-thrown-out-of-homes.

Neve, Geert de. *The Everyday Politics of Labour: Working Lives in India's Informal Economy*. New Delhi: Social Science Press, 2005.

New Delhi High Court. *Naz Foundation v. Government NCT of Delhi*, 160 *Delhi Law Times* 277, July 2, 2009. Accessed December 15, 2011. http://lobis.nic.in /dhc/APS/judgement/02–07–2009/APS02072009CW74552001.pdf.

Niaz, U. "Violence against Women in South Asian Countries." *Archives of Women's Mental Health* 6 (2003): 173–84.

Nigam, Aditya. "'Molecular Economies': Is There an 'Outside' to Capital?" In Nivedita Menon, Aditya Nigam, and Sanjay Palshikar, eds., *Critical Studies in Politics: Exploring Sites, Selves, Power*, 527–59. New Delhi: Indian Institute of Advanced Study and Orient Blackswan, 2013.

———. "Politics, Political Society, and the Everyday." *Kafila*, March 31, 2012. Accessed January 20, 2013. http://kafila.org/2012/03/31/politics-political -society-and-the-everyday/.

———. "Rethinking the Unorganised Sector." *Social Action* 47 (1997): 125–34.

———. "Secularism, Modernity, Nation: Epistemology of the Dalit Critique." *Economic and Political Weekly* 35 (2000): 4256–68.

Nijman, Jan. "Against the Odds: Slum Rehabilitation in Neoliberal Mumbai." *Cities* 25 (2008): 73–85.

O'Connell-Davidson, Julia. *Children in the Global Sex Trade*. Cambridge: Polity, 2005.

Oldenburg, Veena Talwar. *Dowry Murder: The Imperial Origins of a Cultural Crime*. New York: Oxford University Press, 2002.

———. "Lifestyle as Resistance: The Case of the Courtesans of Lucknow, India." *Feminist Studies* 16 (1990): 259–87.

Omvedt, Gail. "Marathwada: Reply to Dipankar Gupta." *Social Scientist* 8 (1979): 51–58.

Padilla, Mark. *Caribbean Pleasure Industry: Tourism, Sexuality, and AIDS in the Dominican Republic*. Chicago: University of Chicago Press, 2007.

Pais, P. "HIV and India: Looking into the Abyss." *Tropical Medicine and International Health* 1 (1996): 295–304.

Parrenas, Rhacel. *Illicit Flirtations: Labor, Migration, and Sex Trafficking in Tokyo*. Stanford, CA: Stanford University Press, 2011.

Patel, Sujata, and Jim Masselos, eds. *Bombay and Mumbai: The City in Transition*. New Delhi: Oxford University Press, 2005.

Patel, Sujata, and Alice Thorner, eds. *Bombay: Metaphor for Modern India*. New Delhi: Oxford University Press, 1996.

———, eds. *Mumbai: Mosaic of Modern Culture*. New Delhi: Oxford University Press, 1995.

Pateman, Carole. "Feminist Critiques of the Public/Private Dichotomy." In S. I. Benn and G. F. Gaus, eds., *Public and Private in Social Life*, 281–303. New York: St. Martin's, 1983.

Pathak, Aditi Nargundkar. "Socio-spatial Exclusion in Urban Spaces: Mumbai City." *The Urban Vision: Expert Diary*, October 10, 2009. Accessed January 30, 2013. http://www.theurbanvision.com/blogs/?p=275.

Pillai, Neetha N. "Women's Work in the Post Reform Period: An Exploration of Macro Data." Occasional Paper No. 52, Center for Women's Development Studies, 2009. Accessed December 12, 2012. http://www.cwds.ac.in/OCPaper /OccassionalPaperNeetha.pdf.

Platts, John T. *A Dictionary of Urdu, Classical Hindi, and English*. London: W. H. Allen, 1884.

Portes, Alejandro, and Josh DeWind, eds. *Rethinking Migration: New Theoretical and Empirical Perspectives*. New York: Berghahn Books, 2007.

"Protocol to Prevent, Suppress and Punish Trafficking in Persons, Especially Women and Children 2000." Article 3 (a). United Nations Crime and Justice Information Network, Center for International Crime Prevention, Office for Drug Control and Crime Prevention. Accessed May 2012. http://www.uncjin .org/Documents/Conventions/dcatoc/final_documents_2/convention _%20traff_eng.pdf.

Rajagopal, Arvind. "Special Political Zone: Urban Planning, Spatial Segregation and the Infrastructure of Violence in Ahmedabad." *South Asian History and Culture* 1 (2010): 529–56.

Rajan, Rajeshwari Sunder. *The Scandal of the State: Women, Law and Citizenship in Postcolonial India*. Durham, NC: Duke University Press, 2003.

Ramberg, Lucinda. *Given to the Goddess: South Indian Devadasis and the Sexuality of Religion*. Durham, NC: Duke University Press, 2014.

———. "When the Devi Is Your Husband: Sacred Marriage and Sexual Economy in South India." *Feminist Studies* 37 (2011): 28–33.

Rangarajan, L. N., ed. and trans. *The Arthashastra / Kautilya*. New Delhi: Penguin Books India, 1992.

Ratliff, E. A. "Women as 'Sex Workers,' Men as 'Boyfriends': Shifting Identities in Philippine Go-Go Bars." *Anthropology and Medicine* 6 (1999): 79–101.

Rege, Sharmila. *Writing Caste, Writing Gender: Reading Dalit Women's Testimonios*. New Delhi: Zubaan, 2006.

Research Centre for Women's Studies and Forum against the Oppression of Women. *Working Conditions and Backgrounds of Women Working as Dancers in Dance Bars*. Mumbai: SNDT University, 2005.

Roy, Arundhati. *The Cost of Living*. New York: Modern Library, 1999.

Saeed, Fouzia. *Taboo: A Ph.D. Girl in the Red Light Area*. Oxford: Oxford University Press, 2002.

Sainath, P. "Farm Suicides Rise in Maharashtra, State Still Leads the List." *The Hindu*, July 3, 2012. Accessed December 1, 2012. http://www.thehindu.com /opinion/columns/sainath/article3595351.ece.

Sakunde, Deepak. "Kareena and Rani to Play Sex Workers in Kamathipura." *Zimbio*, January 9, 2011. Accessed January 2012. http://www.zimbio.com /Bollywood+Movies/articles/CCI10Zta6bM/Kareena+Rani+play+sex +workers+Kamathipura.

Sampada Mahila Grameen Sanstha. "Of Veshyas, Whores, Vamps, and Women." Sangli: SANGRAM, 1999.

Sassen, Saskia. "Informalization in Advanced Market Economies." Geneva: International Labour Office, 1997. Accessed December 20, 2012. http://www.ilo .int/wcmsp5/groups/public/@ed_emp/documents/publication/wcms_123590 .pdf.

Schenk, Hans. "Towards Apartheid? Policies of Segregation and Deprivation in Delhi." In K. R. Gupta, ed., *Urban Development Debates in the New Millennium*, 1:96–114. Delhi: Atlantic, 2004.

Sedgwick, Eve Kosofsky. *Epistemology of the Closet*. Berkeley: University of California Press, 1990.

Sengupta, Anasuya. "Concept, Category and Claim: Insights on Caste and Ethnicity from the Police in India." *Ethnic and Racial Studies* 33 (2010): 717–36.

Shah, Svati P. "Born into Saving Brothel Children." *SAMAR: South Asian Magazine for Action and Reflection*, January 24, 2005. Accessed January 2012. http://samarmagazine.org/archive/articles/190.

———. "Brothels and Big Screen Rescues: Producing 'Prostitution in India' through Documentary Film." *Interventions: Journal of Postcolonial Studies* 15 (2013): 549–66.

———. "Distinguishing Poverty and Trafficking: Lessons from Field Research in Mumbai." *Georgetown Journal on Poverty Law and Policy* 9 (2007): 441–54.

———. "Producing the Spectacle of Prostitution in India: The Politics of Red Light Visibility in Mumbai." *Cultural Dynamics* 18 (2006): 269–92.

———. "South Asian Border Crossings, Migration and Sex Work." *Sexuality Research and Social Policy: Journal of NSRC* 5 (2008): 19–30.

Sharma, Animesh. "Section 377: No Jurisprudential Basis." *Economic and Political Weekly* 43, no. 46 (2008): 12–14.

Singh, Y. N., and A. N. Malaviya, "Long Distance Truck Drivers in India: HIV Infection and Their Possible Role in Disseminating HIV into Rural Areas." *International Journal of STD and AIDS* 5 (1994): 137–38.

Sinha, Chinki. "The Fading Red Light." *Open Magazine*, September 15, 2012. Accessed January 15, 2013. http://www.openthemagazine.com/article/nation /the-fading-red-light.

Srinivas, M. N. "Some Reflections on Dowry." New Delhi: Centre for Women's Development Studies, 1984. Accessed December 14, 2012. http://www .womenstudies.in/elib/dowry/dw_some_reflections.pdf.

Srinivasan, S. "Marathwada: Will Someone Please Pay Attention Here?" Rediff .com, October 6, 2004. Accessed June 15, 2010. http://www.rediff.com/election /2004/oct/06maha1.htm.

Tagore, Rabindranath. *The Home and the World*. New York: Macmillan, 1919.

Tambe, Ashwini. *Codes of Misconduct: Regulating Prostitution in Late Colonial Bombay*. Minneapolis: University of Minnesota Press, 2009.

————. "The Elusive Ingénue: A Transnational Feminist Analysis of European Prostitution in Colonial Bombay." *Gender and Society* 19 (2005): 160–79.

Thacker, Teena. "Bill Gates Foundation to Stop Funding HIV Programs." *Indian Express*, March 25, 2011. Accessed February 15, 2012. http://www .indianexpress.com/news/bill-gates-foundation-to-stop-funding-hiv -programmes/767166/0.

Thappa, Devinder Mohan, Nidhi Singh, and Sowmya Kaimal. "Prostitution in India and Its Role in the Spread of HIV Infection." *Indian Journal of Sexually Transmitted Diseases* 28 (2007): 69–75.

Thompson, E. P. *The Making of the English Working Class*. New York: Random House, 1964 [1963].

Tindall, Gillian. *City of Gold: The Biography of Mumbai*. London: Temple Smith, 1982.

Unique Identification Authority of India. "UIDAI Mandates and Objectives." Accessed January 15, 2012. http://uidai.gov.in/.

United Nations Development Programme. *Human Development Report Maharashtra 2002*. Accessed June 2010. http://hdrc.undp.org.in/shdr/mhdr/.

Vanita, Ruth, ed. *Queering India: Same Sex Love and Eroticism in Indian Culture and Society*. New York: Routledge, 2002.

Varshney, Ashutosh. "Ethnic Conflict and Civil Society: India and Beyond." *World Politics* 53 (2001): 362–98.

"Violent Reactions to Delhi Demolitions." *Business Standard*, December 20, 2005. Accessed March 3, 2013. http://www.business-standard.com/article /Economy-Policy/Violent-reactions-to-Delhi-demolitions-105122001125 _1.html.

Wadke, Rahul. "Maharashtra May Repeal Urban Land Ceiling Act." *Hindu Business Line*, January 21, 2006. Accessed October 15, 2008. http://www .thehindubusinessline.in/2006/01/21/stories/2006012103480100.htm.

Waheed, Sarah. "Women of 'Ill Repute': Ethics and Urdu Literature in Colonial India." *Modern Asian Studies* (forthcoming).

Wald, Erica. "From Begums and Bibis to Abandoned Females and Idle Women: Sexual Relationships, Venereal Disease and the Redefinition of Prostitution in Early Nineteenth-Century India." *Indian Economic Social History Review* 46 (2009): 5–25.

Warner, Michael. *Publics and Counterpublics*. Brooklyn: Zone Books, 2002.

Weinstein, Liza, and Xuefei Ren. "The Changing Right to the City: Urban Renewal and Housing Rights in Globalizing Shanghai and Mumbai." *City and Community* 8 (2009): 407–32.

Wersch, Hubert van. *The Mumbai Textile Strike*. New Delhi: Oxford University Press, 1991.

Whyte, William Foote. *Street Corner Society: The Social Structure of an Italian Slum*. Chicago: University of Chicago Press, 1943.

Zheng, Tian Tian. *Ethnographies of Prostitution in Contemporary China: Gender Relations, HIV/AIDS, and Nationalism*. New York: Palgrave Macmillan, 2009.

Filmography

Born into Brothels. Directed by Zana Briski and Ross Kaufman. New York: Red Light Films, 2004.

Chameli. Directed by Sudhir Misra. Mumbai: Pritish Nandy Communications, 2004.

Chandni Bar. Directed by Madhur Bhandarkar. Mumbai, 2001.

Farmingville. Directed by Carole Sandoval and Catherine Tambini. New York: Camino Bluff Productions, 2004.

Harishchandrachi Factory. Directed by Paresh Mokashi. Mumbai: Mayasabha Productions, 2009.

Jai Bhim Comrade. Directed by Anand Patwardhan. Mumbai, 2012.

Mandi. Directed by Shyam Benegal. Mumbai: Blaze Film Enterprises, 1983.

Rooms of Shadow and Light. Directed by John Webster. Helsinki: Millennium Film Oy, 2001.

Saathiya. Directed by Shaad Ali. Mumbai: Kaleidoscope Entertainment, 2002.

Salaam Bombay. Directed by Mira Nair. Mumbai: Cadrage, Channel Four Films, Doordarshan, 1988.

Split Wide Open. Directed by Dev Benegal. Mumbai: Adlabs Films, 1999.

violence, 42, 213n2; caste markers, 219n18; dowry and, 70–74, 221n3; geographic segregation and, 213n2; goddess dedication and, 20–22; higher education and, 99, 220n21; marital status and, 98–99, 102–3; Nav Buddho community, 54, 55, 56, 84, 98, 100–101, 105–6, 109, 219n18; political society and, 141–43; Scheduled Caste, 207n3, 213n1; Scheduled Tribe, 207n3, 213n1; sexual commerce and, 97–99. See also *dalit* communities

Castles, Stephen, 212n62

Chakla Bazaar, 186

Chakravarti, Uma, 74, 98, 220n21

Chameli (2004), 155, 226n17

Chandni Bar (2001), 155

Chari, Sharad, 39, 110

Chatterjee, Partha, 139–40, 141–44, 146

chawl (worker housing), 165, 172, 174, 182, 226n18

Chennai (Madras), 23, 24–25, 80

child prostitution, 6–7, 18, 149–50, 199–201, 215n18, 228n2

civil society, 143–45

Codes of Misconduct (Tambe), 29

colonial-era India, 26–30, 51, 73–74, 130–34, 151–53

condom use/distribution, 25, 26, 91–92, 121–22, 180, 194, 199, 224n1

consent, 11–12, 31–32

constraint (*majburi*), 124–28, 173, 197–99, 221n5

Contagious Disease Acts, 151

Convention Against Transnational Organized Crime (2000), 11

criminalization: civil society and, 18–22, 129–34, 143–46; conflation of women/child sex workers, 181, 189–205, 200–201; HIV/AIDS and, 20–26, 156–57, 179–80, 209n23, 211n40, 221n2, 223n19; morality and, 143–45; political society and, 113–14, 141–43; visibility and, 79, 132–34, 137–38, 168

dalit communities: use of term, 214n1, 216n22; anticaste movement and, 54, 62–63, 100–102; *naka*-based, 54, 64, 98–100; sexual commerce and, 102, 193; violence against, 59, 66. *See also* caste system

dance bars, 114, 122–23, 128, 132, 135–36, 141, 221n1

Daya (worker), 107, 181, 182–84

De Genova, Nicholas, 52–53, 212n62

de Neve, Geert, 80

Denning, Michael, 82

Deshingkar, Priya, 221n3

detention: lock hospitals and, 210n39; remand homes, 132–33, 181–82, 228n31

devadasi (dedicated girl), 20–22

DeWind, Josh, 212n62

dhanda (profession/sex work), 14, 167, 226n16

dhanda wali (female professional), 14

didi (older sister), 214n9

domestic work, 93–94, 104, 107, 166–67

dowry, 70–74, 221n3

Dutta, Mohan, 199

Echanove, Matias, 50

Edwardes, Stephen, 152

1857 uprisings, 28–30, 51, 212n58

Emergency, the (1975–77), 220n24

Enloe, Cynthia, 212n66

feminism, x, 13–22, 37–39, 50, 74, 98–99, 156–57, 202–5, 222n9

Footloose Labour (Breman), 9, 218n5

Foucault, Michel, 23, 35–36, 48, 111, 142

Fourteenth Lane, 151, 164–65, 172, 174, 181, 182

Fraser, Nancy, 199

Gandhi, Indira, 66, 99, 175, 220n24

Gandhi, Rajiv, 99–100, 220n25

Gandhi, Sonia, 99–100, 220n25

Ganesh Chaturthi (festival), 175, 227n22

garibi hatao (slogan), 99, 220n24

Gates Foundation (Bill and Melinda
Gates Foundation), 157
gender: use of term, 13–16; *hijra* (third
gender, assigned male sex at birth),
ix, 16, 169, 187, 198; migrants (male),
43–44, 211n43; sex work and, ix–x,
15–16, 43–44, 57, 77–79, 189–205, 198,
211n43; spatialization of gendered
hierarchies, 212n66
Ghar Banao Ghar Bachao Andolan
(Build and Save Homes Movement),
49
Gidwani, Vinay, 39, 110
Giri (worker), 46, 47, 67–68, 71–73,
90–91, 108–9
Global Commission on HIV/AIDS,
223n19
Global Fund to Fight AIDS, Tuberculo-
sis and Malaria, 157
Global Sex Workers (Kempadoo and
Doezema), 14–15
Glover, Will, 50–51
Goa Children's Act (2003), 18
goddess dedication, 20–22
Gooptu, Nandini, 218n5
gorey lok (person with racialized privi-
lege), 181, 228n30
Gramsci, Antonio, 140, 142
Gujarat massacre, 38
Gupta, Charu, 28

Habermas, Jürgen, 49–50
Hansen, Thomas Blom, 130
harassment: cyclical nature of, 5; fines,
5, 128, 134, 137, 182; physical attacks,
5, 7, 128, 132, 141, 201–3, 222n7; raids,
6–7, 167, 179–84, 186–87; shopkeeper
harassment, 5, 54–55, 128. *See also*
police
harm discourse, 15, 18, 20, 22, 30, 51,
153, 155, 158, 186–87, 192–93, 201–3
Harriss-White, Barbara, 80
Hart, Keith, 9, 80, 82
Hegel, Georg Wilhelm Friedrich,
144–45

hijra (third gender, assigned male sex
at birth), ix, 16, 169, 187, 198
Hina (worker), 172–74, 220n28
Hinduism, 20–22, 38, 64, 68, 96, 107,
164, 202, 214n1, 216n22, 220n27,
225n4
HIV/AIDS: condom use/distribution,
25, 26, 91–92, 121–22, 176, 180, 199,
224n1; conflation with sex work,
20–26, 156–57, 179–80, 209n23,
211n40, 221n2, 223n19; historiog-
raphy of in India, 22–26; HIV/AIDS
prevention programs, ix–x, 6, 22–26,
38, 91–92, 149–50, 156–57, 185, 199,
208n14; impact of rates of infection
on sex work, x; prevalence data,
25–26; sexual research scholarship
and, ix–x, 6, 20–26, 38, 149–50,
156–61, 199, 223n19
housing: *basti* (settlements), 62, 63–66,
217n35; brothel-based sex workers
and, 7, 164, 165, 173–75, 178–79, 182,
184–87, 226n18; Chakla Bazaar evictions, 186; *chawls*, 165, 172, 174, 182,
226n18; migration and, 45–46, 53–57,
60–70, 75, 106, 116–19, 184–87; naka-
based sex workers, 45–46, 53–57,
60–70, 106; slum demolitions, 62,
66–70, 78, 95–97, 149, 180, 185–86,
223n18; street-based sex workers
and, 116–19, 142–43; Urban Land
Ceiling Act, 68. *See also* slum demolitions; water access

Immoral Trafficking Prevention Act
(ITPA, 1956), 13, 18, 92–93
income-generating strategies: agricultural work, 4, 6, 8–10, 31, 42, 46, 69,
75, 115–19, 141, 197–98, 207n2; *bura
kam* (bad work/sexual services),
14–15, 56–57, 89, 92, 105, 108–9, 120;
construction work, 4–5, 38, 42–45,
55, 80–81, 83, 90, 96, 106–9, 119–20,
124–28, 178–79, 191–92; domestic
work, 93–94, 104, 107, 166–67;

legal frameworks: British colonial era, 26–30, 51, 73–74, 130–34, 151–53; Contagious Disease Acts (CD Acts), 22–23, 30, 210n39; critiques of, 209n23, 222n9; early regulations of sex work, 29, 30–34; following the 1857 uprisings, 28–30, 51, 212n58; Goa Children's Act (2003), 18; Immoral Trafficking Prevention Act, 13, 18, 92–93; international policies, x, 11–13, 36, 156–57, 208n14; Palermo Protocol and, 11–12; slum demolition policies, 68–69; within urban spaces, 51–52. *See also* criminalization; police
Levine, Philippa, 151
Lewis, Clara, 180
LGBTQ political movements, xi–xii, xv–xvi, 129, 156–57, 222n8, 223n19
Lina (worker), 116, 121–22, 139
livelihood strategies: agency and, 145, 197–99; agricultural work, 4, 6, 8–10, 31, 42, 46, 69, 75, 115–19, 141, 197–98, 207n2; assessment of viability of sex work, 124–28; *bura kam* (bad work/ sexual services), 14–15, 56–57, 89, 92, 105, 108–9, 120; dowry savings and, 70–74, 221n3; engagement in multiple jobs/worksites, 161–63, 167, 190–92; *jabardasti* (force), 124, 125, 197–99; legitimized/stigmatized, 4, 16–17, 22–30, 89–90, 97–109, 114–15, 160–61, 192, 200–201; *majburi* (constraint), 124–28, 173, 197–99, 221n5; *marzi* (choice), 31, 110, 112, 160, 163–64, 171, 173, 197–200; sex for work, 78, 84–86, 92–93, 167, 177–78; sex work as exceptional, 201–3; solicitation as, 4–7, 34–38, 42–45, 48–53, 75–76, 80–82, 111–12, 124–28, 171, 191–93; stability of income, 124–28; stigma and, 4, 16–17, 22–30, 89–90, 97–109, 114–15, 160–61, 192, 200–201. *See also* income-generating strategies; wage negotiation
"Locating HIV/AIDS and India" (Karnik), 24–25

lock hospitals, 22–23, 29, 30, 210n39
Lucknow, 28–29

Madras (Chennai), 23, 24–25, 80
Maharashtra Industrial Development Corporation (MIDC), 226n21
majburi (constraint), 124–28, 173, 197–99, 221n5. *See also* agency; livelihood strategies
Mandal Commission, 99, 220n21
Mandi (1983), 155
mangalsutra (necklace for women signifying marriage), 107, 220n28
Mani, Lata, 74
Manto, Sadat Hasan, 211n55
Marathwada, 45–46, 53–61, 69, 70, 216n25
marital status: brothel-based sex workers and, 175; caste and, 98–99, 102–3; gay marriage, xi; *mangalsutra*, 107, 220n28; remittances/dowry savings and, 70–74, 221n3; *rishtey*, 102–6; sexual slavery and, 20, 20–21; sex workers and, 20–21, 51–52, 220n28; widows, 6, 71, 84–85, 116
marzi (choice), 31, 110, 112, 160, 163–64, 171, 173, 197–200. See also *jabardasti*
Masselos, Jim, 130
Massey, Doreen, 212n66
Meena (worker), 168–72
Meeta (organizer), 45–48, 60–61
methodology: use of terms, 13–16; ethnographic conventions, 36–39, 161; interview process, 164, 168, 170–71; research fatigue, 161, 168, 194–96; silence/speech reticence, 194–96
migration/migrant workers: use of term, 31; abjection and, 52–53, 208n16; abolitionist discourse and, 203–5; agency and, 31–33, 197–98, 212n62; agricultural work, 4, 6, 8–10, 31, 42, 46, 69, 75, 115–19, 141, 197–98, 207n2; Bargi Dam project, 69; dowry and, 70–74, 221n3; housing and, 45–46, 53–57, 60–70, 75, 106, 116–19; impact of police harassment on,

117–19; internal vs. international, 221n3; of Kamathis to Bombay, 225n4; landless migrants, 8–9, 33, 46, 70–74, 141–43, 213n7; from Marathwada, 53–61, 216n25; permanent migration, 66–70, 75, 105–6; remittances and, 32, 38, 42–43, 70–74, 116–17, 120, 162–63, 173–74, 187, 221n3; seasonal migration, 54, 75, 104–6, 116, 117–19; slavery discourse and, 18–22, 209n24; as spatiotemporal process, 31–33; trafficking vs., 31
Miller, Mark J., 212n62
minors, 6–7, 18, 149–50, 199–201, 215n18, 228n2
Modern Asian Studies (Waheed), 28
morality: brothel-based sex work and, 151–53; *bura kam* (bad work/sexual services), 14–15, 56–57, 89, 92, 105, 108–9, 120; criminalization and, 143–45; as framework for defining urban spaces, 13, 17–30, 48–53, 92–93; *izzat* (honor), 14, 78, 83, 84, 85, 95, 102, 109, 119–20, 166, 203; legal frameworks for, 13, 17–30, 48–53, 92–93, 129–34, 143–45; morality/ immorality, 23, 141; naka-based sex work and, 89–90, 102–6; of non–sex workers, 145; origin narrative and, 161; policing and, 129–34, 141; political society and, 141–43; red-light districts and, 151–56; rescue narratives and, 154, 181, 198–99, 200; streetbased sex work and, 113–14, 128–29; victim framework and, 198–99
Mukhu, 86–90, 100–102
Muslim communities, 28, 101–2, 164–65, 166, 216n25

Nair, Janaki, 34–35
Nair, Mira, 155
Najma (worker), 163–70
naka-based sex work: abject-as-self, 53; age, 82–83; agricultural work, 115–16, 117, 119, 207n2; bribes, 69; *bura kam* (bad work/sexual services),

14–15, 56–57, 89, 92, 105, 108–9, 120; condom use/distribution, 91–92, 194; construction work vs. sex work, 124–28; fines, 5; housing, 45–46, 53–57, 60–70, 75, 106; *izzat* (honor) and, 84–86; marital status and, 70–74, 84; morality and, 89–90, 102–6; multiple jobs/worksites of, 162–63, 191–92; open secret and, 5, 110, 196–97; remittances/dowry savings and, 70–74, 221n3; sex for work, 84–86, 92–93; social mobility of, 82–83; solicitation, 4–7, 34–38, 42–45, 48–53, 75–76, 80–82, 111–12, 124–28, 193; stigma and, 89–90, 97–109; visibility of, 83–84, 86–95
nakas (day wage labor markets): use of term, 42–45, 207n2; anticaste movement and, 54, 62–63; *bura kam* (bad work/sexual services), 14–15, 56–57, 89, 92, 105, 108–9, 120; caste/class social segregation, 47–48; construction work contracts, 4, 124–28; as heterotopic space, 48–50; multiple uses of, 3–7; NGOs within, 56, 65; open secret of sexual commerce within, 4–5, 110, 196–97; as public spaces, 48–53; sex work within, 82–86; silence/speech about sex work, 194–95; skilled/ unskilled labor, 4–5, 207n2; slum demolitions, 62, 66–70, 78, 95–97; solicitation, 4–7, 34–38, 42–45, 48–53, 75–76, 80–82, 111–12, 124–28, 193; spatiotemporality of, 35–36, 55–57; visibility of, 79; women as laborers within, 4–5. *See also* informal economies; wage negotiation
Narmada River dam projects, 69, 216n33
National AIDS Control Organization (NACO), ix, 25, 157
National Alliance of People's Movements, 49
National Human Rights Commission, 18
National Sample Survey of India, 81

Nav Buddho community, 54, 55, 56, 84, 98, 100–101, 105–6, 109, 219n18
nawab/nawabi (nobility), 28, 29, 211n53
Nigam, Aditya, 9, 68, 81, 137–38, 139–40
nongovernmental organizations (NGOs): abolitionist discourse and, 149–50, 160–61, 168, 176, 179; condom distribution and, 114–15, 121–22, 180, 224n1; HIV/AIDS programs, ix–x, 6, 22–26, 38, 91–92, 149–50, 156–61, 185, 199, 208n14; Indian Foreign Contribution Regulation Act and, 226n15; legal/illegal activities, 92–95; public health mobile clinics, 164–65, 172, 182–83; sex research tourism, 156–63, 168, 194–96; watershed development, 46, 59, 61
North American Task Force on Prostitution, 24–25

Oldenburg, Veena Talwar, 28, 74
origin narratives: LGBTQ political discourse, xi–xii; sex work discourse, 161, 162–63, 200, 211n49

Palermo Protocol (2000), 11–13
Patel, Sujata, 130
Patwardhan, Anand, 213n2
PEPFAR (President's Emergency Plan for AIDS Relief), 12–13, 157
Periyar, E. V. R., 216n22
Piru (worker), 122, 123
Platts, John T., 211n53, 221n5
police: bribes, 69, 122–23, 128–29, 132, 133–34, 167; critiques of, 131; fines, 5, 128, 134, 137, 182; history in India, 130–32; legal frameworks for, 92–93, 129–30; legislation, 209n23; morality and, 129–34, 141; physical violence of, 5, 7, 128, 132, 141, 201–3, 222n7; raids, 6–7, 167, 179–84, 186–87. *See also* legal frameworks
political society, 141–43
Politics of the Governed, The (Chatterjee), 141–42

Portes, Alejandro, 212n62
Prema (worker), 86–90, 102
President's Emergency Plan for AIDS Relief (PEPFAR), 12–13, 157
Prison Notebooks (Gramsci), 140, 142
private space: *bura kam* (bad work/sexual services), 14–15, 56–57, 89, 92, 105, 108–9, 120; as gendered, 212n66
Promise of the Metropolis (Nair), 34–35
prostitutes/prostitution: use of term, 13–16, 17; as ahistorical category, 17–22; colonial-era development of, 26–30, 51, 73–74, 130–34, 151–53; courtesans (*tawā'if*), 26–30, 155, 211n55, 228n1; as economic abjection, 48–49, 78, 193; as evidence of women's oppression, 201–2; as exceptional livelihood strategy, 201–2; political society and, 141–43. *See also* sexual commerce
Prostitution Pledge (U.S.), 12–13, 208n14
Protocol to Prevent, Suppress and Punish Trafficking in Persons, Especially Women and Children (2000), 11
public health: lock hospitals and, 210n39; mobile clinics, 164–65, 172, 182–83; sex workers and, x
public space: use of term, 48–53; as gendered, 212n66; geographies of sexual commerce and, 4; heterotopic space, 48–50; normalizing gaze, 77–78; open secret and, 4–5, 110, 196–97; silence/speech about sex work, 194–95; solicitation and, 4–7, 18, 34–38, 42–45, 48–53, 75–76, 80–82, 111–12, 124–28, 132, 171, 191–93

Radha (worker), 117, 118, 119–20, 124, 126, 128
Rajdhani anecdote, 1–3
randi (whore), 14
red-light districts: development of, 26–30, 147–48, 150–53; brothel owners and, 29, 133, 175–77, 181–82,